Mineral Economics and Basic Industries in Asia

Other Westview Special Studies on China and East Asia

Women in Changing Japan, edited by Joyce Lebra, Joy Paulson, and Elizabeth Powers

Cadres, Commanders, and Commissars: The Training of the Chinese Communist Leadership, 1920-45, Jane L. Price

Mineral Resources and Basic Industries in the People's Republic of China, K. P. Wang

The Problems and Prospects of American–East Asian Relations, edited by John Chay

The Chinese Military System: An Organizational Study of the People's Liberation Army, Harvey Nelsen

The Medieval Chinese Oligarchy, David G. Johnson

Chinese Foreign Policy after the Cultural Revolution, 1966-1977, Robert G. Sutter

The Politics of Medicine in China: The Policy Process, 1949-1977, David M. Lampton

The Story of a Chinese People's Commune, Gordon Bennett

Perspectives on a Changing China: Essay in Honor of Professor C. Martin Wilbur, edited by Josh Fogel and William Rowe

River Management in Modern China, Charles Greer

China's Oil Future: A Case of Modest Expectations, Randall W. Hardy

A Theory of Japanese Democracy, Nobutaka Ike

North Korea: Government and Politics in the Democratic People's Republic of Korea, Jung-Gun Kim

Intra-Asian International Relations, George T. Yu

Other Westview Special Studies on South and Southeast Asia

Indira Gandhi's India: A Political System Reappraised, edited by Henry C. Hart

Southeast Asia and China: The End of Containment, Edwin Martin

Intra-Asian International Relations, George T. Yu

Westview Special Studies on China and East Asia/South and Southeast Asia

Mineral Economics and Basic Industries in Asia
K. P. Wang and E. Chin

This book reviews resource potential, mineral trade and consumption, the role of minerals internally and in world supply, the nature of minerals enterprise, major mineral industries, labor and infrastructure (as it affects industrial development), national attitudes and plans, and the general economic outlook for twenty-six countries. A mineral-supply data tabulation and a basic mineral-location map is provided for most of the countries reviewed. There are also more than a hundred additional mineral or industrial maps and photographs. A general regional view of Asia's people, history, products, economies, resources, basic industries, and development problems is accompanied by charts and tabulations describing each area's relative importance as a mineral producer, consumer, importer, and exporter.

Each country-chapter is organized according to the following categories: significance of minerals, mineral supply position, nature of mineral enterprise, principal mineral industries, mine and industry workers, mineral transport, energy and power, and summary outlook.

K. P. Wang, a supervisory physical scientist with the U.S. Bureau of Mines, is a specialist in international resources and mineral economics. Previously adjunct associate professor in mineral economics at Columbia University, Dr. Wang has also served on several occasions as a consultant to the UN in the areas of mineral economics and the application of science and technology in developing countries.

E. Chin is presently with the Far East Area Office of the U.S. Bureau of Mines. He was formerly a commodity analyst in nonferrous metals and the bureau's representative to the Interior Department's Law of the Sea Advisory Group.

Mineral Economics and Basic Industries in Asia

K. P. Wang and E. Chin

Routledge
Taylor & Francis Group
LONDON AND NEW YORK

First published 1978 by Westview Press

Published 2018 by Routledge
52 Vanderbilt Avenue, New York, NY 10017
2 Park Square, Milton Park, Abingdon, Oxon OX14 4RN

Routledge is an imprint of the Taylor & Francis Group, an informa business

Library of Congress Cataloging-in-Publication Data
Wang, Kung-Ping, 1919-
Mineral economics and basic industries in Asia.
Bibliography: p.
1. Mineral industries-Asia. 2. Mines and mineral resources-Asia. I. Chin, Edmond, joint author. II. Title.
HD9506.A652W36 338.2 77-25267
ISBN: 0-89158-411-0

ISBN 13: 978-0-367-02096-5 (hbk)
ISBN 13: 978-0-367-17083-7 (pbk)

Contents

Figures

Tables

Preface

Mineral developments in Asia and the Far East, particularly in Japan and the People's Republic of China, have been increasingly in the news. Japan's purchases of crude minerals around the world and its exports of metal and industrial products affect the economies of many countries. The surge in Japanese demand and the efforts of Japanese technicians to obtain raw materials have promoted the discovery and development of numerous deposits all over the world. With the minerals and fuels acquired for processing and utilization in ultramodern smelters and industrial plants, Japan has emerged as the world's third largest producer of finished mineral and metal goods (after the United States and the Soviet Union). Japanese-made tankers and ore carriers sailing the international shipping routes far outnumber those produced by any other country.

China came into prominence more recently, although it had quietly made significant progress even before the 1970s, uncovering many deposits and developing many mines in the process. The coal, salt, tungsten, tin, and antimony industries have long been famous. In 1973, China broke into the news when it purchased many large nitrogenous fertilizer plants. Then the world petroleum crisis brought to light that China's oil and gas potential may be great and that it had achieved the status of a medium-sized world producer of these fuels. In 1975, spurred by the greater use of fuels and progress in industrial development, the country started to import very large quantities of metals in international markets. The Tangshan earthquake in 1976 occurred after Chou En-lai's death and before Mao Tse-tung passed from the scene. Tangshan is in the middle of China's foremost producing coalfield, near the Takang oil field, and not too far from Tientsin and Peking.

Development of minerals is important in India's effort to raise living standards. Coal production rivals the United Kingdom and West Germany, and a much greater surplus of iron ore can be developed. The country has large resources of manganese, bauxite, and mica. Various nonferrous mines and smelters are being built from a hitherto uncertain resource base. Southeast Asia, better known historically as the land of rice, coconuts, and spices, is now noted for tin, tungsten, copper, fluorspar, low-sulfur oil, and offshore potential. The two Koreas and Taiwan in Northeast Asia have become significant in industry and are consuming increasing quantities of minerals, metals, and fuels, much like smaller-scale Japans.

Accuracy of information varies in this report from a very open Japan to a rather secretive North Korea. There are also problems of data availability for the "Indochina" countries and some other areas. However, reasonably good evaluations can be made for most countries, because significant developments seldom escape the attention of the international press and because there are many travelers and observers. Care has been taken when plotting and defining locations in the maps, knowing that place-names can be spelled in various ways. The emphasis in country names is geographical rather than political. Thus, names such as China, Mongolia, North Korea, South Korea, and Taiwan are used. All tonnages in this report are in metric tons when not otherwise defined, and the metric system is used for most other measures as well. All monetary figures are in U.S. dollars unless otherwise noted.

The authors wish to express their appreciation and gratitude for the encouragement and assistance of Rose K.

Wang, Lee Ngon Win Chin, Sherry Anderson, Garrett R. Hyde, Gordon L. Kinney, Charles B. Kenahan, Roger L. Shockey, Linda M. Arsenault, Maurice A. Johnson, Michael L. Lawson, and J. Thomas Jones in the preparation of this report.

Symbols Used on Base Maps and in Tables

Italicized symbols denote metals or processed minerals.

Symbol	*Commodity*	*Symbol*	*Commodity*
Ag	Silver	Gyp	Gypsum
Al	Bauxite	Jade	Jade
Al	Aluminum, refined	K	Potassium
Asb	Asbestos	Kao	Kaolin
Au	Gold	Ky	Kyanite
Ba	Barite	Lime	Limestone
Be	Beryllium	LL	Lapis lazuli
Bi	Bismuth	Marb	Marble
C	Coal	Mg (Mag)	Magnesite
Cem	Cement	Mica	Mica
Clay	Clay	Mn	Manganese ore
Co	Cobalt	*Mn*	Manganese metal
Cr	Chromite	Mo	Molybdenum
Cu	Copper, mine	Ni	Nickel, mine
Cu	Copper, refined	*Ni*	Nickel, refined
D	Diamond	Oil	Petroleum, crude
Dol	Dolomite	*Oil*	Petroleum products
F	Fluorspar	P	Phosphate rock
Fe	Iron ore, iron sands	P	Apatite
Fe	Pig iron	*P*	Phosphates
FeNi	Ferronickel	Pb	Lead, mine
Fert	Fertilizer	*Pb*	Lead, refined

Gas	Natural gas	Per	Perlite
Gem	Gemstone	Pyr	Pyrite
Gra	Graphite	R	Rutile
Gran	Granite	Salt	Salt
Sands	Sands	Talc	Talc
Sb	Antimony, mine	Ti	Ilmenite, rutile
Shale	Shale	*Ti*	Titanium
Si	Silica sands, quartz	U	Uranium
Sn	Tin, mine	W	Tungsten, mine
Sn	Tin, refined	Zn	Zinc, mine
St	Steel	*Zn*	Zinc, refined
Steel	Steel ingot	Zr	Zircon

Exchange Rates

Country	*Date*	*Currency equivalent to US $1*
Afghanistan	1/77	45 Afghanis
Bangladesh	2/77	15.58 Taka
Bhutan	1/77	8.85 Ngultrum
Brunei	1/76	2.45 Brunei dollars
Burma	9/76	6.78 Kyats
Cambodia	1/76	1,280 Riel
China	3/77	1.90 Ren-min-bi
Hong Kong	4/77	4.65 Hong Kong dollars
India	4/77	8.74 Rupees
Indonesia	5/77	386 Rupiahs
Japan	7/77	269 Yen
Laos	1/76	1,360 Kip
Macao	9/76	5.1 Pataca
Malaysia	4/77	2.49 Ringgits
Mongolia	1/76	3.31 Tugriks
Nepal	1/77	12.5 Rupees
North Korea	1/76	1.06 Won
Pakistan	4/77	9.76 Rupees
Papua New Guinea	2/77	0.91 Kina
Philippines	4/77	7.44 Pesos
Singapore	4/77	2.47 Singapore dollars
South Korea	4/77	476 Won
Sri Lanka	2/77	8.71 Rupees
Taiwan	1/77	38 Taiwan dollars
Thailand	4/77	20.4 Baht
Vietnam	—	Dong (No current quotation)

Conversion Factors

Metric ton (mt) equals 2,204.6 pounds or 1,000 kilograms.

Metric ton (mt) also equals 1.1023 short tons (st) or 0.9842 of a long ton (lt).

Tpy and tpd are tons per year and tons per day.

Ton-unit means one percent of content in weight.

Hundredth weight, or cwt, means 1 percent of a gross ton.

Kiloliter equals 6.29 U.S. barrels; and liter equals 0.264 of a U.S. gallon.

Barrel equals 42 U.S. gallons and 34.97 imperial gallons.

Bpd and bbl are abbreviated for barrels per day and barrels.

Bpd multiplied by 50 is roughly equivalent to mtpy.

For most crude oils, a metric ton equals 7.2 to 7.6 barrels.

For cement, a barrel equals 376 pounds, or four 94-pound bags.

Cubic meter equals 1.308 cubic yards and 35.31 cubic feet.

Kilometer (km) equals 0.62137 of a mile.

Meter (m) equals 1.0936 yards and 39.37 inches.

Kw and kwh are abbreviated for kilowatt and kilowatt-hours.

Dwt means deadweight tons in shipping.

1
Asia's Role in the World Minerals Economy

Asia has unique mineral characteristics. It is not an Africa rich in crude minerals in widely separated areas and little else, an Australia or a Canada with abundant resources but limited markets, a Latin America with spotty enclaves of resources and industries but a relatively homogeneous population, a Europe with a mineral economy lacking in adequate resources but possessing advanced technology and large markets, nor a United States or U.S.S.R. with high levels of both mineral production and consumption. Rather, Asia is heterogeneous and densely populated in some regions, underdeveloped and resource-rich in other areas, and moderately industrialized and high in mineral consumption in still others. There are about half a dozen races of people, the literacy rate in many countries is higher than normally believed, and Asia is the cradle of various religions. The riches of Southeast Asia and the industry of Northeast Asia contrast sharply with the agrarian economy of coastal, continental Asia and the poverty of the subcontinent. In this book "Asia" excludes the Middle East and Soviet Asia.

Many minerals, metals, and fuels are produced in significant quantities in Asia and the Far East. Table 1 and table 2 show the leading producers and their combined output of various minerals. The area provides (see figure 1*) more than two-fifths of the world output of tin, tungsten, anthracite, graphite, mica, pyrophyllite, and high-grade refractory chromite; more than a fifth of the bituminous coal, pig iron, steel, cement, salt, fluorspar, magnesite, kyanite, antimony, bismuth, zinc metal, and titanium; and 10-20 percent of the refined oil (not crude), nitrogenous fertilizers, iron ore, mine zinc, refined copper, aluminum, cadmium, metallic nickel, manganese, columbite-tantalite, pyrite, barite, soapstone, and rare earths.

Asia and the Far East are famous not for the major basic minerals but for exotic minerals (see figure 2). The People's Republic of China (PRC) leads the world in tungsten, both Koreas and Thailand are also important producers of tungsten, and the list extends to Burma, Laos, Japan, Vietnam, and Mongolia as well. Malaysia is in a class of its own in tin, but after Bolivia come Indonesia, Thailand, and China. China had a special position in antimony during World War II, and it still ranks with South Africa and Bolivia in the big three; Thailand is the world's fifth largest producer. India is by far the world's largest producer of natural mica. The Philippines has a unique role as the world's foremost producer of high-grade refractory chromite. Magnesites from North Korea and northeast China are massive and high-grade. North Korea, South Korea, and China are all within the first five in amorphous graphite, and Sri Lanka also produces a very high-unit-value graphite. Nearly half the world's anthracite comes from the Far East, mainly from North Korea, South Korea, and China. Southeast Asia is well known for gemstones. Because of surpluses, most of these minerals are exported and well known in world markets. The mineral self-sufficiency position of Asia and the Far East is shown in table 3.

However, Asia produces large tonnages of basic minerals

*All figures appear at the ends of chapters.

TABLE 1. Relative importance of Asia in world mineral output, 1974 (Thousand metric tons)

Commodity	% World output	Asia tonnage	Major Asian producers (% of world)			
Aluminum, refined	11	1,500	Japan	(8%)		
Antimony, mine	25	17	PRC China	(17%)	Thailand	(7%)
Asbestos	4	180	PRC China	(4%)		
Barite	15	700	PRC China	(5%)	Thailand	(4%)
Bauxite	5	4,200	India	(2%)	Indonesia	(2%)
Bismuth, refined	31	1	Japan	(21%)	PRC China	(7%)
Cadmium, refined	18	3	Japan	(17%)		
Cement	21	150,000	Japan	(10%)	PRC China	(4%)
Chromite	8	650	Philippines	(7%)		
Coal, anthracite	40	70,000	N. Korea	(18%)	PRC China	(11%)
Coal, bituminous	23	530,000	PRC China	(18%)	India	(4%)
Copper, mine	7	560	Philippines	(3%)		
Copper, refined	14	1,230	Japan	(11%)		
Fluorspar	22	1,000	Thailand	(8%)	PRC China	(6%)
Graphite	41	160	N. Korea	(19%)	S. Korea	(11%)

TABLE 1 (Cont.)

Iron ore	10	90,000	PRC China	(6%)	India	(3%)
Iron, pig	27	130,000	Japan	(18%)	PRC China	(6%)
Lead, mine	8	300	PRC China	(3%)	N. Korea	(3%)
Lead, refined	12	510	Japan	(5%)	PRC China	(2%)
Magnesite	30	2,700	N. Korea	(19%)	PRC China	(11%)
Manganese ore	12	2,600	India	(7%)	PRC China	(4%)
Mercury, refined	10	900	PRC China	(9%)		
Nickel, mine	3	20	Indonesia	(2%)		
Nickel, refined	15	105	Japan	(15%)		
Nitrogen, fixed	14	7,000	Japan	(7%)	PRC China	(6%)
Petroleum, crude	5.5	160,000	Indonesia	(2.5%)	PRC China	(2.5%)
Petroleum products	12	350,000	Japan	(8%)	PRC China	(2%)
Pyrite	17	4,000	PRC China	(8%)	Japan	(6%)
Salt	21	35,000	PRC China	(15%)	India	(4%)
Talc, pyrophyllite	50	2,700	Japan	(30%)	S. Korea	(8%)
Tin, mine	63	128	Malaysia	(31%)	Indonesia	(10%)
Titanium, refined	20	9	Japan	(20%)		
Tungsten, mine	40	16	PRC China	(22%)	S. Korea	(7%)
Zinc, refined	20	1,200	Japan	(14%)	PRC China	(2%)
Zinc, mine	10	600	Japan	(4%)	N. Korea	(2%)

NOTE: The Middle East and Soviet Asia have not been included.

TABLE 2. Asia's share of world mineral production, 1974

Mica	70%	Nickel, refined	15%
Tin, mine	63%	Barite	15%
Talc & pyrophyllite	50%	Copper, refined	14%
Graphite	41%	Nitrogen, fixed	14%
Anthracite	40%	Petroleum, refined	12%
Tungsten, mine	40%	Lead, refined	12%
Bismuth, refined	31%	Manganese ore	12%
Magnesite	30%	Aluminum, refined	11%
Iron, pig	27%	Iron ore	10%
Antimony, mine	25%	Mercury, refined	10%
Steel ingot	23%	Zinc, refined	10%
Coal, bituminous	23%	Chromite	8%
Fluorspar	22%	Lead, mine	8%
Salt	21%	Copper, mine	7%
Cement	21%	Petroleum, crude	6%
Titanium, refined	20%	Bauxite	5%
Zinc, refined	20%	Asbestos	4%
Cadmium, refined	18%	Nickel, mine	3%
Pyrite	17%		

NOTE: The Middle East and Soviet Asia have not been included.

TABLE 3. Relative importance of Asia in world mineral consumption, 1974 (Thousand metric tons)

Commodity	% World	Asia	Adequacy
Aluminum, refined	15	1,950	Shortage
Antimony, mine	12	9	Large surplus
Asbestos	15	600	Large shortage
Barite	12	500	Surplus
Bauxite	7	7,000	Large shortage
Cement	21	150,000	Adequate
Coal	30	690,000	Small shortage
Copper, mine	16	1,250	Large shortage
Copper, refined	15	1,200	Adequate
Fluorspar	15	700	Large surplus
Graphite	30	120	Surplus
Iron ore	26	220,000	Large shortage
Lead, mine	18	430	Shortage
Lead, refined	12	510	Small shortage
Magnesite	11	1,000,000	Large surplus
Nickel, mine	13	100	Large shortage
Nickel, refined	18	130	Shortage
Nitrogen, fixed	20	6,000	Small surplus
Petroleum, crude	13	380,000	Large shortage
Phosphate rock	10	11,000	Large shortage
Pyrite	15	4,000	Adequate
Salt	25	42,000	Small shortage
Talc and pyrophyllite	43	2,300	Small surplus
Tin, mine	23	50	Large surplus
Tungsten, mine	13	5	Large surplus
Zinc, mine	21	1,300	Large shortage
Zinc, refined	20	1,200	Adequate

NOTE: The Middle East and Soviet Asia have not been included.

also. In world coal, China ranks third and India about sixth; Northeast Asia, on the other hand, is very short of coking coal, particularly Japan. India has very large tonnages of high-grade iron ore, and China has extensive low-grade materials. But the Far East as a whole is short over 100 million tons of iron ore per year, mainly because of Japan's massive requirements. Yet there is a sizable surplus of steel products, owing again to Japan. The Far East is weak in nonferrous metal ores. Only the Philippines has a surplus of copper, but Japan brings in nonferrous ores from around the world for smelting in its ultramodern smelters. Lateritic ores bearing aluminum and nickel are abundant in Southeast

Asia and the Pacific islands, and Northeast Asia has the metal plants. Japan's production of most major metals ranks within the world's first three, a fact that raises averages for all of Asia. China has recently been buying large tonnages of copper and aluminum in world markets, indicating that it has not yet been able to develop its own resources adequately. It produces very large tonnages of salt, making it second only to the United States. Aside from major producers such as Japan, China, and India, the area has half a dozen countries each producing 4 to 10 million tons of cement annually. Asia without the Middle East is currently very short of oil, except for Southeast Asia and China, but the near shore and offshore potential in various areas seems good.

The Far East is relatively industrialized, particularly the northern and central coastal areas. South Korea, North Korea, and Taiwan compare favorably in industrial and commercial strength with the smaller European countries, and such cities as Manila, Hong Kong, Singapore, Bangkok, and soon Jakarta have many light industries and growing basic industries as well. The data on coal, oil, steel, and cement shown in figure 3 reflect general industrial needs for minerals and metals in Asia and the Far East.

The relative standing of this very densely populated area of the world, in terms of gross national product (GNP) and mineral output value (MOV), is shown in table 4. Japan's GNP is roughly twice that of China and six times that of India. China is by far the most important in mining output, and India is prominent in iron ore, coal, manganese, and mica. On the other hand, Japan overshadows all other countries in mineral and metal processing, leaving even China, the next most important Asian country, far behind. The Koreas and Taiwan are small-scale Japans. Brunei's small population is very rich per capita because of the oil. Tin is of great importance to Malaysia, copper and gold are vital to the Philippines, and in Indonesia oil has created both a bonanza and a scandal. Oil provides China with foreign exchange to buy metals and equipment. Japan accentuates the "value added" part of mineral activity. In Thailand, minerals are still far outranked by agricultural

TABLE 4. Gross National Product (GNP)
and Mineral Output Value (MOV) of
Asian Countries, 1975
(Estimated in million U.S. $)

Country	GNP	MOV [1]	Mineral Value Added
Afghanistan	1,600	70	Insignificant
Bangladesh	8,000	25	Small
Brunei	1,200	1,000	Small
Burma	3,000	150	Small
China	250,000	20,000	Over 10,000
Hong Kong	7,200	15	Insignificant
India	85,000	5,000	Possibly 3,000
Indonesia	30,000	7,000	Small
Japan	500,000	2,000	Possibly 50,000
Laos	Small	10	Insignificant
Malaysia	8,100	800	Small
Mongolia	820	65	Insignificant
North Korea	10,000	1,900	Under 500
Pakistan	9,000	70	Small
Philippines	15,500	700	Under 200
Singapore	5,800	Small	500
Sri Lanka	3,100	40	Insignificant
South Korea	18,700	500	1,000
Taiwan	14,300	260	800
Thailand	14,800	200	Moderate
Vietnam	5,000	200	Small

1/ Mine output value only, including oil and gas.

products.

Historically, the U.S. connection in the Orient with regard to minerals and related fields has been minimal, except in the Philippines, where Americans began the initial development of the mining industry. However, U.S. investments have been significant in general business and manufacturing in many countries. U.S. involvement in Asian resources has not been greater because of colonial rights by other Western countries, the general instability of the area, and the emergence of Japan as an influential country. The end of World War II brought great changes, but U.S. firms were still hesitant about Asia, and the United States soon became involved in Korea and Vietnam. During the early post–World War II years, the United States did important basic private and industrial planning work in Japan through the natural resources advisory groups. Subsequently, the U.S. government made a contribution to mineral development in the Far East through the technical assistance program. U.S. steelmen and oilmen played vital roles in introducing the best of technology to the early steelworks and refineries built in Japan, the forerunners of an exponential plant construction program.

However, U.S. mining companies left Philippine minerals for Japanese firms to help develop, although they took an important part in the unlocking of Australia's mineral storehouse. The investment climate in Southeast Asia has been difficult except in Indonesia, which attracted many international petroleum and mining firms in the 1960s because of advantageous "work contracts." But even Indonesia with its good mineral potential is having trouble sustaining this reputation. The prospects for hard-rock mining have improved somewhat in the Thai-Malay archipelago in terms of potential, but the political situation is not stable. Northeast Asia does not have large mineral deposits, China has been a "closed door" so far, and India is leaning toward more state enterprises. Nonetheless, U.S. mining, construction, and equipment firms are becoming interested in China and are learning more about the other areas of the Orient as well.

The outlook for mineral development in Asia is uneven: there is good potential for oil in coastal Asia; hard-rock mining is not particularly attractive, except in the Philippines and except in China and India, which want to develop the minerals themselves; industry and mineral markets are sizable and expanding; and opportunities are good with regard to introducing mineral and metal and fuel technology, consulting and plant construction, and business and manufacturing related to mineral and metal processing and fabrication, chemicals and fertilizers, and general engineering.

Illustrations for Chapter 1

Figure 1 Index map of Asia

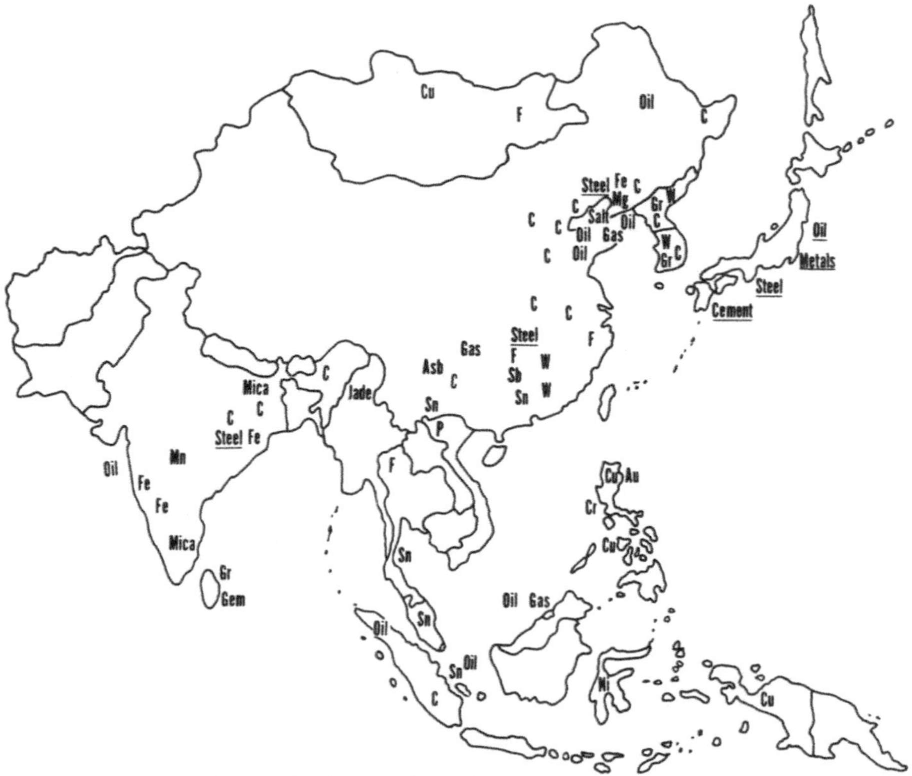

Figure 2 Major minerals in Asia and the Far East

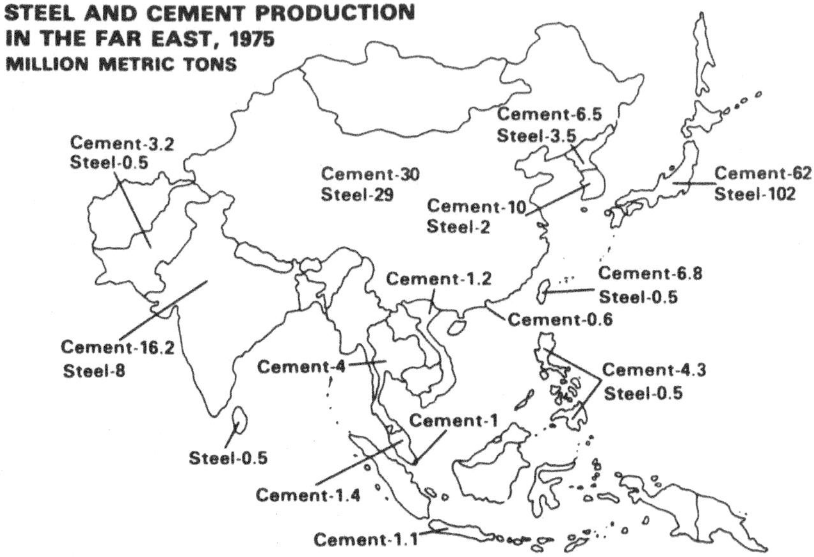

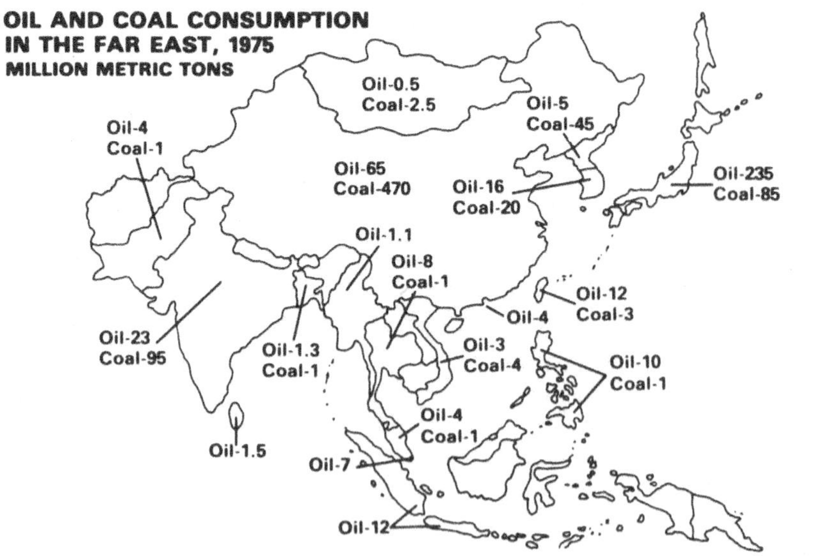

Figure 3 Steel, cement, and fuels in Asia and the Far East

2
Asia's Economic Geography and Industrial Base

Geography

The area encompassed by the political entities included in this study comprises 8.3 million square miles, or about 14 percent of the total earth's land area. The bulk of the region is contained on the Asian continental land mass. The islands of New Guinea, Borneo, Sumatra, and Honshu are among the largest in the world. Collectively, they constitute a land area of 0.86 million square miles, or an area about one-fourth the size of the United States.

The region is noted for its great rivers. The Yangtze, Huang (Yellow), Amur, and Mekong are respectively the fifth, sixth, eighth, and eleventh longest rivers in the world. The Ganges-Brahmaputra has created the world's largest delta, which covers 30,000 square miles. Abutting East Asia are the Sea of Japan, East China Sea, South China Sea, Bay of Bengal, and Arabian Sea. The continental shelf adjacent to the region constitutes a large proportion of the world's readily accessible shelf area. On the other hand, the Philippine and Java trenches and, further out, the Mariana Trench reach to formidable, abyssal depths, downward to 6,000 fathoms. Contrasting to this is Mount Everest, the Parnassus of the East, which reaches a lofty 29,028 feet. And there is Tibet, whose high plateaus have been called the roof of the world.

The man-made feats are just as impressive. One of the world's deepest mines is in India. Excavation for gold at Kolar, Mysore, has approached depths of 11,500 feet. The majestic Great Wall of China, completed during the reign of Shih Huang-ti, was built to insulate the Middle Kingdom. The main sections of the Great Wall from Shanhaikuan to Kansu meander for some 2,100 miles, averaging heights of twenty-five feet. In contrast, the rectangular "Forbidden City" in Peking measures 1,050 yards by 820 yards and is surrounded by moats having a total length of 3,600 yards.

Population

Asia is unique for the sheer size of its population. This tremendous resource is currently estimated at 2.1 billion persons, or about 53 percent of the total world population. China is first, with a citizenry of over 850 million; some place the figure at more than 900 million. India is next with 600 million persons, followed by Indonesia and Japan with 130 million and 110 million, respectively. Aside from Macao, the least populated area is Brunei, with resident inhabitants of only 150,000. Bhutan has a population of 1.1 million and Mongolia, 1.4 million.

Quite naturally, the highest population density occurs in the city-states of Hong Kong, Macao, and Singapore, with Macao having 44,300 persons per square mile, the densest population in the world. Political entities whose population density ranges between 500 and 1,300 persons per square mile include Bangladesh, Japan, South Korea, Sri Lanka, and Taiwan. On the other end of the scale is Mongolia, whose population density is the world's lowest—2.3 persons per square mile.

The region's average annual growth rate in population is estimated at 2 percent. In absolute numbers, the area can be expected to add nearly 45 million persons to the world's population annually. High rates of population growth, around 3 percent per year, are projected for Brunei, Cambodia, Pakistan, Philippines, and Thailand, compared with a 1.2–1.4 percent growth in China, Japan, and Singapore. By the year 2000, the region's population is expected to reach 3.5 billion.

Income and Wages

Traditionally, the economies of the region were all agrarian and pastoral, except for Macao and the entrepôt ports of Hong Kong and Singapore. Significantly, Japan and the two Koreas are among the states whose industrial output accounts for 40 percent of their respective gross national products. By contrast, countries whose agricultural sector accounts for more than 40 percent of the gross national product include Afghanistan, Bangladesh, Bhutan, Cambodia, India, Indonesia, Laos, Mongolia, Nepal, and Vietnam. China, Indonesia, the Koreas, Malaysia, the Philippines, and Taiwan are actively seeking to increase industrial output and have made significant gains in this respect. In terms of per capita income, only wages in Japan and Singapore compare favorably with Western standards. All other countries have an individual income level of less than $1,000 per year. Moreover, the average annual personal income in Bangladesh, Burma, Cambodia, and Laos averages $60-80.

Organizations and Aid

The Asian Development Bank (ADB) was formed in 1966 to help member nations obtain monies for development projects. One of the ADB's main priorities is lending in the agricultural sector, mostly for water resources development. There are twenty-five member nations in the bank. Bhutan, Brunei, China, Macao, Mongolia, and North Korea are currently not members of the ADB. During 1975, the ADB approved loans totaling $660 million to its members. The loans were distributed as follows (in percent): agriculture, 37.2; industry, 19.5; public utilities, 28.8; transportation and communications, 12.4; and education, 2.1.

In addition, the World Bank and the International Development Association have provided low-interest loans and interest free credits in the region. By June 30, 1976, the cumulative total of loans and credits for Asia was close to $14 billion. Agricultural development received the largest portion of the funding—$3.2 billion. The transportation sector followed with $3.0 billion, and electric power generation projects received $1.9 billion. Financial assistance for industry was as follows (in million dollars): fertilizers and chemicals, 763; iron and steel, 189; mining, 54.5; pulp and paper, 4.2; and other, 5.6. Loans and credits for telecommunications totaled $557.3 million. By country, loans and credits were as follows (in million dollars): India, 5,872; Indonesia, 1,459; Pakistan, 1,473; Philippines, 949; Thailand, 919; Japan, 863; Malaysia, 734; Bangladesh, 701; Singapore, 181; Sri Lanka, 177; Burma, 166; and other, 148.

The countries of the region also belong to international or local groups that provide additional measures and security for economic growth. For instance, the Association of South-East Asian Nations (ASEAN) was formed on August 8, 1967, by Indonesia, Malaysia, Philippines, Singapore, and Thailand. Through collaboration and mutual assistance, particularly in investments and trade, each member nation has increased both its per capita income and its purchasing power and foreign exchange earnings. Mongolia is the only country in the region that is a member of the Council for Mutual Economic Aid. The International Tin Council (ITC) is composed of two memberships—one for tin-producing countries and the other for tin-consuming countries. Indonesia, Malaysia, and Thailand collectively hold nearly three-quarters of ITC producer votes, although a major producer, China, is not a member. Japan and India are the only Asian members of the tin-consuming group.

Indonesia is a member of both the International Bauxite Association and the Organization of Petroleum Exporting Countries. India is a member of the Association of Iron Ore Exporting Countries. Japan is the only Asian country represented in the Organization for Economic Cooperation and Development, or OECD. This group, composed of twenty-four nations, was formed in 1960 to promote stable economic growth in member countries and the world at large, and to help expand free trade. Brunei, the two Koreas, and Taiwan are not members of the United Nations. The UN Economic and Social Council has a regional Economic Commission for Asia and the Pacific, which has thirty-one member countries. China, a permanent member of the U.N. Security Council, and Japan are the only countries in the region that are assessed to contribute to the annual, regular budget of the UN. Most countries are members of the World Bank and the International Monetary Fund.

Agriculture

During 1976, rice production in Asia approached 210 million tons, or 90 percent of the world's rice output. China was the largest producer, accounting for 78 million tons, followed by India with 47 million tons. Bangladesh, Indonesia, Japan, and Thailand each produced between 10 and 15 million tons. Total world production of wheat in 1976 was estimated at 389 million tons. The U.S.S.R. was the largest producer with an output of 101 million tons, followed by the United States, 56 million tons, China, 42 million tons, and India, 27 million tons. The remainder of the wheat production in Asia was 10 million tons and was principally from Pakistan, Bangladesh, and Japan, in that order. The world output of coarse grains was around 700 million tons; Asia's production was around 131 million tons (compared with 221 million tons for the United States and Canada). China and India were again the area's largest producers, accounting for 81 million and 29 million tons, respectively. Exports of wheat and coarse grains from Asia in 1976 were about 3 million tons, and imports were 41 million tons. Japan was the largest buyer, importing about 19 million tons, followed by India with 6.5 million tons, and China, 2.6 million tons.

The area's limited cocoa output comes largely from Papua New Guinea and Malaysia. The main Asian producers of coffee are Indonesia, India, and Papua New Guinea, and tea is primarily from China, India, and Sri Lanka. Black pepper comes mainly from India, Malaysia, and Indonesia; Malaysia and Indonesia also produce white pepper. Other spices produced and traded include cardamom, cassia, lignin, clove, and turmeric.

India produces around 10 million tons of oil seeds annually, principally groundnut and cottonseed. Nearby Sri

Lanka and the Philippines produce copra and coconut oil. Palm oil is a major foreign exchange earner for Malaysia and Indonesia, and China and India account for about 40 percent of the total world supply of rapeseed.

Asia produces about 90 percent of the world's natural rubber. Although current output is modest compared with past production, natural rubber production and consumption are expected to rise owing to the increased use of radial tires by the automotive industry and owing to the higher price of synthetic rubber due to the increased cost of petroleum products. In the early 1970s the rubber plantations of Malaysia were reconditioned, and rubber production is now one of its major foreign currency earners. Thailand has also increased its output of rubber in recent years.

Fuels and Energy

The production of crude oil throughout Asia was over 170 million metric tons in 1976. China and Indonesia together account for about 86 percent of the total output. The remainder is from Brunei, India, Malaysia, and Burma, in that order.

China is also the largest producer of natural gas in the area, with output rising to perhaps 80 billion cubic meters in 1976. The only other significant producers of natural gas are Brunei, which produced about 8 billion cubic meters in 1976; Pakistan, whose output was around 4 billion cubic meters; and Indonesia, with 2 billion cubic meters.

Total coal production in Asia now exceeds 650 million metric tons. The production of bituminous coal accounts for nearly 90 percent of the total output. China is the largest producer, with an estimated output of 480 million tons in 1976. Other major producers are India, North Korea, Japan, and South Korea, in that order. In 1976 combined production by these four countries was about 177 million tons, or 27 percent of the area's output. Other coal production is nominal, coming from Afghanistan, Indonesia, Mongolia, Taiwan, and Vietnam.

Only Brunei, China, and Indonesia can be considered self-reliant in terms of domestic energy supply. Conversely, Hong Kong, Laos, Macao, the Philippines, and Singapore import virtually all of their energy requirements. Other areas that import 70 percent or more of the energy consumed include Japan, Nepal, Sri Lanka, Thailand, and Taiwan.

To meet future energy requirements, nuclear power plants have been constructed and are being planned in India, Japan, Pakistan, Philippines, South Korea, and Taiwan. Three small units with a total output of 600 net megawatts are in operation in Bombay and Kota, India, and another five units, each with a net capacity of around 200 megawatts, are being constructed. Japan has thirteen medium-size nuclear reactors in operation, generating a total of 7,170 megawatts of electrical energy. Japan is now constructing eleven additional units, which should add 9,130 megawatts to existing nuclear power generation. Five of these latter units have generating capacities between 1,000 and 1,100 megawatts. Three medium-size reactors are being planned for Genkai, Monju, and Ikato-cho.

Korea Electric Co. is constructing three medium-size reactors, two near Pusan and the third at Ulsan. The first is scheduled for completion in late 1977 and the two others in 1982. Output from these plants will total 1,798 megawatts. Pakistan has a 125-megawatt, pressurized heavy-water reactor near Karachi. This unit has been operating commercially since the end of 1972. Philippine National Power Corp. is planning the construction of twin units (626 mw each) at Bagac. Taiwan Power Co. is constructing three twin nuclear reactor plants with a total output of 5,140 megawatts—two near Keelung in the north (2 x 636 mw, and 2 x 985 mw) and one near the southern tip of Taiwan (2 x 950 mw). The first Keelung plant will probably be completed by 1978, and the second perhaps by 1982; both plants will have boiling-water reactors. The southern plant, with pressurized water reactors, is scheduled for completion in about 1984.

The following countries were operating research reactors as of early 1977: India, four; Indonesia, one; Japan, twenty; Pakistan, one; Philippines, one; South Korea, one; and Thailand, one. In addition, Japan had three research reactors under construction. India is presently constructing a fast-breeder thorium research reactor. The status of nuclear power programs in the centrally controlled economies of the region is largely unknown.

Minerals and Metals

Asia and the Far East have large surpluses of tin, tungsten, antimony, bismuth, mica, fluorspar, magnesite, talc, and graphite. Tin occurs in the Malay Peninsula granite ranges—from Southwest China south through Burma, Thailand, and Malaysia to Indonesia's tin islands. Tungsten and by-product bismuth come from Southeast China (mainly Kiangsi), the central Korean peninsula, and isolated spots in Thailand and Burma. Mica is India's special product, and talc and magnesite occur in the basic rocks of the Liaotung and Korean peninsulas. Korean graphite is associated with anthracite.

In the face of expanding energy demand, Asia (without the Middle East) is very short of oil and slightly short of coal. However, China's fuel position is strong across the board, and Indonesia is rich in oil and has recently found some coal. The two Koreas have no oil, but have major anthracite deposits. India's coal position is good, and oil shows hope. Thailand relies totally on foreign oil, although oil shale is present and gas has been found. The Philippines has few fuel resources. Japan's massive requirements for fossil fuels are met primarily by imports. Taiwan is a small-scale Japan. East Asia has some of the world's best refineries and petrochemical plants. Offshore oil and gas show promise in many areas.

Asia produces and consumes large tonnages of cement and steel products, which reflects primarily the industrial progress in East Asia, particularly in Japan. Cement raw materials are derived locally from many Far East countries. Japan imports most of its iron ore and is the world's leading steel exporter. China does not produce enough steel to meet demand, and local iron ores are generally low-grade. India is the only country in the region with large surpluses of iron ore. Generally, Asia has a growing number of large steel centers and cement plants.

The region is a large net importer of nonferrous base metals and ores, although East Asia has many modern smelters and refineries. Japan is combing the world for metal ores, and South Korea and countries farther south are also building up on smelters. The Philippines has surplus copper, and India and Indonesia, surplus aluminum raw materials. Southeast Asia and the Pacific have become more important in lateritic nickel. However, the overall metal shortage is increasingly apparent, particularly in China, which has imported large tonnages of nonferrous metals in recent years. There are also severe deficiencies in fertilizer raw materials, such as phosphates and potash. China and Japan are large producers of nitrogenous fertilizers; Japan provides its surpluses to China. Asia is short in salt and grossly deficient in asbestos.

Economic Development

The most immediate challenge to the nations of the Orient is to establish their industrial strength. The natural resources of the area are in general still underdeveloped, and the human resources are underutilized. Japan is singular in the region and compares well commercially and industrially with the United States, the U.S.S.R., and West Germany. Its industries are large, multifarious, and sophisticated. Japan is a modern country in outlook and prestige, although it still has many Oriental traditions and shibboleths.

The status and progress of China's construction programs are largely veiled to the outside world. However, the late Chou En-lai maintained that China's ascendancy was predicated upon achieving "comprehensive modernization of agriculture, industry, national defense, science, and technology." For agriculture, the model was the productivity of the terraced hills of Tachai. For industry, the model was the oil fields of Taching. China continues to expand its railways and road system, which are essential for transport and communication. The total rail network is currently estimated at 31,000 miles of track—compared to a nationwide highway mileage of close to 500,000 miles. The capacity of

China's nine major harbors continues to be enlarged. Forty deepwater wharves were reportedly completed in the country's ongoing port expansion program. In 1976, an oil wharf capable of handling tankers in the 100,000-ton class was completed at Darien.

Singapore and Hong Kong are the great trading posts of the East, and Macao thrives solely on its tourism. Less than a dozen countries profit from heavy industries and light manufacturing; most of the region remains dependent on agricultural output. East Asia and Southeast Asia are economically stronger than the old Indochina countries. To the west, India's growth and progress exceed that of its neighbors.

Afghanistan, Bhutan, Laos, Mongolia, and Nepal are landlocked countries. Bhutan and Nepal have just recently been open to developing a tourist trade. Afghanistan's potential lies in the development of its iron ore and petroleum finds. Laos, on the other hand, is the poorest of the Indochina countries. It has no railways, and the prospect of developing the sylvanite-potash deposit in the Vientiane Plain (or for that matter any other project) is formidable. Because of Erdenet, Mongolia is destined to be a significant producer and exporter of copper and by-product molybdenum. Other newly rich countries are Brunei, because of its commercial exploitation of oil and natural gas; and Papua New Guinea, because of its copper and associated precious metals.

Bangladesh is faced with controlling a bulging population and alleviating poverty. As in Cambodia, the budget allocation is highest for agricultural development and related activities. Similarly, Burma has primarily an agrarian economy. However, it is developing its small oil industry to reduce imports of fuels. Pipelines are being constructed, and oil barges and tugs are being acquired; domestic crude production can then be increased and flow steadily from wellhead to refinery. A major thrust in India's development program is in the energy sector. The coal industry is entirely nationalized, and the oil industry is also being nationalized. A significant development is the initial production of oil from the Bombay High offshore oil field. The Oil and Natural Gas Commission plans to have about ninety wells drilled, and by 1980 production of oil from the Bombay High fields is expected to reach 200,000 barrels per day. Increased output of coal is further encouraged to boost the possibilities of greater coal exports.

The ASEAN member nations continue to forge ahead economically through mutual cooperation. These countries are among the world's largest producers of rubber and lumber, spices, vegetable oils, rice, fruits, fish, and many other commodities. The region is also noted for its petroleum, tin, copper, gold, and chromium.

Taiwan is now completing its ten major development projects, which include an iron and steel complex, highway construction, an international airport, and nuclear power plants. South Korea is planning to expand Pusan and Mukho ports. Major emphasis is placed on the transport sector: railway service is increasing and national and provincial roads are being lengthened and paved. Industrial estates are being established throughout the country to increase the output of semimanufactures and consumer goods for export. Meanwhile, North Korea has been overly zealous in developing its industries and is faced with financial difficulties owing to an increase in its trade deficit and posting payments on past foreign purchases.

Vietnam is faced with a massive task of reconstruction and new construction. Bridges, roads, and railways are being repaired and built. Irrigation projects are being constructed in the Mekong delta and central Vietnam, existing canals are being dredged, and new reservoirs and watercourses are being dug. The wharf at Danang has been repaired, and construction on a shipyard has just started. Significant progress has reportedly been made in restoring the country's infrastructure since reunification, even though reconstruction requires tremendous amounts of steel, cement, and other construction materials.

3
Afghanistan

Afghanistan is a landlocked Muslim country of 17 million people surrounded by the Soviet Union, China, Pakistan, and Iran. Its economy is primarily agricultural; it has little industry. Afghanistan is world-famous for lapis lazuli, but other minerals are of little consequence by world standards. Natural gas heads the list of minerals extracted. Other industries are coal and salt. Small amounts of marble, barite, and talc are also produced for local consumption. There are two small cement plants and one fertilizer plant. However, Afghanistan has promising mineral potential. Important iron ore deposits are slated for future development, oil prospecting is active, and several million tons of copper ore have been uncovered around Ainak near Kabul, the capital.

Significance of Minerals

Afghanistan's GNP was about $1.6 billion in 1975. The mineral industry has traditionally accounted for less than 5 percent of the GNP.

Mineral Supply Position

Natural gas is Afghanistan's principal mineral export. In 1975, approximately 99 billion cubic feet of gas was exported to the Soviet Union, earning nearly $47 million in foreign exchange. Afghanistan also exports its entire output of lapis

TABLE 5. AFGHANISTÁN: ROLE IN WORLD MINERAL SUPPLY
(Thousand metric tons, unless otherwise noted)

Major Commodities (Map Symbols)	Production			World Output Share, 1975	Trade in 1975 Exports or Imports	Reserves (or Raw Materials)
	1976	1975	1974			
Nonmetals						
Barite (Ba)............	5	5	10	Minute	Small imports	50
Cement (Cem)...........	167	140	146	Minute	Exports--56	(Local materials)
Fertilizer (Fert)......	45	45	25	Minute	Imported	(Natural gas)
Lapis lazuli (LL kilograms)	7,400	8,000	8,500	80 %	Exports--8,000	Sizable
Talc...................	5	6	3	Minute	Neither	170
Fuels						
Coal (C)...............	164	160	153	Minute	Neither	400,000
Oil, crude (Oil).......	---	---	---	---	Imports--285	4,500
Natural gas (Gas, billion cu. ft.).....	110	106	102	Minute	Exports--99	3,500

lazuli, principally to West Germany. Cement is the country's only other mineral export of consequence; approximately 40 percent of the cement produced is exported to the Soviet Union and Iran. Refined petroleum is Afghanistan's leading mineral import, and almost all of this comes from the Soviet Union. In 1975, Afghanistan's imports of petroleum products amounted to about 285,000 tons.

Nature of Mineral Enterprise

Almost all mineral industries are owned and controlled by the state. In recent years, the Afghan government has invited international bids for the exploration and development of minerals in certain parts of the country. The Foreign and Domestic Private Investment Law of 1967 permits investment agreements in mineral exploitation between the government and any investor, including foreigners. This law was revised in 1974 to require that all new ventures be at least 51 percent Afghan-owned and that all existing ventures conform to this stipulation in due time.

No mining code or petroleum code has yet been adopted by the Afghan government, although complete drafts have been prepared for both. In 1975, a law was passed creating the Afghanistan National Oil Company (ANOC), whose responsibilities include the completion and implementation of a national petroleum law and the negotiation of oil and gas exploration and production rights with foreign firms. ANOC's charter includes the provision that it own at least 51 percent of any joint venture.

Principal Mineral Industries

Natural gas production generally exceeds 100 billion cubic feet per year. The five main gas fields—Khwaja-Gogirdak, Yatim Tag, Khwaja Borhan, Juma, and Jarqduq—are all situated in northwest Afghanistan just south of the Soviet border, and they have been developed with Soviet financial and technical aid. Almost all of the natural gas produced by Afghanistan, except that used for making fertilizers, is exported to the Soviet Union. The Soviets doubled the price paid for Afghan gas in 1975, thereby greatly increasing Afghanistan's export earnings. The Soviets also helped build two new gas treatment plants—at Khwaja-Gogirdak and at Jarqduq.

The mining of lapis lazuli at the world-famous mines in northeastern Badakhshan dates from 1934. Salt production was about 60,000 tons in 1975. Approximately two-thirds of this is rock salt from opencast mines near Tallequan in Takhar Province, and the balance is brine salt from the salt lakes near Herat, Kandahar, and Andkhoi. Afghanistan's coal comes from the Karkar, Ishpushta, and Darra-i-Suf mines, all in the northeast. Consideration has been given to the construction of a third cement plant ($50 million, 1,600 mtpy in the Kandahar region) to complement the ones at Ghouri and Jabal-i-Seraj north of Kabul. Afghanistan's fertilizer plant, which produces urea and ammonium phosphate, is located at Mazar-i-Sharif.

Mine and Industry Workers

Afghanistan has little mining and industry. At most, 10 percent of the work force is engaged in such activities.

Mineral Transport

Inadequate transportation facilities (no railroads and only 8,000 km of roads) have been partly responsible for the limited development of Afghanistan's mineral resources. Most commodities are either trucked directly to the Soviet Union and Iran or transferred to Peshawar in Pakistan, where they are shipped by rail to Karachi for export. Foreign aid has helped improve infrastructure. Natural gas is transported across the Amu Darya River by a new surface pipeline linking the Khwaja-Gogirdak wells of Afghanistan to Soviet Turkmenistan. A significant recent development is Iran's offer to finance the construction of a railway system linking landlocked Afghanistan with Iran's transport network and its Persian Gulf ports. This project is scheduled for completion in 1983.

Energy and Power

Most of Afghanistan's petroleum requirements are met by the Soviet Union. Natural gas from the northwest fields is mostly sold to the Soviet Union, but a small part is used domestically by a fertilizer plant and a 36,000-kilowatt (will be expanded to 48,000 kw) thermal power plant at Mazar-i-Sharif. In November 1975, a new 33,000-kilowatt hydroelectric plant was opened at the Kajakai Dam in Helmand Province. The rest of Afghanistan's power-generating capacity of about 207,000 kilowatts consists of hydropower, mostly from the Kabul area.

Summary Outlook

The most important recent addition to Afghanistan's mineral inventory is the Hajigak iron ore deposits, situated in the Hindu Kush mountains northwest of Kabul. A branch line of Afghanistan's railway system will be built to open up the deposits, whose reserves of 60 percent Fe ore amount perhaps to 2 billion tons.

Other nonfuel minerals being actively explored in Afghanistan include copper, chromite, beryl, fluorite, asbestos, lead, mica, fuller's earth, and gemstones. Here again, the Soviets are helping in exploration. The Mazar-i-Sharif chemical fertilizer plant reportedly started to produce at full capacity of 300 tons daily in early March 1977.

Oil has recently been discovered at the Angut and Aq Darya fields in the southern part of Jowzjan Province, and exploration for additional oil and gas in these and other fields is continuing. In 1975, the government granted an exploration license to France's Compagnie Française des Pétroles for a tract of 20,000 square kilometers in the southwest Katawaz basin. Plans have been made to build a 4,000-bpd refinery (in the Jarqduq area of Jowzjan Province) with Soviet assistance.

Illustrations for Chapter 3

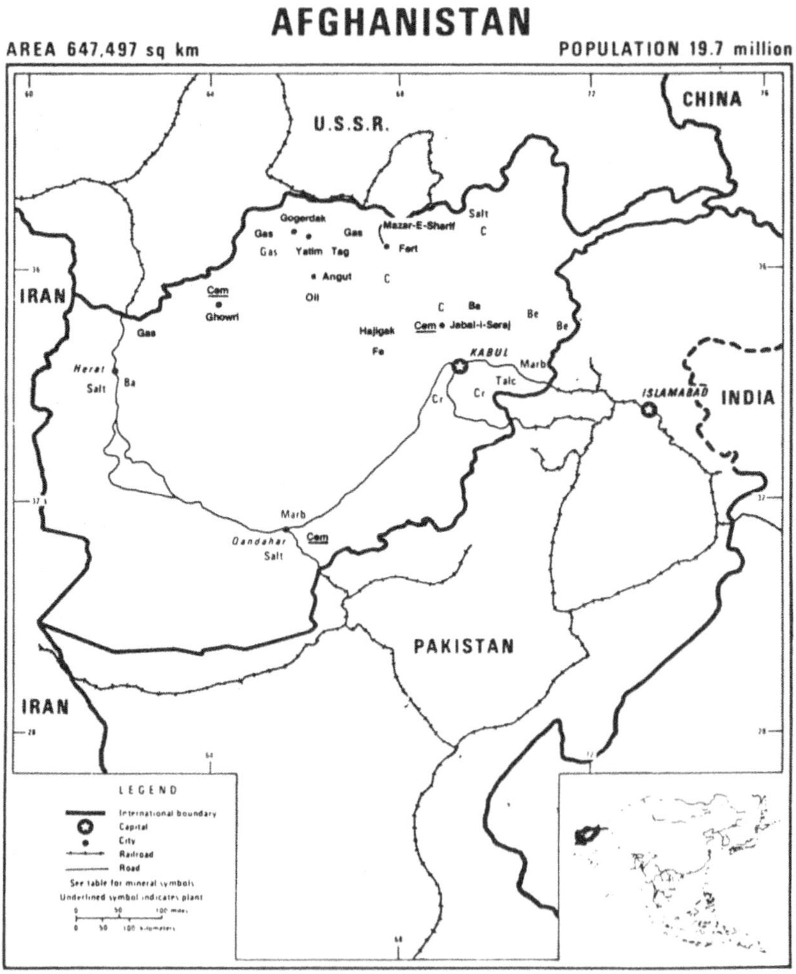

Figure 4 Map of Afghanistan

Figure 5 General scenes of Afghanistan (Courtesy Embassy of Afghanistan)

4
Bangladesh

Bangladesh's five-year plan launched in July 1973 was upset by the world oil crisis, and little progress has been made in industrial production since that time. Population growth has been more than 2 percent yearly, and prices have increased fourfold since independence on March 26, 1971. Gross underutilization of industrial capacity has sharply curtailed employment. The jute industry (backbone of the economy) has been producing at only two-thirds of the 1969-1970 level. The balance-of-payments deficit in 1975 was about $1.2 billion. However, the foreign investment situation greatly improved in 1976, although there was little interest in minerals and metals. Bangladesh had bumper harvests of jute and food grains in 1975 and 1976.

Significance of Minerals

1975 GNP was U.S. $8 billion. Natural gas was the only mineral of consequence, with an annual output at about a billion cubic meters. Bangladesh also produced 175,000 tons of nitrogenous fertilizers, 750,000 tons of salt, and 91,000 tons of cement in 1975.

Mineral Supply Position

Bangladesh does not export minerals. However, oil imports exceeded $50 million in 1975 and $100 million in

1976. Most coal needs were met by imports, including nearly 700,000 tons from India in 1975. The fertilizer produced from natural gas is consumed locally, and much more could be used. The roughly 80,000 tons of steel produced in 1975 was based mainly upon imported scrap. Small quantities of construction materials are produced and consumed.

Nature of Mineral Enterprise

Bangladesh has only a limited number of gas fields, some small mines, a few mineral and industrial plants, and one fair-sized oil refinery. Sizable additional natural gas resources and a coal deposit can be developed. Various mineral-related industrial plants are planned, and government corporations will be the principal vehicle for production. There is a proposal to build a large limestone mine and cement works in Jaipurhat, Bogra District.

Principal Mineral Industries

Natural gas has been produced at Semutang north of Chittagong port from reserves totaling possibly 300 billion cubic meters. National resources may be three to four times as much if the gas fields found in the Chittagong Hill Tract in 1973 are any indication. A 340,000-tpy urea plant located at Ghorasal produced at half capacity in 1975. The Indian government has entered into a joint venture with the Bangladesh government to build a 2,200-tpd fertilizer plant in Bangladesh.

There is a 1.5 million-tpy oil refinery near Chittagong, which has been worked far below capacity because of the high cost of importing Middle East crude. In 1975, Bangladesh imported about 770,000 tons of crude oil and 470,000 tons of refined oil. Onshore oil is known to occur in the Chittagong Hill Tract and in Sylhet. Drilling for oil was started in the Bay of Bengal in October 1975 by a subsidiary of the Japan Petroleum Development Corp. Five other international oil companies have been engaged in preliminary exploration.

There are a 250,000-tpy scrap-based steel plant and a small cement plant at Chittagong. The Indians have offered to help build a 500,000-tpy direct-reduction sponge iron plant based upon natural gas. The Bangladesh Mineral Development Company has been investigating the Jamalganj coal deposit.

Mine and Industry Workers

Bangladesh has hardly any mines and mine workers. Only a limited number of workers are employed at the few gas fields and industrial plants in the country. New workers will have to be trained for new projects. The Indians are providing some special help.

Mineral Transport

Bangladesh has about 3,000 kilometers of railroads, 6,000 kilometers of roads, numerous waterways (including the Ganges and Jamuna rivers), and the big industrial port city of Chittagong. Few heavy minerals have as yet been produced. Access roads will be a future problem. The natural gas of the Chittagong Hill Tract should be important to industrial development in the southeastern coastal region.

Energy and Power

Energy demand is mainly met by natural gas and imported fuels. Annual needs for oil and coal are about 1.5 million tons each for both minerals. For 1977, Iran has agreed to supply 400,000 tons of crude oil and the United Arab Emirates, 600,000 tons. Electric power output has been only about 1 billion kilowatt-hours yearly, reflecting a very low standard of living.

Summary Outlook

Further development of natural gas and related industries (fertilizers and direct-reduction steel) will have an important bearing on the economy. The effort to produce coal at Jamalganj should be of some significance. At least six international oil firms are engaged in offshore exploration, and the Soviets are helping onshore as well. The severe inflation could possibly be alleviated by expanding production. Larger industries will be mostly government-run, and funds for capital investment are a critical problem. Oil capital is available through production-sharing contracts, and success in oil search will be of great significance.

In March 1977, it was announced that the Union Oil Company of California's wholly owned subsidiary struck gas in the Bay of Bengal about fifty miles offshore and sixty miles southwest of Chittagong at a depth of about 8,750 feet. The well—Kutubdia No. 1—in twenty-seven feet of water, tested gas at a rate of 18 million cubic feet per day through a three-quarter-inch choke. Another well being drilled by Ina-Naftaplin of Yugoslavia is also most promising. Onshore gas at Muladi in Barisal District and at Begamganj in Noakhali District appears to be promising, too. Thought has been given to installation of liquefied natural gas (LNG) facilities—with a view toward earning foreign exchange.

Illustration for Chapter 4

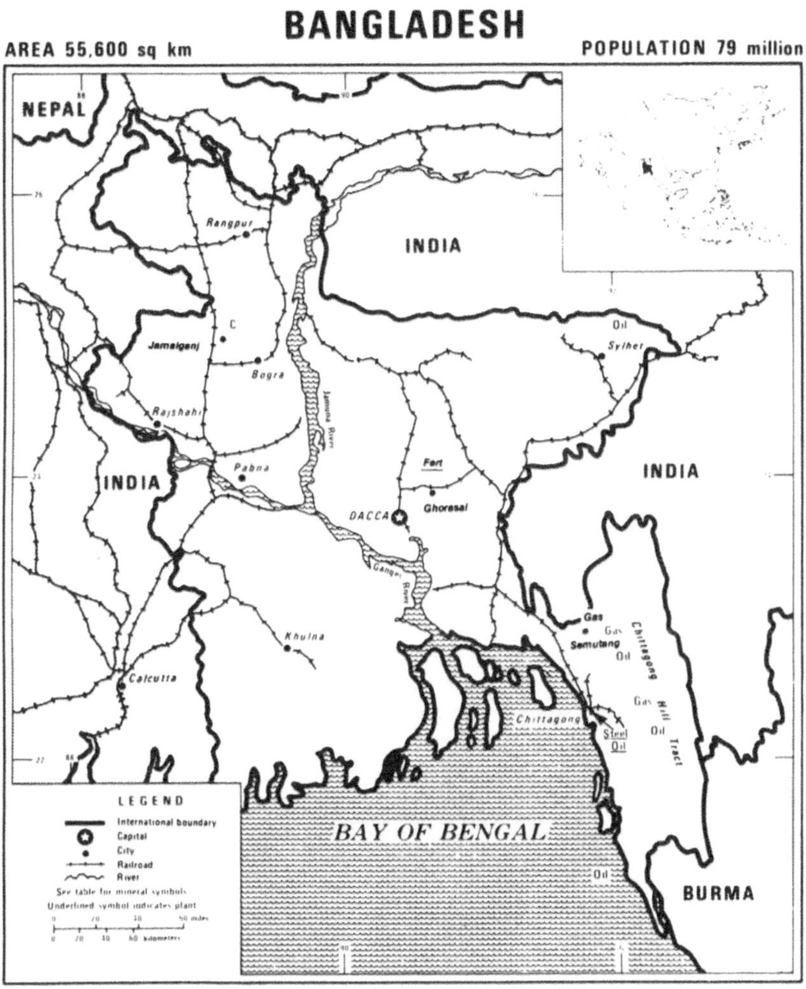

Figure 6 Map of Bangladesh

5
Bhutan

The Kingdom of Bhutan, with just over a million people, is a landlocked Himalayan country bounded by China's Tibetan plateau and the Assam-Bengal plains of northeastern India. Bhutan has an agrarian and pastoral economy, with the weather varying with the altitude. It relies heavily on foreign financial aid and technical assistance, mainly through the Colombo Plan. Although its people's racial and cultural affinities are with Tibet and Nepal, Bhutan's close economic links today are with India rather than Tibet.

The use of Bhutanese and Indian currency is replacing barter as the principal means of exchange. India has been financing Bhutan's recent economic development plans, and its pledge for the Third Five-Year-Plan (1971-1976) was $47.2 million, compared with $26.6 million for the Second Five-Year-Plan.

Forests, meadows, and grasslands cover much of Bhutan. The country is self-sufficient in food, however, and rice, wheat, barley, and maize are the main crops. The economy is primitive, and there are no GNP estimates. Bhutanese postage stamps remain the major source of foreign exchange. There is hardly any mineral industry. The hydropower potential is fairly good. The 18,000-kilowatt Jaldhaka River plant provides power to West Bengal and southwestern Bhutan. Another project is under construction—a 300,000-kilowatt plant at Chukha.

Illustrations for Chapter 5

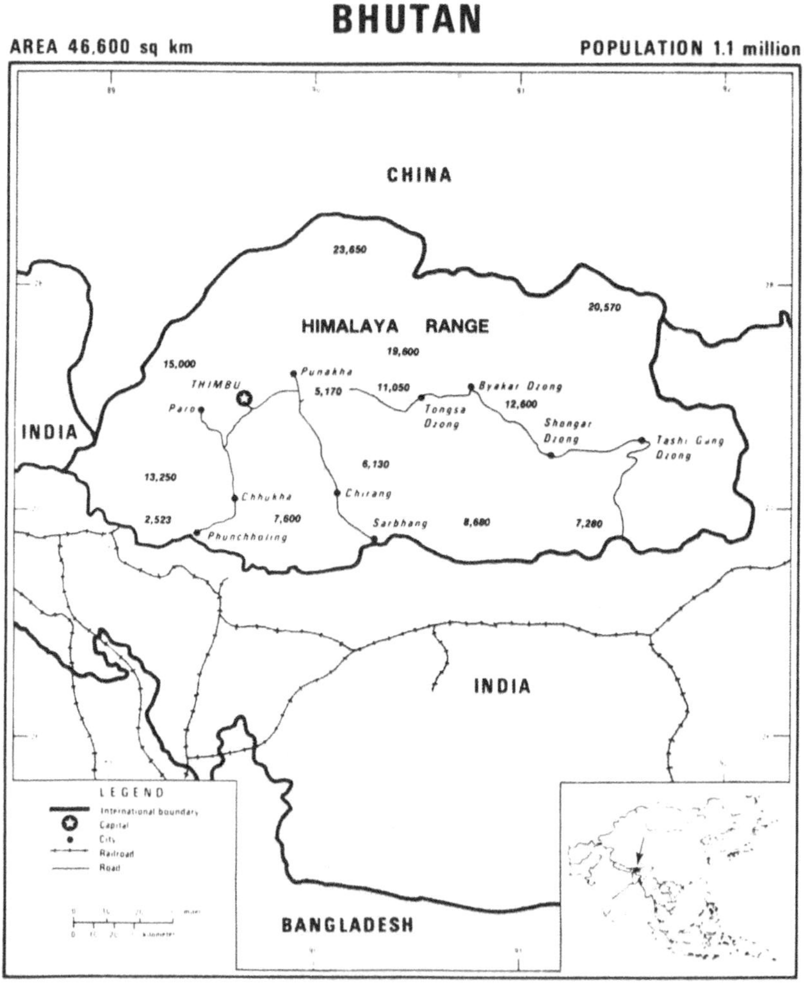

Figure 7 Map of Bhutan

Thimpu's Tashichho Dzong

"Tiger's Nest" at Taksang

Figure 8 Scenes from the mountainous kingdom of Bhutan

6
Brunei

The Sultanate of Brunei, a British protectorate with only 150,000 people, is located in northeastern "Borneo." Brunei is divided into two separate parts, each surrounded by Sarawak and the South China Sea. For many years, Brunei produced nothing but a little rubber and timber. However, its first oil field was discovered in 1920, and within a few years, Brunei became one of the richest states per capita in Asia. Brunei holds the distinction of being the first Far Eastern country to produce liquefied natural gas (LNG).

Significance of Minerals

GNP in 1975 was about $1.2 billion, predominantly from oil and natural gas, which overshadowed rubber and timber. Brunei's oil output represents about a third of a percent of the world's total, especially significant for a small country. Brunei is one of the few LNG producers of the world.

Mineral Supply Position

Brunei exports by far the bulk of the crude oil, liquefied natural gas, and petroleum products produced. Its oil and gas products already earn nearly $1 billion annually of foreign exchange, and crude output is scheduled to be more than doubled within five years. Brunei imports almost all the foodstuffs, manufactured products, machinery, and luxury items that it uses.

Nature of Mineral Enterprise

Brunei's only mineral industries are related to oil and gas. Brunei Shell Petroleum, a subsidiary of Royal Dutch Shell and 25 percent owned by the government of Brunei, operates the country's oil fields and the only gas field (offshore). In the near future, Brunei Shell will also "take delivery of new offshore oil and gas production packages." Royal Dutch Shell is associated with Japan's Mitsubishi enterprise in the LNG project, which is scheduled to deliver $2.6 billion worth of LNG to Japan under a twenty-year contract.

Principal Mineral Industries

Brunei's predominantly offshore oil fields together produced just over 200,000 barrels per day (equal to over 10 million metric tons) of crude oil in 1975 and 1976. Oil reserves were approximately 150 million tons in early 1977. The Ampa (S.W. Ampa) field produces more than the other three put together (Champion, Fairly, and Seria). The nine new platforms working in 150 feet of water are designed for 30,000 bpd each. Brunei's crude is mostly exported as such, but a part first goes to the nearby 60,000-bpd Shell refinery at Lutong in Sarawak, Malaysia. Natural gas production, now more than 750 million cubic feet per day (or 20 million cubic meters per day), comes mainly from the offshore operation at Bintula. The gas is piped to the onshore LNG plant at Lumut within the country. Brunei also produces over 3 million barrels (about 400,000 metric tons) of natural gas liquids yearly.

Mine and Industry Workers

Fewer than two-thirds of the population are Brunei citizens. There is a shortage of skilled workers, most of whom are foreign nationals. Additional Brunei workers for new projects must be specifically trained and lured away from other, possibly more attractive, occupations.

Mineral Transport

A terminal was completed in 1972 at Seria; it permits crude oil to be exported directly instead of being first piped to

Malaysia's Lutong refinery. Offshore gas is piped to the LNG plant onshore, which loads special LNG vessels.

Energy and Power

Indigenous oil and natural gas and the electric power produced therefrom, of course, can easily support the small industry and population of Brunei.

Summary Outlook

Shell maintains an exploration and development drilling program in Brunei with a view toward more than doubling the production of oil and gas by 1980. The government has asked for tenders for a cost and feasibility survey on setting up a national shipping company.

Illustration for Chapter 6

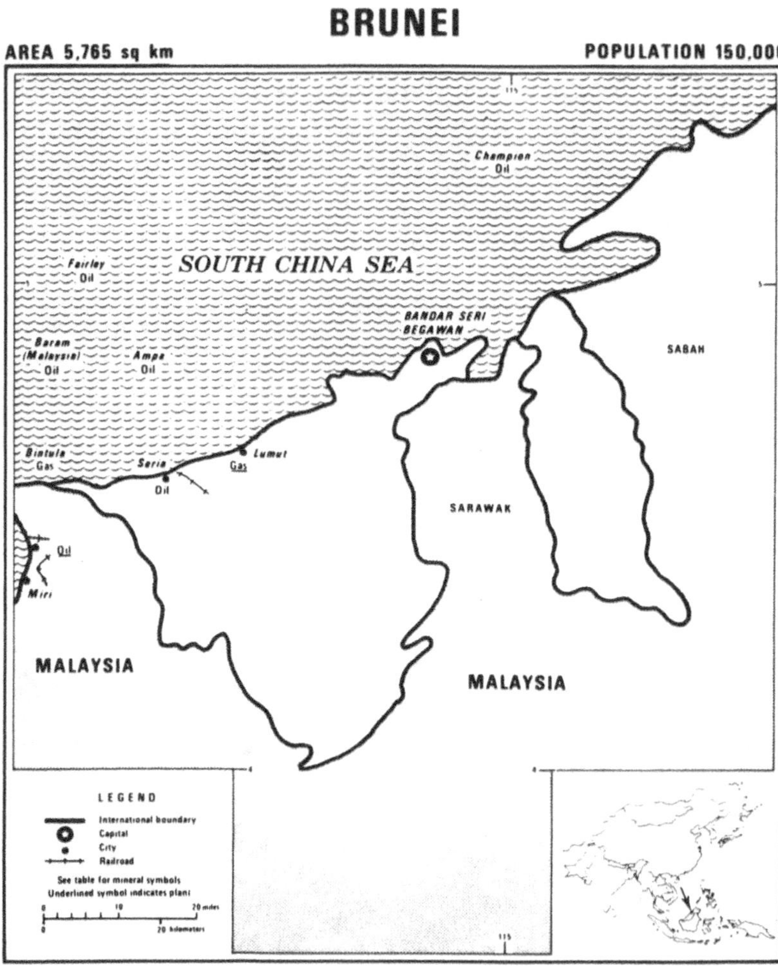

Figure 9 Map of Brunei

7
Burma

Burma has long been known as a promising mineral country, starting from the days when President Herbert Hoover helped develop the fabulous Bawdwin lead-zinc-silver mine, whose ores contained one-third metal. Another premier mine—Mawchi—was famed for its tin-tungsten. Burma was also one of the first countries to produce oil in Asia. Today, however, the rich ores are depleted, and new mines have not been developed. In fact, Burma's mineral economy has literally been at a standstill since the end of World War II. Although there is good potential for developing new mineral prospects, this gives only hope and no comfort for the present.

This country of 30 million people, with a 60-percent literacy rate, has been isolated and poor, despite the fact that it is one of the world's rice bowl areas. Rice output has been down ever since the local Chinese rice growers left the trade. Foreign investment has not been encouraged. The Burmese citizen does not want for food, but neither does he have much purchasing power and money to buy imports. Burma has not had much economic contact with the outside world for decades. However, a $40-million loan from Western banks to help finance an oil pipeline was sought in early 1977. There is little industry, and mineral requirements are low. Burma still has insurgency problems that affect its political stability.

TABLE 6. BURMA: ROLE IN WORLD MINERAL SUPPLY
(Thousand metric tons, unless otherwise noted)

Major Commodities (Map Symbols)	Production 1976[e]	1975	1974	World Output Share, 1975	Trade in 1975 Exports or Imports	Reserves (or Raw Materials)
Metals						
Lead, refined (Pb, tons)..	3,200	9,700	9,000	0.3%	Exports--9.5	(10^6 mine lead)
Silver (Ag, 10^3 oz).......	211	775	722	0.3%	Exports--560	Moderate
Tin, mine (Sn, tons)......	500	700	650	0.3%	Exports--700	Moderate
Tungsten, mine (W, tons)..	300	400	400	1 %	Exports--400	Moderate
Zinc, mine (Zn, tons).....	2,200	4,000	4,200	0.1%	Exports--4.0	5×10^5 plus tailings
Nonmetals						
Cement (Cem)..............	239	228	180	Minute	Small imports	(Adequate)
Fuels						
Oil, crude (Oil)..........	1,100	900	1,100	Minute	Imports--120(1974)	12,000
Oil, refined (Oil)........	1,200	1,000	1,000	Minute	Imports--100 (1974)	(Moderate)

e estimated

Significance of Minerals

Burma's 1975 GNP was about $3 billion, and mineral output value was estimated at $37 million. Real GNP growth has been minimal in the last decade, and real mineral output value has not changed much either.

Burma's metallic minerals have always been exported. But the reduced tonnage now produced and exported does not earn much foreign exchange. Local oil has been helpful to the economy, but output has not been adequate in recent years.

Mineral Supply Position

Under British rule, Burma was a true mineral exporter, exporting at its peak 40,000 tons of mine zinc annually, 80,000 tons of refined lead, 2,500 tons of tin and 1,500 tons of tungsten contained in mixed tin-tungsten concentrates, and 3,000 tons each in clean tin and tungsten concentrates. As an independent country in the post–World War II period, Burma exported the same minerals but at less than one-fifth the historic peak levels.

Nature of Mineral Enterprise

All important mineral organizations are run by the government. The Ministry of Mines of Burma was reorganized in April 1975. It now comprises the Minister's Office, Planning and Inspection Department, Geological Survey and Exploration Department, Myanma Oil Corporation (MOC), Myanma Bawdwin Corporation, Myanma Mineral Development Corporation, Myanma Tin and

Tungsten Corporation, and Industrial Mineral Corporation. The former Myanma Oil Corporation Refinery and Petroleum Products Sales Corporation are now under the Ministry of Industry.

The government intends to step up production of minerals during the Second Four-Year-Plan, which started in 1975/76, and envisages an annual 4-percent growth rate. Burma also hopes to achieve self-sufficiency in oil during the second plan and to export oil as well.

Without much domestic funds and international investments, Burma has had to accept technical aid and foreign grants in the form of small projects. The United Nations helped the Bawdwin mine with exploration some years back, and now the West Germans are rendering assistance to double output. The UNDP has started a $1.3-million, three-year tin exploration program in the Tenasserim region and will help drill the Monywa copper deposit, which has 80 million tons of low-grade reserves indicated.

The West Germans are also helping to modernize the Heinda tin mines in the northern Shan states and are involved with a natural gas project. The Soviets are still helping to rebuild Mawchi, and the Japanese are studying the Monywa copper project in terms of milling and smelting. The United Nations Industrial Development Organization is assisting the Syriam Oil Refinery in training personnel. The British will provide a 1.9-million-pound grant to buy trucks and spares for the rig transport and supporting bulldozers required for onshore oil production.

Principal Mineral Industries

The Bawdwin enterprise near the Burma Road is burdened with old equipment and is reportedly operating at a loss. Underground ore reserves may be about 6 million tons, and open-pit reserves may be 10 million tons. Annual output is about 160,000 tons of ore, containing 7 percent lead, just under 4 percent zinc, much silver, and some copper, antimony, and nickel. There is an old, but large, lead smelter with by-product recovery facilities, but zinc is sold as concentrates. The West Germans made a commitment to spend 65 million marks to convert the mine from underground to open-pit operations so as to double output, but unsettled security conditions may divert the money to other uses. Bawdwin also has rich zinc tailings.

The Mawchi enterprise in Kayah State, once the largest single tin-tungsten producer in the world, is producing only 600 to 700 tons of mixed concentrates annually. The Soviets are trying to help raise output to 1,800 tons, with no apparent success as yet. The UNDP project on the Tenasserim coast partly involves a tin dredge offshore, but again the insurgency problem makes the status of the project uncertain. In fact, Burmese and Thai operators are sporadically involved in smuggling activities both ways across the border.

Burma's small oil industry is producing at about 21,000 bpd from about 520 wells. The new wells at Mann provide 60 percent of current output. When a fifty-two-mile, ten-inch pipeline is completed between the new Letpando field and Chauk, national production could be doubled. There are two small refineries, one at Yenangyaung near the oil fields and another at Syriam, 300-odd miles to the south, near Rangoon. An old pipeline connecting the two areas was destroyed during World War II and never rebuilt. Burma has four production-sharing offshore contracts with Cities Service, France's Pétroles, a Japanese consortium, and a subsidiary of Esso. No offshore oil has yet been found, with roughly ten wells drilled. A third refinery of 25,000 bpd will be built at Mann with a $100-million loan from Japan.

Mine and Industry Workers

There are few industrial workers in Burma. The Bawdwin enterprise has about 6,000 workers, about half at the mines. No statistics are available for the other projects, but Mawchi and Tenasserim each has "thousands of workers," and the oil industry may have up to 10,000 workers.

Mineral Transport

Burma's only important railroad is from an area near the Bawdwin enterprise to Rangoon, but this railroad has been disrupted from time to time. For the tin-tungsten areas, the shipment of concentrate presents no problem. However, transport of equipment is difficult; besides, the security situation is bad. Oil is shipped south on the Irrawaddy River and by railroad, and there are some pipelines in the oil field area. The cement plants are not too far from Rangoon and are accessible by both roads and railway. Developing the Monywa copper deposit in the north would be difficult. Overall, transport facilities are rather inadequate.

Energy and Power

Burma could supply its own oil needs from domestic resources. There is a small lignite deposit. The low levels of industrial activity require little fossil fuel. Electric power-generating capacity is only about 400,000 kilowatts, mostly in Rangoon but some at the different mining centers as well. New industrial projects would need auxiliary power plants. Burma produces and consumes about 850 kilowatt-hours of electric power annually.

Summary Outlook

Burma has not been able to reassert itself as a mineral producer under present conditions. Insurgent activities make carrying out projects in most areas of the country uncertain. Funds for evaluating Burma's true mineral potential have not been forthcoming. The government has little money to invest, and foreign companies cannot participate except on a consulting basis. Some worthwhile work has been done by the United Nations, East and West Europe, and Japan. During the last decade, Burma's state investments were minimal, totaling possibly $100 million, and combined outside commitments are considerably less than $50 million. Thus, unless the mining climate is markedly improved, no great upturn in mineral production should be expected. The outlook for oil looks a little more hopeful, since something might be done at least onshore. Offshore, various oil firms are making serious exploration efforts, although not on an extensive scale.

Illustrations for Chapter 7

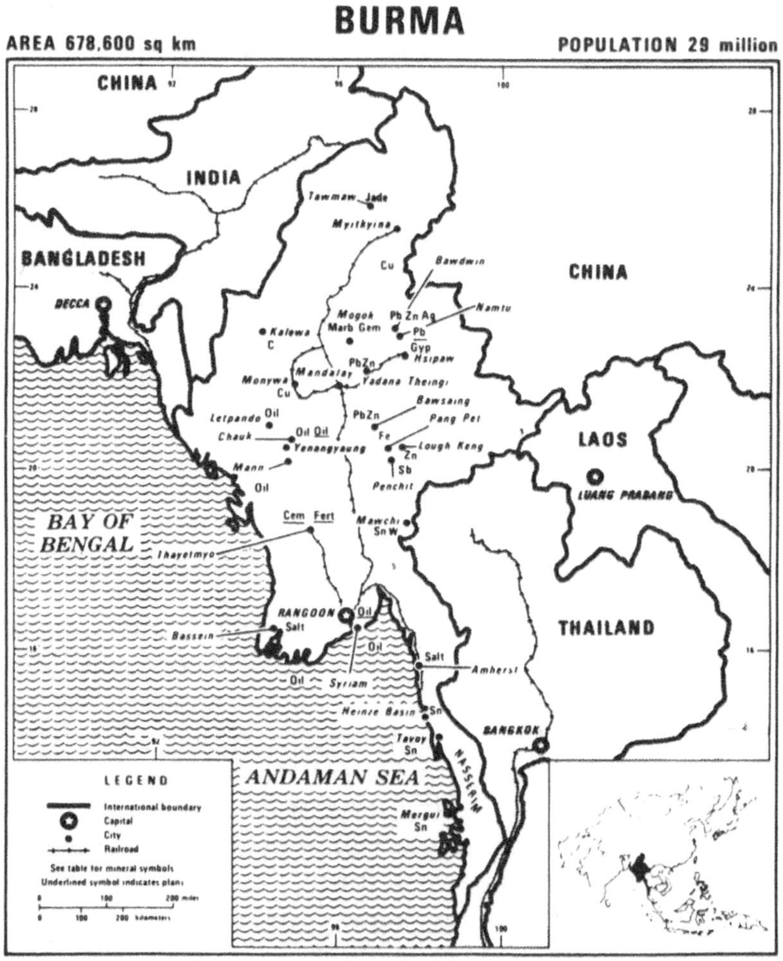

Figure 10 Map of Burma

Figure 11 Buddha and temples in Burma

Figure 12 General scenes of Burma

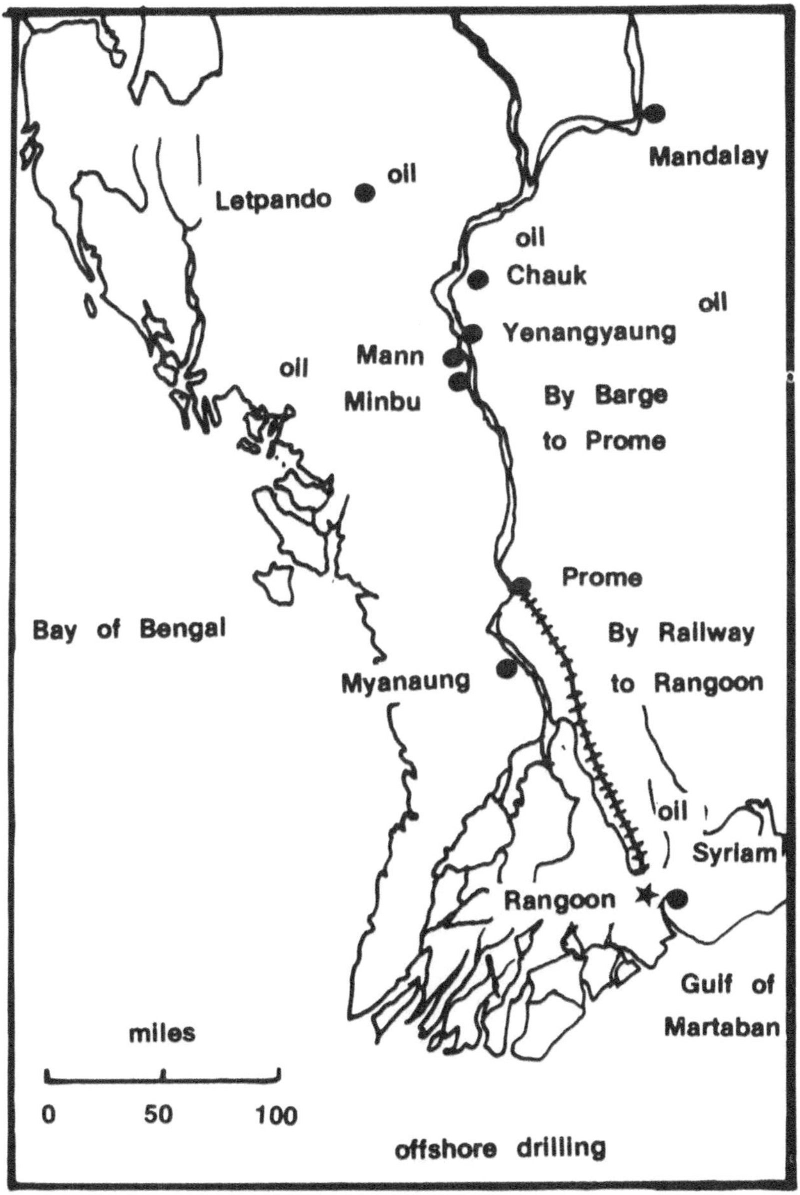

Figure 13 Oil facilities in Burma

8
Cambodia

Cambodia was formerly a rich, rice-surplus country, roughly comparable to West Malaysia in both population and land area. It is also half covered with dense forests and jungle areas. Until April 1975, however, it was embroiled in an internecine war, which disrupted economic activity and caused rampant inflation. On January 5, 1976, a new constitution was adopted by the Khmer Rouge government, and the country was renamed Democratic Kampuchea. Massive foreign aid from France, West Germany, the United States, and the People's Republic of China has been sustaining the economy. Cambodia has potentially promising mineral resources capable of supporting moderate levels of production.

Significance of Minerals

Even before the war, minerals and industries played a role secondary to agriculture. Under stable conditions, however, a variety of minerals can be developed for local and foreign markets. The only significant minerals produced so far are phosphates, refined oil, cement, and salt. All foreign properties and major industries have been nationalized since the war.

Mineral Supply Position

Cambodia does not produce any minerals for world markets, except for small amounts of gemstones. It imports refined oil products because its oil refinery at Kompong Som is reportedly inoperable. It extracts some construction materials for the local market and buys limited quantities of foreign metal products.

Nature of Mineral Enterprise

Commercially viable deposits of phosphates, iron ore, bauxite, manganese ore, silica, gold, gemstones, and pagotite have reportedly been identified. However, only the phosphate deposits at Tuk Meas in Kampong Province and at Mongkol Borei and Phnom Sampou in Battambang Province have been tapped from reserves totaling "hundreds of thousands of tons." It can be expected that fertilizers will receive priority attention. Copper lodes found years ago in Kompong Thom are still not worked. To the north near Phnom Deck, three iron ore deposits with combined reserves of 5 million tons have been reported. Coking coal occurs near Talat. There is also manganese ore in Kompong Thom Province. There was talk about building a small steel wire and bar plant. Studies have been made on bauxite found in the early 1960s north of Battambang and smelting possibilities. The government's role may well be vital in any large mineral and industrial project.

Principal Mineral Industries

There is an oil refinery at Kompong Som built with French help in 1968; it is said to have been severely damaged during the war. This refinery had an installed output capability of 400,000 tons of oil products annually, which is adequate for present needs. A 100,000-ton cement plant utilizing local limestone from Charey Ting is in operation. Small quantities of sapphires and rubies have been produced in Pailin, Battambang.

Mine and Industry Workers

For lack of mines and industry, Cambodia will have to

train additional workers for new enterprises. Basically, Cambodians do not have much industrial experience.

Mineral Transport

The only railroad starts along the coast, passes through Phnom Penh, and heads northwest into Thailand. The Mekong River extends inland to Laos. Building roads into the dense forests where the minerals occur is difficult. Mine development will have to be coordinated with road construction (often more than just access roads).

Energy and Power

Cambodia's energy resources have not been carefully surveyed. Two wildcat oil wells were drilled by France's Elf-ERAP offshore before the Khmer Republic fell to the present Khmer Rouge government. However, the question remains whether there is offshore oil near the contested islands of Wai. There are a hydropower plant at Sambaur and a big potential site in Stung Treng. Cambodians will probably work on small hydroelectric stations in the beginning. Generally, power facilities are sadly inadequate, and this area of endeavor should receive high priority.

Summary Outlook

Cambodia's first job is to stabilize the economy, then to rebuild infrastructure and normalize agricultural and manufacturing production. Minerals and industry should receive increasing attention. There seems to be an open mind toward foreign aid from industrialized countries. The fact that Peking has extended a $1 billion loan (spread over five to six years) indicates the Chinese influence and the likelihood of emphasizing basic industries to complement agriculture.

Illustrations for Chapter 8

Figure 14 Map of Cambodia

The world famous Angkor Temple. Angkor, the ancient capital of Kampuchea, is made up of magnificent stone structures and exquisite stone bas-reliefs.

The Kompong Kandal Saltfield run by women.

Phnom Penh, capital of Democratic Kampuchea, is located on the banks of the Mekong.

Figure 15 Cambodia's Angkor Wat and other scenes

9
China

Chinese mineral developments, especially petroleum, have been increasingly in the news. Oil and gas may have great potential, and a very large coal industry is already in existence. The steel industry ranks fifth or sixth in the world. The People's Republic of China (PRC) is also prominent in iron ore (low-grade), fertilizer, cement, and salt production. Various export minerals and metals are well known, including tungsten, tin, antimony, talc, and fluorspar. China is a medium-sized producer of asbestos, magnesite, graphite, and barite. A large diamond deposit reportedly was discovered recently, and the country already produces synthetic diamonds. Considerable quantities of rare earths and rare metals are extracted. The country is also buying heavily in world markets in nonferrous base metals, particularly copper, aluminum, and nickel.

Like the United States and the Soviet Union, and unlike Japan, Canada, and Australia, China is both a large producer and a large consumer of minerals and metals. Development of the rich mineral resources has been essential to the growth of both agriculture and industry. An industrious and disciplined population has been successfully mobilized to work the land efficiently, harness the waters, uncover and extract the resources, and produce the necessary goods and services. Much more can be accomplished, but there is already no question that the Chinese are enjoying a higher

TABLE 7. CHINA: ROLE IN WORLD MINERAL SUPPLY
(Thousand metric tons, unless otherwise noted)

Major Commodities (Map Symbols)	Production 1976	Production 1975	Production 1974	World Output Share, 1975	Trade in 1975 Exports or Imports	Reserves (or Raw Materials)
Metals						
Aluminum, ingot (Al)..	200	200	200	1.5%	Imports--400+	(Sizable, off grade)
Antimony, mine (Sb)...	12	12	12	15 %	Exports--6 (1974)	Perhaps world's leader
Copper, refined (Cu)..	150	150	150	2 %	Imports--140 (1974)	(Moderate, undeveloped)
Iron ore, 50% Fe (Fe).	65,000	65,000	60,000	5 %	Imports--minor	Large, low grade
Iron, steel ingot (St)	27,000	29,000	27,000	4 %	Neither	(Mainly primary)
Lead, refined (Pb)....	100	100	100	2 %	Imports--32 (1974)	(Not plentiful)
Tin, refined (Sn).....	20	22	20	10 %	Exports--15.5	(Large, lode and placer)
Tungsten, mine (W)....	9	9	8.5	20 %	Exports--5.5 (1974)	Largest in world
Zinc, refined (Zn)....	100	100	100	2 %	Imports--8 (1974)	(Possibly recent finds)
Nonmetals						
Asbestos (Asb)........	150	150	150	4 %	Exports--small	Considerable
Barite (Ba)...........	300	250	200	5 %	Exports--125 (1974)	Perhaps extensive
Cement (Cem)..........	35,000	30,000	25,000	3 %	Little trade	(Extensive)
Fluorspar (F).........	350	350	300	7 %	Exports--300 (1974)	First rank
Graphite (Gr).........	30	30	30	7 %	Little trade	Moderate
Magnesite (Mag).......	1,000	1,000	1,000	10 %	Exports--small	First rank
Phosphate rock (P)....	4,000	4,000	3,000	3 %	Imports--400 (1974)	Extensive, uneven grade
Pyrite (Py)...........	2,000	2,000	2,000	8 %	Neither	Moderate
Salt..................	30,000	30,000	25,000	15 %	Exports--1,000	Large, plus seawater
Fuels						
Coal, hard............	480,000	470,000	450,000	17 %	Exports--small	First rank
Natural Gas, 10^6 cu m.	80,000	70,000	60,000	1 %	Neither	Possibly first rank
Oil, crude (Oil)......	90,000	80,000	65,000	2 %	Exports--small	Possibly first rank
Oil, refined (Oil)....	75,000	65,000	60,000	2 %	Exports--small	(Low sulfur, high wax)

NOTE: All data estimated.

standard of living. China's industrial progress was slowed in 1976 because of a series of earthquakes, transportation difficulties, and major political developments.

"Walking on two legs" has been a fundamental policy to develop both large and small industries simultaneously, which creates localized economic strength, cuts down on transportation requirements, and enables industry to serve agriculture better. The Chinese know that small-scale operations can also be worked efficiently. Most Chinese live in the eastern, coastal third of the country, where the markets are and where many of the resources and industries have been developed, particularly in the north and northeast. Since 1971, a new factor has entered Chinese industrial planning—the concept of dispersing industry for strategic reasons.

During the Fourth National People's Congress in January 1975, the PRC's long-term development goals were stated as follows: (1) before 1980, the last year of the Fifth Five-Year Plan, China should have established a relatively independent and integrated industrial system, and (2) before the end of this century, it should become a modern power in all respects.

Significance of Minerals

GNP in 1975 was about $250 billion, placing the PRC solidly in the first ten by world standards. Minerals represented possibly 7-9 percent of GNP. Oil value was close to $7 billion ($8-9 billion in 1976), coal perhaps $5 billion, and metals, nonmetallics, and fertilizers and chemicals on the order of $2 billion each. It is difficult to estimate value added for the mineral industry, but the figure should be sizable. The People's Republic of China knows the importance of mineral resource development to the economy and has placed considerable emphasis in this field.

China is one of the world's rich mineral areas, fully capable of supporting a modern, first-rank industrial economy. Its relative importance should grow significantly in the decade ahead, judging from the resource potential and the developments already under way. As befits a large country with a huge population, China produces a great variety of minerals and metals and ranks within the first three world producers in eight commodities and within the first five world producers in an additional ten commodities. If all minerals are added together for a combined output value, the PRC ranks within the world's first five for crude minerals, and only a little behind the first five in terms of total value added for processed minerals and metals.

Mineral Supply Position

Overall 1975 trade was slightly higher than the $14 billion estimated for 1974, and the balance-of-payments gap was cut down in comparison. However, China sharply reduced imports of agricultural products and complete industrial plants and raised imports of various metals. It imported nearly 5 million tons of finished steel products and exported possibly 10 million tons of crude oil in 1975. Trade circles have reported that the PRC bought well over 400,000 tons of aluminum from abroad during 1975. Imports of copper-lead-zinc and nickel have also been sizable. Recently, China contracted to buy moderate quantities of copper concentrates and high-grade iron ore. There was a lull in mineral and metal imports in 1976, partly because of the difficulty in selling oil, although overall trade was still about $14 billion.

Minerals, metals, fuels, chemicals, fertilizers, mineral-related products, and equipment and plants for mineral and metal development, extraction, and processing are very important components of China's overall trade. Out of the approximately $7.5 billion the PRC imported in 1974, $1.3 billion probably went to complete industrial plants, $900 million to steel products, $400 million to fertilizers and raw materials, $200 million to nonferrous metals, $200 million to ferrous metals, and perhaps $200 million to machinery and equipment for the mineral industry. Of the roughly $6.5 million the PRC exported in 1974, $550 million was oil, $150 million was "export metals," and $10 to $15 million each was salt, fluorspar, coal, talc and magnesia, and other nonmetallics.

Partly in order to avoid another balance-of-payments

deficit, the purchase of complete industrial plants in 1975 was cut by nearly $1 billion over 1974. Steel imports were up at least $300 million, nonferrous metal imports were up perhaps $300 million, and machinery and equipment purchases were above the 1974 levels. The PRC's minister of foreign trade told Peking visitors near the end of 1976 that large-scale foreign trade would be resumed in 1978, particularly purchases of complete plants.

China has become a very large consumer of minerals and metals, as shown by the fact that little of the coal, cement, and salt are exported and only 10-15 percent of the oil is exported. As already mentioned, large quantities of metals and fertilizers are imported to supplement the already sizable output. The approximate tonnages of consumption for 1975 are estimated as follows (in million metric tons): coal, 470; cement, 30; salt, 30; oil, 60 plus; iron and steel (as equivalent ingot), 35 plus; aluminum, close to 0.4; and copper, 0.3. Spurred by the big oil push now under way, Chinese consumption of minerals should increase steadily in the years ahead.

Nature of Mineral Enterprise

China is self-sufficient in most minerals, has large surpluses of many, and is deficient in only a few. No country can be totally independent of raw materials from abroad, nor is it necessarily desirable for this to happen, and China is no exception. The Chinese have done well in fuel supply: they are outstanding in coal and at least moderately good in oil. Iron raw materials are extensive but often low-grade. Fluxing and refractory materials are more than adequate. The PRC is self-sufficient in cement and would like to sell some salt. It is short of sophisticated steel products and very short of copper, aluminum, and nickel.

The technological achievements for Chinese mineral industries have been uneven. For larger and newer facilities, the basic engineering is basically good, but there is room for increased mechanization. Smaller and less efficient facilities serve local needs. The best of the smaller plants are expanded into more conventional operations. China has some of the world's largest and best-designed underground coal mines, but it is weak on open pits. Large iron mines are reasonably efficient, but small ones are crude. Except for some special metals, Chinese metallurgical and fabrication facilities are considerably behind world levels. The Chinese do well in chemicals and refineries.

The government owns and runs virtually everything. It utilizes the design institute to plan and construct; the mines and combines to help carry out the industrial program; the technical conference to exchange and disseminate information countrywide; the schools to test and produce things as well as to impart the concept of emulation among worker groups; the ideas of the workers in technical management; and established industrial complexes to help develop new centers. Specialized areas such as nuclear science, missiles, and computers are not ignored.

The Chinese do well in basic geology, prospecting, and drilling. They drill out oil fields, gas fields, and coalfields thoroughly before development and extraction. A national magnetic survey was completed a few years ago. There are "tens of thousands" of workers engaged in geological surveys. Over a dozen geological institutes are in existence in addition to geology departments in universities. Many worker-peasant-soldier students are enrolled in geology. Great importance is attached to mobilizing the masses to report on ore findings, and many large deposits are discovered this way. People look for mineral deposits while engaged in other work. Many factories make geological equipment and instruments. The Chinese geological force prospects from "the air, sea, land, and underground," and owns considerable drilling equipment. Three important geological maps were published in 1977: a geologic map of China, a tectonic system map of China, and a geologic map of Asia.

Principal Mineral Industries

Extensive coal reserves can support a much larger output. China has some of the world's largest coal bases. About eight produce more than 10 million tons of mine-run coal annually; one of these—Kailan (Kailuan)—normally turns out more than 20 million metric tons, and three others—Tatung, Fuhsin, and Fushun—are in the range of 12 to 18 million tons. Most of the Kailan mines, particularly Tangshan near Tientsin, recently went through severe earthquakes. Tatung will be substantially expanded. There has been a rapid development of coal mines south of the Yangtze River, mostly of medium and small mines.

Chinese oil potential could be great, both onshore and near shore in Pohai Bay. The best producing oil fields so far are continental rather than marine in origin. However, offshore oil discoveries in the south are marine sediments. The three largest oil fields—Taching, Shengli, and Takang—are already producing at high levels, and apparently several others now being developed will also turn out to be important, including the new Yingkou-Chinchou oil field in Liaoning and the Huapei oil field in Hopei. Taching has several large subdivisions, which should soon have a combined annual capacity of perhaps 40 million tons. Shengli and Takang are potentially in the range of 15-20 million tons.

The PRC's steel and cement industries are comparable to those of West Germany, France, Italy, and the United Kingdom. However, the steel industry may not move too fast during the rest of the 1970s, and it only has one large steel base—Anshan—barely within the world's first twenty. In fact, Chinese steel output suffered a setback in 1976. On the other hand, the cement industry is gaining fast on those of the U.S.S.R., the United States, and Japan. China has only four cement plants of 1 million tons annual capacity, but it has a rapidly growing small-scale sector that already produces as much cement as the large plants do.

Most of China's export metals have been famous for decades. China is again the "king of tungsten," and Hsihuashan and Kiangsi are well known in wolframite trade circles. The U.S.S.R. has been the foremost buyer of Chinese tungsten in recent years. Antimony from Hsikuangshan,

Hunan, dominated the world market in World War I, but now China finds itself in the company of South Africa and Bolivia—with not much money to be earned. Kuchiu in Yunnan is one of the largest tin centers of the world, and more high-quality Chinese tin is coming into the United States. There was a lull in Chinese exports of tungsten, tin, and antimony in 1976. Mercury, bismuth, and manganese are difficult to sell abroad.

China has been a major world factor in fertilizer output, consumption, and international trade for more than five years. It produces about 3 million tons of nitrogen (N) annually and consumes over 4 million tons; it is Japan's largest customer by far. The phosphate potential is good, but output is less than one-tenth that of the United States, the world leader. Shantung Province has become a very important producer of various fertilizers. The Chinese "seawater" salt industry is gaining ground on U.S. salt production. The PRC is prominent in pyrite. Northeast China is famous for magnesite and talc. China is a medium-sized producer of asbestos, graphite, fluorspar, and barite.

Mine and Industry Workers

By tradition Chinese workers are diligent, conscientious, and hardworking. They are now disciplined and they are therefore a great asset to the PRC's program of industrial and mineral development. A whole new work force has been trained in the last two decades around the many mines and factories that have been developed. Students and other future technical managers are getting practical experience, and the workers also have an opportunity to learn about technology and management. Another interesting aspect of the Chinese industrial work force is that many women are employed.

For emergencies and new projects, the Chinese are able to mobilize the mine and industry labor force on a national scale. When Tangshan of the Kailan Combine was hit by the recent earthquakes, rescue crews from most other large coal combines pitched in. Workers from the old Yumen oil field helped build the famous Taching field, which in turn dispatched workers to aid the Shengli and Takang oil fields and so on. Mine safety is stressed as part of the socialist doctrine of improving the lot of workers. Workers help to improve the environment and food supply of mining and industrial communities. Generally speaking, the Chinese do not seem to have any particular difficulty in organizing a suitable labor and technical work force for planned projects, except for certain sophisticated areas of technology in which they have had no experience.

Mineral Transport

Although the Chinese intend to build up the west slowly (as exemplified by the effort in Sinkiang), the principal resource and industry locations, the markets, and the population concentrations are still in the eastern third of the country. Generally, transportation facilities are not quite adequate even here, particularly railroads, and this partially explains the Chinese policy of developing "local" industries. Yet, heavy minerals such as coal, iron ore, and construction materials are moved fairly effectively. Before the recent construction of quite a number of pipelines, oil was transported partly in railroad tankers. Highway development has been good, and a push is clearly under way with the greater availability of oil and gas. Internally, China is somewhat short in mineral transport facilities, and externally it is grossly inadequate.

In the eastern part of the country, there are many rivers, which run primarily west to east, and a north-south canal system parallels the coast. Coastal shipping by vessels up to 30,000 dwt has expanded considerably, and the Chinese recently completed a 50,000-dwt ship. Moreover, they are also making "cement" boats in order to save steel. But China is not well equipped with large ports for international shipping. Shanghai has become mainly an inland port. Several northern oil ports have been built to connect with pipelines and accommodate medium-sized ships. If the PRC is to engage in heavy ore traffic, special deep-channel facilities will have to be built.

Energy and Power

China has large resources of coal, oil, gas, hydropower, and nuclear raw materials. Hence, the basic problem is to develop these resources prudently, under clearly defined policies. So far, the program has been fairly successful. Coal has thus far been the foundation of electric power and the principal energy source for cement manufacture. Hydropower has been developed wherever possible. With the greatly increased production of oil and gas, additional facilities of this type are being added to coal-firing facilities. The energy and power "mix" is thus undergoing significant change.

The electric power capacity of the PRC has undergone important growth, but the total is still less than one-tenth of U.S. capacity. Installed hydropower capacity is only 7 to 9 million kilowatts, which is a mere fraction of the potential. The Chinese feel that building large hydrofacilities is expensive. Thermal capacity is about four times the hydrocapacity. The largest hydroelectric generator is 300,000 kilowatts, as compared with 200,000 kilowatts for thermal units. During the 1970s, the Chinese built many medium-sized hydroplants and more than 60,000 small hydroplants around the country, particularly in south and southwest China. A significant recent development is the emphasis on purchasing gas-turbine generating units from Canada and Japan, a development that reflects China's emergence as a significant gas producer and consumer.

Summary Outlook

Chinese mineral trade and purchases of industrial equipment are of great interest. But to the PRC, these are means to an end. Much more important is the production of minerals and metals for internal use—that is, in order to build an economy with viable industries in support of agriculture. The large tonnages already produced are having a profound impact abroad as well as within China and, in due time, should elevate the country to a status comparable with that of the United States, the U.S.S.R., Japan, and Western Europe. Barring internal political problems, China's industry in general and mineral industry in particular can be expected to make steady, if not spectacular, progress.

The country's oil production is at least medium-sized, and a decade from now China may well be producing 200 million metric tons of oil annually. New oil fields being developed seem to be as promising as the producing fields. The natural gas potential is also excellent, considering both the Szechuan gas fields and the gas from oil fields. There is shale oil, too. Much greater consumption of oil and gas is transforming the economy. Exports of petroleum should steadily increase, although China is not expected to become a major oil exporter. The sharp rise in oil prices a few years ago clearly represents a windfall to China.

The coal industry is already comparable to those of the United States and the U.S.S.R., and annual output could well reach 700 million tons by 1985. The problem is to develop more coal in the known areas of the north, particularly major mines, and to develop the many scattered deposits in the south and southwest that could serve local industries. The Chinese understand the interenergy relationships and regional development of fuels and power in conjunction with agriculture, local industries, and electric power. Despite excellent potential, massive hydropower and nuclear power seem to be reserved for the future. Why not? There is oil, gas, and coal for the present.

The steel industry could be producing 60 million tons yearly a decade from now. Magnetic iron is already being recovered from the "taconites," and work has begun to float the hematites or the silica gangue associated with the taconites. Iron resources are extensive but generally low-grade. The ore supply to steelworks is being stabilized, and more high-grade concentrates and sinter are being produced. The country is also rich in manganese, tungsten, molybdenum, magnesite, and fluorspar needed in steelmaking. The coking coal position needs to be improved through better planning. The main problem of the steel industry is capital investment. Without a concerted effort to build from within or to make substantial purchases from abroad, the Chinese steel industry will have to develop slowly. The key is a policy decision in the light of growing balance-of-payments difficulties, which can be resolved only through much expanded oil production and exports.

Nonferrous base metals are a weak link in the Chinese mineral economy. "Export metals" only earn moderate amounts of foreign exchange. The shortage of nickel and chrome may result from a geological deficiency. For other metals (aluminum and copper), the solution of the resource problem may lie in large-scale extraction coordinated with integrated operations and complemented by imports of reasonably priced materials. The annual output of copper and aluminum might be raised to 300,000 and 500,000 tons a decade from now. South and southwest China need to be explored for lead and zinc. The requirements for nonferrous metals continue to mount, and there is no recourse in the next five years except to buy from abroad in substantial quantities.

In nonmetallics, fertilizers to support agriculture are fundamental. Either China itself must produce enough, or monies must be spent abroad to purchase chemical fertilizers and the equipment necessary to expand production. A compromise is in effect now, but in a decade construction already under way will easily raise fertilizer output to more than 8 million tons of contained nitrogen per year. In construction materials, the outlook is for continued rapid expansion of productive facilities, both large and small, and for increasing use of fuel oil and natural gas in the process. Yearly cement output should easily surpass 50 million tons within a decade. Salt output may one day reach U.S. levels. China seems to have good insulating materials, refractories, and clays. Oil drilling requires barite, the output of which can be stepped up. Graphite for foundry use will also grow. Fluorspar has been mainly an export product, but domestic use is expanding as the steel, aluminum, and chemical industries are expanding.

Figure 16 Map of China

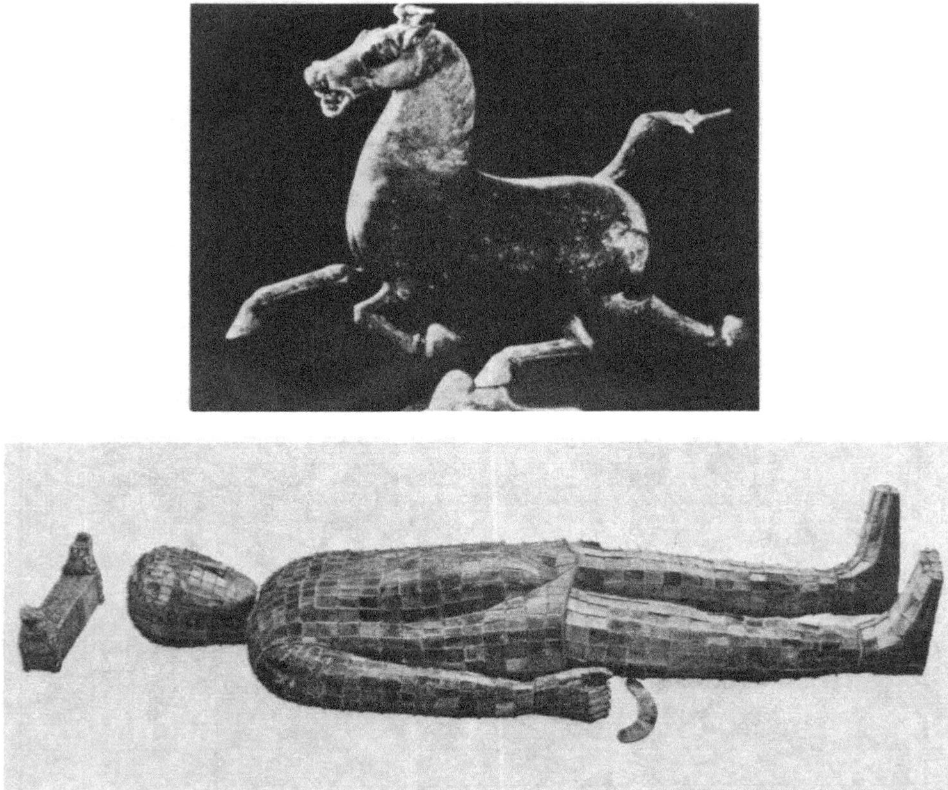

Figure 17 Antiquity of China: a gilded jade suit and a bronze flying horse

Figure 18 The Great Wall in North China

Figure 19 Palace Museum of Peking, with posters

Figure 20 Mourning for Chairman Mao Tse-tung

Figure 21 Mechanization of agriculture will be pushed in China

A team of women fitters laying a new pipeline

An extraction worker

These women are in a refinery maintenance team

The Taiyangsheng Pumping Station, which sends Taching crude oil to the rest of the country, is operated by women

A woman geologist (second from left) discusses plans for opening up a new field with a worker and cadres

On the drilling platform

Figure 22 Chinese women workers in the oil industry

Unloading of coal is highly mechanized at the port of Shanghai

Newly-built crude-oil dock at Chinwangtao

New harbor for 100,000-ton class oil tankers at Talien

Berth which can accommodate two 10,000-ton vessels at Tientsin's Hsinkang

Figure 23 Deepwater berths of China (Shanghai, Talien, Chinwangtao, and Tientsin

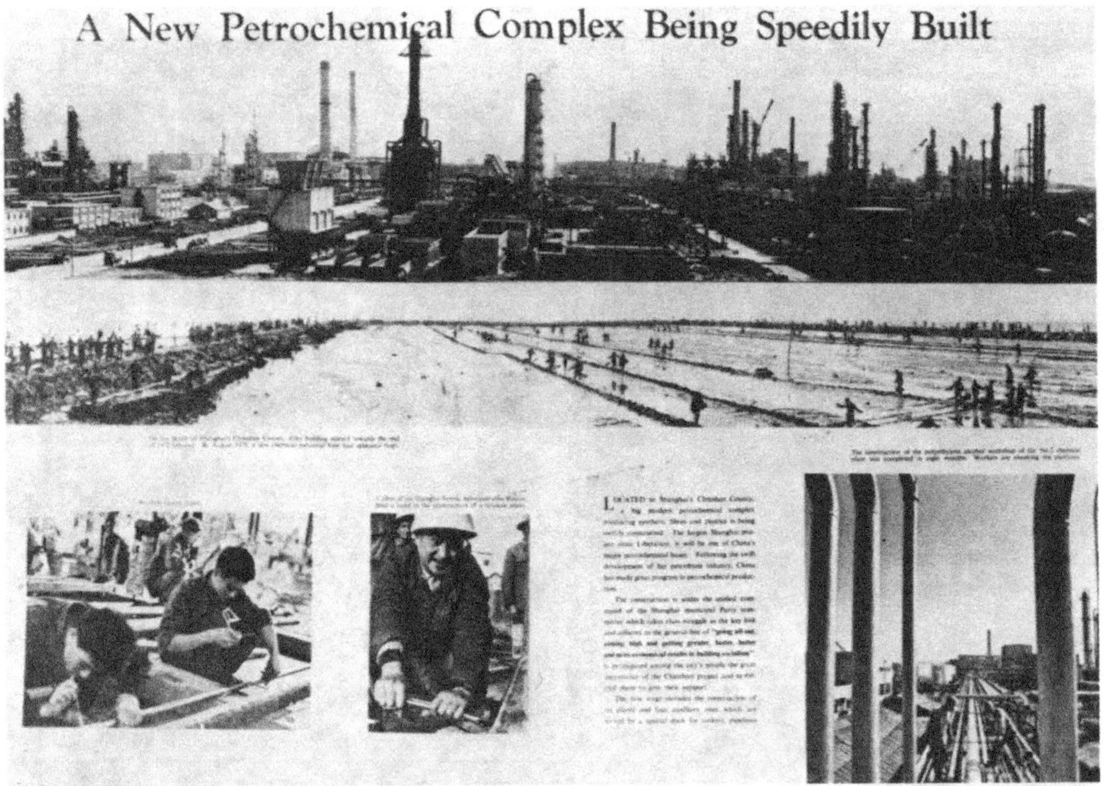

Figure 24 Shanghai's Chinshan refinery and petrochemical complex

Figure 25 New million-ton fertilizer plant in Szechuan based upon natural gas

Figure 26 Tatung Colliery in Shansi—soon to become China's biggest coal base

Figure 27 New Paoting coal base in Southwest China

Figure 28 The Mowming (Maoming) oil center in Kwangtung, South China

Figure 29 One of China's steelworks at night

Shovel working at one of Anshan's iron mines

New million-ton Chisan iron mine near Nanking

Ore dressing plant at Ta-yeh iron mines near Wuhan Steelworks

New iron beneficiation plant of the Capital (Peking) Steelworks at Chiennan

Figure 30 Iron mining in China

Figure 31 The Peimu saltfield in the South China Sea

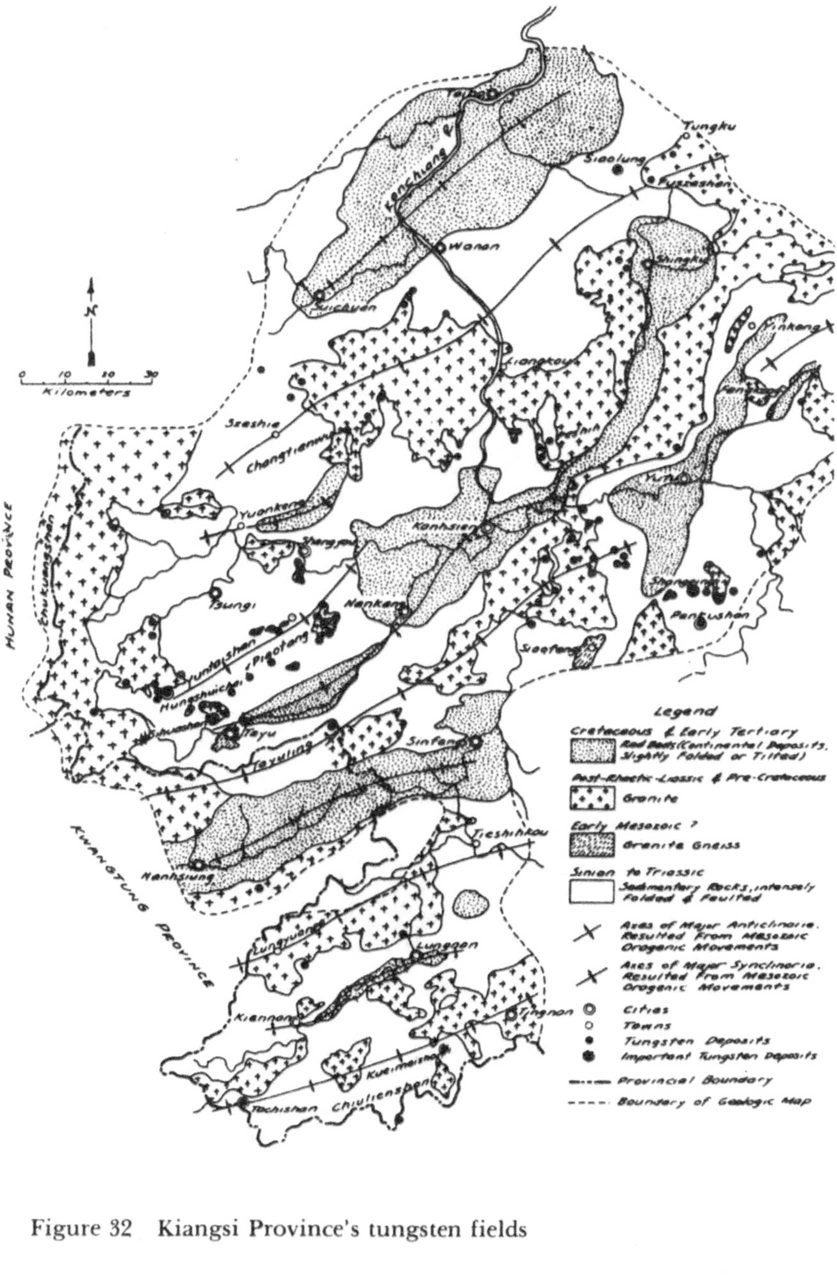

Figure 32 Kiangsi Province's tungsten fields

Figure 33 Industrial and mineral bases—a map in Chinese characters

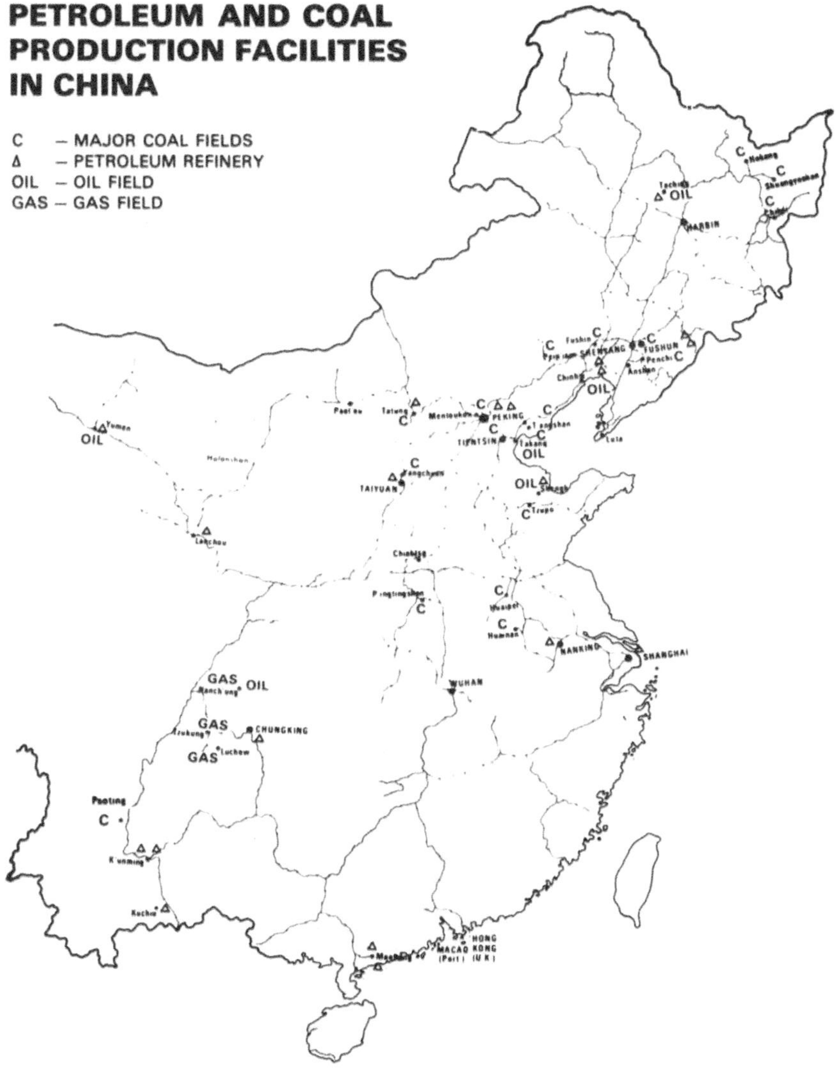

Figure 34 Petroleum and coal facilities in China

Figure 35 Minerals and metals of China

10
Hong Kong

The British Crown Colony of Hong Kong comprises Hong Kong Island, Kowloon Peninsula, Stonecutter's Island, and the New Territories. Under the provisions of the ninety-nine-year lease ratified at the Second Convention of Peking in 1898, most of the land area of the colony will revert to China in 1997, and Hong Kong Island and Kowloon Peninsula remain British in perpetuity. A longtime entrepôt, Hong Kong entered into a period of industrialization in the early 1950s. Presently, the manufacture of textiles and clothing, electronics, plastic products, and toys plays an important role in its economy. Mineral production is understandably rather limited. However, the use of imported fuels has been increasing. Hong Kong is establishing closer economic ties with the People's Republic of China. GNP gained 16 percent in 1976, and the predicted growth in 1977 is 7 percent.

Significance of Minerals

Hong Kong's gross national product in 1975 was $7.2 billion. The largest inputs by sectors were manufacturing, $2.1 billion; social services, $1.54 billion; tourism, $1.52 billion; and transport and storage, $0.43 billion. The value of mining and quarrying—primarily stone aggregate and iron concentrate—was $14.4 million. GNP in 1976 was $9.5 billion.

Mineral Supply Position

Gross imports were valued at $6.7 billion in 1975 and $5.6 billion in 1976, with food, paper products, fabrics, and machinery and transport equipment accounting for over 60 percent. The value of mineral fuels imported for consumption was $425 million in 1975 and $544 million in 1976. Hong Kong's manufacturing industries produce mostly light consumer goods. Textiles, electronics, and plastic products account for more than 70 percent of total exports, which were valued at $6.3 billion in 1975 and $8.5 billion in 1976.

Nature of Mineral Enterprise

The only significant mineral activities in Hong Kong are cement manufacture and the production of iron concentrate. Most of the cement is consumed domestically. In the past, smelting facilities were lacking, and the iron ore produced was exported to Japan.

Principal Mineral Industries

Hong Kong produces modest quantities of cement, iron ore, clays, feldspar, and quartz. Cement is produced by the Green Island Cement Co. in Hung Hom, Kowloon, from imported clinker. Rated at 790,000 tons, Hong Kong's only cement plant produced only 575,000 tons of cement in 1975. The Ma On Shan iron mine in the New Territories, which produces about 150,000 to 170,000 tons of product annually, is nearing the end of its life. An oil refinery has been proposed for Pok Liu Chau Island.

Mine and Industry Workers

Hong Kong's total industrial employment in 1976 was estimated at 774,000 workers, of whom 50 percent were engaged in the garment and textile industries. The plastics and electronics industries were the next two largest employers. Mining and quarrying accounted for only 4,000 workers.

Mineral Transport

The colony is serviced by the Canton-Kowloon railroad,

owned by the Hong Kong government on the Hong Kong side, which handles a substantial proportion of all goods imported from the People's Republic of China. This railroad has been bringing oil from China since August 1974 and has the potential to transport more than 2,000 tons per day. The total length of roads maintained by the Hong Kong government throughout the colony is 1,074 kilometers, of which 341 kilometers are on Hong Kong Island, 317 kilometers in Kowloon, and 416 kilometers in the New Territories. Hong Kong has a natural harbor, which ranges from one to six miles in width and encompasses an area of twenty-three square miles. Hong Kong can handle modern shipping and is a pivotal port in Southeast Asia.

Energy and Power

Hong Kong is dependent on imported fuel, particularly oil, for its energy requirements. During 1976, Hong Kong imported about 1.8 million tons of oil for consumption, possibly 300,000 tons of it from China. The Hong Kong Electric Company, the China Light and Power Company, and the Cheung Chau Electric Company—all fossil-fuel-fired power plants supplying electricity throughout the colony—have a combined capacity of 2,600 megawatts. The Hong Kong and China Gas Company supplies manufactured gas to the urban areas.

Summary Outlook

Hong Kong is not noted for mineral production, but consumption of cement and other construction materials is sizable for a small area. The output of iron ore is phasing out. Hong Kong will continue to depend on foreign fuel and metal supplies. It is well known as an international trade center and in recent years has developed many light industries specializing in the manufacture of consumer goods.

Illustrations for Chapter 10

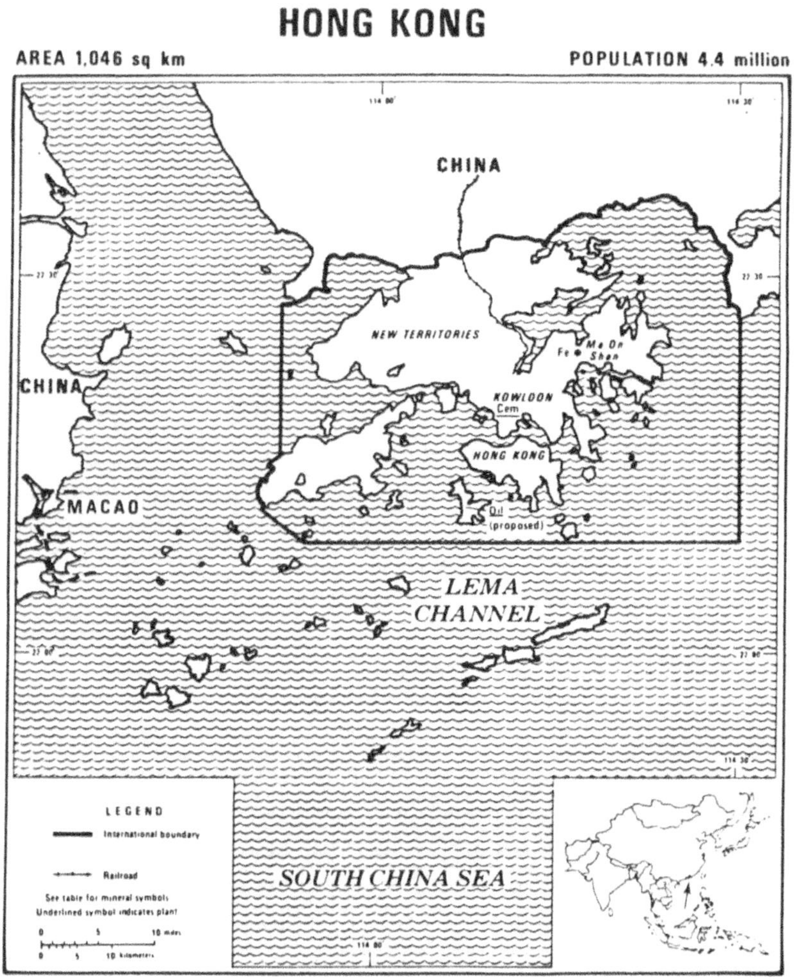

Figure 36 Map of Hong Kong

Business district of Victoria

Aberdeen, fishing junks and high-rise housing estates

Figure 37 Two views of Hong Kong

Figure 38 Crowded market in Kowloon

11
India

India is a mineral producer and consumer of moderate importance, ranking about twentieth in the world in both instances. On the basis of per capita output, the country must be considered poor. However, India is richly endowed with basic resources for industrialization, especially with iron, coal, and construction raw materials. More recently, moderate quantities of oil have been found. Coal production is sizable by world standards. There are also large quantities of high-grade iron ore available for domestic consumption and export. India is greatly lacking in nonferrous base metals, although more indigenous resources can eventually be developed to alleviate this deficiency.

Mineral development is being promoted as a matter of national policy. The Fifth Five-Year Plan, ending in 1979, seeks to raise the production of coal to 125 million metric tons (revised), iron ore to 60 million tons, steel to possibly 10 million tons, cement to 25 million tons, and oil up to 20 million tons. Many nonferrous mines and smelters are planned for development and construction, and it is hoped that capacity can be doubled in a few years' time and that foreign exchange expenditures for imports can thereby be reduced.

To achieve these objectives, government involvement has been stressed in mixed state-private enterprises in recent years, an involvement made necessary by the lack of adequate private capital, the complexities of individual state programs, and the difficulty of overcoming Indian traditions, which have somewhat restrained industrialization. The results of the March 1977 elections may well cause modifications or delay of some industrial programs now being planned, especially for coal.

India maintains neutrality in international affairs and in economic activities as well. For example, India welcomes Japanese, U.S., and Iranian investments and other foreign joint ventures but also has numerous ties through trade and technical assistance with the Soviet Union and East European countries. Many of the foreign undertakings in India are in the minerals and metals field.

Significance of Minerals

India's GNP during fiscal year 1975/76 was $85 billion. Minerals are obviously important; coal production alone is worth at least $2 billion at world prices, and the value added of iron ore and steel together was possibly $1 billion. In addition, the gross value in output for cement and other construction materials, ferroalloys, and ores such as bauxite is considerable, as is the value added for nonferrous metals, chemicals and fertilizers, and miscellaneous minerals such as mica. Most of the coal, construction materials, steel products, and fertilizers and about a third of the iron ore are used locally. These materials are very important for the industrial progress the country has thus far achieved, especially for power generation and transportation.

In terms of world output, India ranks about sixth in coal, iron ore, and manganese; first in mica; close to tenth in cement; and within the first twenty in steel. India is in the process of expanding its basic mineral industries, including crude oil production and refining.

Mineral Supply Position

India is one of the world's important exporters of iron ore, comparable in the lower quantity range of exporting countries like Australia, U.S.S.R., Canada, and Brazil. In

TABLE 8. INDIA: ROLE IN WORLD MINERAL SUPPLY
(Thousand metric tons, unless otherwise noted)

Major Commodities (Map Symbols)	Production 1976	1975	1974	World Output Share, 1975	Trade in 1975 Exports or Imports	Reserves (or Raw Materials)
Metals						
Aluminum, bauxite (Al)....	1,430	1,270	1,113	1.7%	Small exports	1,500,000
Aluminum, ingot (Al)......	211	167	129	1.3%	Insignificant	Not applicable
Copper, refined (Cu, tons)	24,699	21,940	16,000	0.3%	Unknown	Small
Iron, ore (Fe)............	42,600	41,297	35,306	4.7%	Exports--25,000	10,500,000
Iron, pig iron (Fe).......	10,000	8,390	7,340	1.7%	Neither much	(Domestic iron ore)
Iron, steel ingot (St)....	9,230	7,900	6,900	1 %	Neither	(Local pig mainly)
Manganese, ore (Mn).......	1,697	1,531	1,474	7 %	Mostly exported	200,000
Rutile (Ru, tons).........		3,330	3,400	1 %	Neither	Not known
Zinc, mine (Zn, tons).....	25,500	23,600	16,600	0.4%	Neither	Moderate
Nonmetals						
Barite (Ba)...............	NA	171	140	3 %	Large exports	Moderate
Cement (Cem)..............	18,500	16,200	14,300	2 %	Neither	(Extensive)
Kyanite (Ky, tons)........	NA	50,300	45,300	10 %	Sizable exports	Sizable
Mica (tons)...............	NA	11,200	18,200	65 %	Bulk exported	Very extensive
Phosphate rock (P)........	613	429	434	0.4%	Imports--1,100 in 1974	Moderate
Salt......................	NA	7,000	6,000	2 %	Little either way	Moderate
Fuels						
Coal, hard................	101,000	95,000	88,000	4 %	Nominal exports	115,000,000
Oil, crude (Oil)..........	8,569	8,282	7,500	0.3%	Imports--13,930	Undetermined
Oil, refined (Oil)........	22,000*	21,000	20,000	1 %	Imports--2,180	(Mostly imports)

NA Not available
* 1976 refinery crude oil input was 22.762 million metric tons.

1975, iron ore exports were about 25 million tons valued at over $250 million. India's export position for manganese ore is similar; it competes with countries such as the U.S.S.R., South Africa, Brazil, Gabon, and Australia. India's coal exports may have reached 2 million tons in 1976. The country has provided as much as two-thirds of all of the world's best mica and splittings, but international markets on mica are softening.

The country is rather deficient in many nonferrous metals, particularly in this interim period when local resources are not fully developed. During the next few years, India will need to import about 20,000 to 30,000 tons of copper and zinc and 10,000 to 15,000 tons of lead every year. Nickel, tin, and tungsten are almost entirely imported. The combined yearly cost of India's needs for these metals may amount to $100 million. In 1974 India imported about 1.3 million tons of steel products valued at more than $200 million. The country is also deficient in various nonmetallics, includng chemical fertilizers, diamonds, phosphates, sulfur, fluorspar, and asbestos. However, the most striking shortage for the moment is petroleum, and the oil import bill for 1976 was estimated at $1.5 billion.

India is consuming increasing tonnages of minerals. It is estimated that in the next few years it will need annually about 25 to 30 million tons of oil, over 100 million tons of coal, 10 to 15 million tons of steel, up to 300,000 tons of aluminum, 50,000 tons each of copper and zinc, 20,000 tons of lead, 3,000 tons of nickel, 2,000 tons of tin, and 1,000 tons of tungsten.

Nature of Mineral Enterprise

India's mining started from the little-mechanized coal mines of the Bengal-Bihar belt. The new surge in coal demand, spurred by the steep rise in oil prices, will bring more mechanized mines into production in Madhya Pradesh, Maharashtra, Andhra Pradesh, Orissa, and Bengal-Bihar. Cement plants have been constructed as needed near many cities and industrial areas. Fertilizer operations are being built up. As a result of rising energy requirements and costs,

India's oil search, particularly offshore, is being intensified. The steel industry had an early start with the Tata enterprise, but new plants are mainly government projects. India still imports sizable quantities of steel products. Meanwhile, the rich and abundant iron ore deposits of Kiriburu, Bailadila, Goa, and elsewhere have been developed, mainly for export to Japan. This trade should grow along with greater consumption by domestic steelworks. Manganese production was once totally oriented toward exports, but there is now a desire to conserve reserves for domestic consumption. The best manganese deposits are north of Nagpur. Mica, mainly from Bihar, is India's unique resource for world markets. Bauxite from Bihar and elsewhere feeds plants at Renukoot and Belgaum. Very extensive gibbsitic bauxite reserves have been delineated in the eastern Ghats region. India has relatively small copper, zinc, and lead mines and smelters and is deficient in these metals. However, copper deposits in Rajasthan may be significant. India's mines and mineral facilities are generally uneven in technical proficiency, and many operations are relatively labor-intensive.

Private industry is losing ground in India's mineral enterprise. Tata Iron and Steel Co. has the country's only important private steel plant. Aside from Tata, the private sector does not have a single sizable iron mine. Likewise, most large coal mines are not under private auspices. The Neyveli Lignite Corporation runs the lignite deposits of Tamilnadu. Excluding Karnataka State Government's Mysore Minerals Ltd., Sandur Ltd. is the only important private manganese mining company. Private companies run the aluminum industry, such as Hindustan Aluminum (Kaiser affiliation) and India Aluminum (Alcan affiliation), but government companies will be in charge of the important new alumina and reduction plants. Indian Copper Complex was taken over by the government in 1972. One of the two leading zinc firms is private, namely, Cominco-Binani Zinc Ltd. The small mica operations are mostly private, and there is a privately owned synthetic rutile plant. Various cement plants are privately owned.

Well-known government groups engaged in the management and operations of the mineral industry include the Atomic Energy commission, Oil and Gas Commission, Coal India, Ltd., Steel Authority of India, Ltd. (SAIL), National Mineral Development Corporation, Mineral Exploration Corporation, Minerals & Metals Trading Corporation, Manganese Ore (India), Ltd., Bharat Aluminum Co., Hindustan Copper, Ltd., Hindustan Zinc, Ltd., and Mica Trading Corporation. The nuclear energy program is a government undertaking, and petroleum is produced by the government and by foreigners with production-sharing contracts similar to those used in Indonesia. The Indian government is moving toward a total take-over of the oil-refining industry. The National Mineral Development Corporation, a subsidiary of SAIL, is the dominant influence in iron ore mining, and Coal India and its subsidiaries have become the dominant force in making large investments in coal projects. Coal India and the state of Andhra Pradesh own Singareni Collieries, thus illustrating the additional aspect of individual state involvement. The federal government is also engaged in the fertilizer and construction materials industries.

Principal Mineral Industries

In early 1977 India's coal industry was capable of producing 100 million tons of coal per year—three-fourths under ground and the rest on the surface. There are plans to double coal output in a decade, with some emphasis on coking coal and opencast mines. The vast coal reserves afford industry a tremendous potential for expansion. The main region is the Bengal-Bihar belt, but outlying coalfields will be developed to produce up to half of India's total output. Coal India and its predecessor, the Coal Mining Authority, have been responsible for the recent increases in production. Soviet help is important in the present expansion program. However, Bharat Ltd., which produces the bulk of coking coal, suffers from a shortage of power and transport problems. Current programs indicate that coal exports could reach 5 million tons by 1980.

India recently discovered offshore reserves at Bombay

High, 100 miles off the coast, capable of bringing in annually 10 million tons of crude oil (barrels per day equals metric tons per year divided by fifty) and 10 billion cubic meters of gas. By the end of 1977, offshore oil output may reach 4 million tons. Oil India, Ltd. (government and Burmah Oil) currently produces 60 percent of Indian crude from fields inland from the west-central coast. The country's oil-refining capacity was 568,000 bpd (or 28.4 million tons) in late 1976. The Burmah Shell plant at Bombay is rated at 120,000 bpd; Cochin Refineries in Kerala and the Hindustan Petroleum refinery in Bombay are both 70,000 bpd; and India Oil has three refineries rated at 50,000 to 80,000 bpd. India's oil-refining facilities may come totally under government ownership by the 1980s.

India hopes to expand iron ore output by 50 percent, to 60 million tons per year, by the end of the 1970s; 35 million tpy may then be available for export. Reserves of high-grade ores are extensive, and the country is already a medium large producer by world standards. There are three types of mines: captive mines run by steelworks, state-owned mechanized mines, and privately owned small mines. The main producer is the Steel Authority, with the Kiriburu and Bailadila mines. India has a 210-million-ton, twenty-eight-year contract with Iran, which will provide a $630 million loan to develop the Kudremukh deposit (exclusively for the Iranian market) and supporting port facilities. The Minerals and Metals Trading Corp. and Chowgule and Co. control all iron ore exports. Nippon Kokan may help develop the Bababudan deposit 110 kilometers from the port of Mangalore.

The steel industry, with an output capacity of 9 million tons per year, is likely to be expanded to 14 million tons by 1981. Tata, the pioneer of the industry, is the only private steel company left, and its plans to expand output from 2 to 4.5 million tons yearly have been deferred because of financial constraints. The newly established Steel Authority controls the Bhilai, Rourkela, Bokaro, Durgapur, and other steelworks. Bhilai is being expanded from 2.5 to 4 million tons with Soviet help. Rourkela is undergoing diversification, and Bokaro is being expanded from 1.7 to 4.7 million tons. The 1.6-million-tpy Durgapur plant has been faring badly owing to high power costs. India is still somewhat short of steel products, particularly in sophisticated specialty items. In ferroalloys, India is well known in world markets for manganese ore and ferromanganese.

Although the country has large reserves of bauxite, it possesses only a 200,000-tpy-capacity aluminum industry, which is undergoing expansion. Hindustan, Indian, and Bharat are the three leading aluminum companies. There is only one small copper smelter, and the government-owned Hindustan Copper Ltd. has been given the assignment of developing copper mines. Hindustan Zinc, with one of the two zinc smelters, is putting up a new 30,000-ton plant near Visakhapatnam to process imported ore. Cominco-Binani Zinc has the second smelter near Cochin and uses imported ores also. Tundoo is the only lead smelter. India is now very short on all nonferrous base metals, but it has plans to build a series of smelters based upon domestic ores from mines that are still being developed.

India has a cement industry consisting of about fifty-two units with a combined capacity of 20 million tpy. These plants draw their limestone requirements from about a hundred locations. Madras Cement Limited has a new 1,200-tpd, dry-process, four-stage preheater kiln. About four more kilns of this size are being built, and various units of larger sizes are being planned. Coal is the main fuel for cement plants, and every year about 5 million tons of coal are shipped 1,000 kilometers for cement manufacture. New Delhi, Calcutta, Madras, and Bombay are the main consumption centers.

Among the nonmetallics, India is the home of the special Bengal ruby mica and is by far the largest world producer. Bihar is the principal producing area, followed by the Guntur and Rajasthan. Synthetics and transistorization in electronics have cut sharply into the demand for India's mica. Diamond pipes have recently been found in the Krishana and Panna areas. India, moreover, has a phosphate industry of some importance.

Mine and Industry Workers

India may have a large population, but the trained work force suitable for mining and industry is relatively small. The Indian is a hard worker but faces many obstacles due to social traditions. There is no shortage of potential workers, and the key to India's industrial success is to train people in a wide range of technologies. Coal mining has had a long tradition and hence possesses at least a good core of underground miners. Moreover, the number of workers experienced in noncoal opencast operations is increasing. Indian operations are more labor-intensive than those in industrialized countries. For example, much iron ore still comes from nonmechanized mines.

For the major industries and services as of late 1974, there were about 780,000 workers in mining and quarrying (660,000 in the public sector, the rest private), 1,100,000 workers in construction (1,000,000 public), and 5,000,000 in manufacturing (1,000,000 public). The coal industry has a work force of approximately half a million.

Mineral Transport

Transport of heavy materials in this large country is difficult and expensive, especially where modern facilities are lacking. The Bengal-Bihar belt in the east around Calcutta is the country's leading industrial and population base and has most of its major coal mines and steel plants. The New Delhi–Rajasthan complex inland and to the north is becoming more important as a consumption center. Madras is the gateway to the south, and Goa and nearby areas are very important iron ore regions. Calcutta is connected by railroads with these areas and with Bombay on the western coast as well. There is a coastal railraod servicing the entire east coast. The Ganges River, which flows into Calcutta, serves northern India. However, the road system is somewhat weak; therefore, truck transport is not too important.

India has 37,000 miles of railroads, of which 2,300 miles are electrified. It has 740,000 miles of roads, of which 460,000 miles are considered improved. The railroads have a close relationship with mineral traffic. At the beginning of 1975, the total number of railway wagons loaded was about 1,000,000, of which 300,000 carried coal and coke, 100,000 carried iron ore, 60,000 carried cement, 40,000 carried iron and steel, and 10,000 carried manganese ore. Significantly, the railroads often cannot handle all the coal traffic.

Minerals are also shipped by coastal vessels to different parts of India. There are many small ports, particularly on the east coast. Calcutta is a fair-sized port, and Vishakhapatnam is being expanded to accommodate larger ships. Currently, many of the ports either handle iron ore or are being developed for this purpose; the best-known ports are Goa and Paradip. Generally, inadequate port facilities are a restraint to iron ore exports. However, the Japanese industrialists have rendered aid in this regard.

Energy and Power

India's overall plan is to develop the coal industry so that it will increasingly help meet the country's expanding energy needs. A rough estimate of India's hydropower potential is 50 million kilowatts, of which only about 15 percent has been developed. Considerable expansion is thus possible in hydropower, but capital costs are high and have restricted progress in this area. The country's objective in regard to oil is to attain self-sufficiency without greatly expanding its use. There is also considerable potential in the production of associated natural gas. The current nuclear program provides for further construction of CANDU-type heavy-water reactors using indigenous uranium. If the fast-breeder reactor eventually becomes environmentally and economically viable, India's extensive thorium resources will be a basic fuel.

The country's electric power capacity is approximately 20 million kilowatts, which is soon to be raised to 23 million. In 1975 electric power production was about 75 billion kilowatt-hours, of which 60 percent was provided by steam plants (coal-fired plants), 35 percent by hydroplants, 3 percent by nuclear plants, and the rest from oil and gas. About 600,000 kilowatts of generating capacity were recently added to the northern region. Three nuclear plants with a combined capacity of 1.2 million kilowatts were having either construction or teething problems. Regional grids between individual states will eventually be incorporated into a national grid pattern. Various interstate lines are being built, and special thermal power stations will be built near coal pitheads to reduce transport expenses.

Summary Outlook

India's mineral economy is making headway in raising living standards. The output of coal, iron ore, steel, cement, and power has increased steadily in the last decade. Recent offshore oil discoveries give hope that imports can be reduced. Phosphate extraction is being stressed to cut down on dependence on foreign fertilizers. Plans are under way to greatly expand bauxite, alumina, and aluminum production. Integrated development of nonferrous metal production facilities on a moderate scale will be pursued. Iron ore exports will be substantially raised, and coal exports will be promoted.

India is a medium-sized producer and consumer of mineral products. Generally, increased production has been aimed at meeting the combined domestic and any export demand, thereby saving foreign exchange. Much of the mineral development work is being done by national groups, particularly by government corporations and agencies. India's mixed state–private enterprise system is heavily government-oriented, and the trend is not expected to change in the near future. Foreign aid has come from Eastern Europe and private Western companies. Some joint venture and production-sharing contracts have been arranged. Japan has extended contracts for future deliveries of metal ores. India has negotiated a long-term loan and iron ore delivery contract with the Iranians.

For the immediate past and the near future, the oil crisis and world recession have delayed many expansion plans. In fact, the Fifth Five-Year Plan (1974-1979) started with a serious limp. But the overall economic situation is promising, and India can be expected to make good progress once again in its program of industrialization.

Illustrations for Chapter 11

Figure 39 Map of India

Dress of Punjab

Holy man

Taj Mahal

Color throwing on "Holi" day

Figure 40 Taj Mahal and people of India (Courtesy Embassy of India)

Figure 41 Ganges River, "Mother of India," sacred to all Hindus

Hindustan machine tool factory
at Bangalore

Woolen textile plant at Dhariwal

Hindustan aircraft factory at Bangalore

Bombay high oil platform

Medium section mill at the
Durgapur steelworks

Figure 42 Industries of India (Courtesy Embassy of India)

Bhihai steelworks built with Soviet help

Rourkela steelworks built with West German help

Figure 43 Two major Indian steelworks

Crushing plant

Trucking from mines

The Bonai Range subsection

Mining equipment

Figure 44 India's Kiriburu iron project

Panoramic view of a
beneficiation plant

Collecting beach sands for ilmenite,
zircon, rutile, and monazite

Electromagnetic separator

Movable weighing scale
and bagging

Sand products en route
to shipping point

Loading from small boats
to ship

Figure 45 Mineral sands operations near Quillon, Travancore, South India

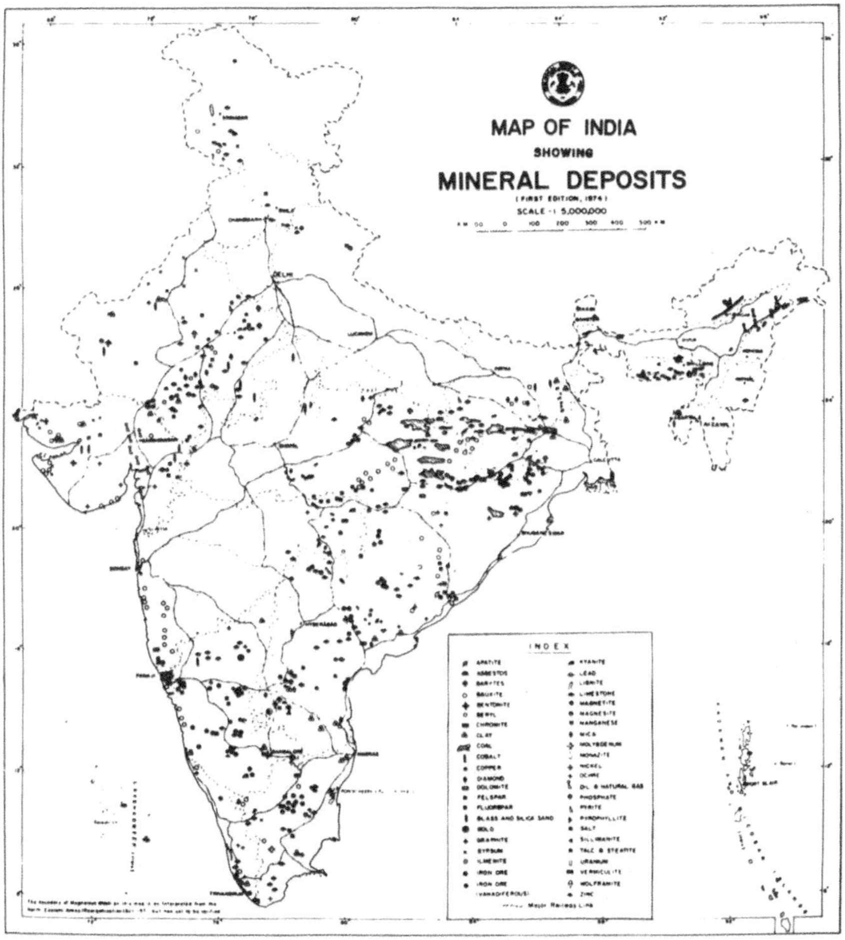

Figure 46 Mineral deposits of India (Courtesy Geological Survey of India)

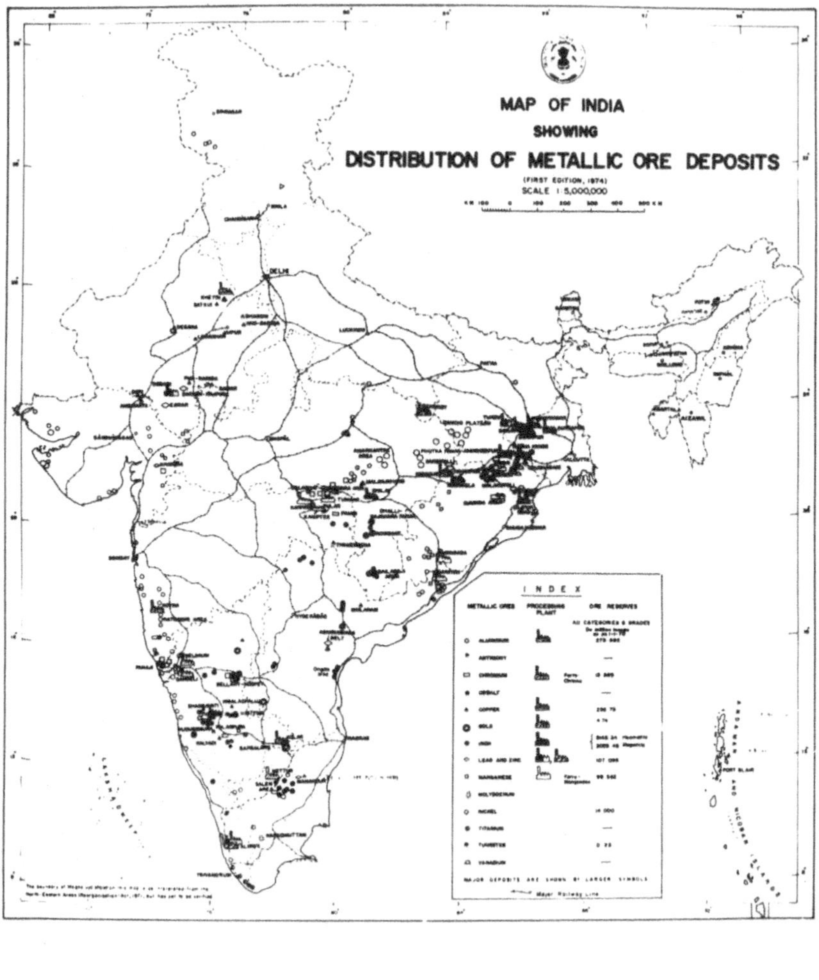

Figure 47 Metallic ore deposits of India (Courtesy Geological Survey of India)

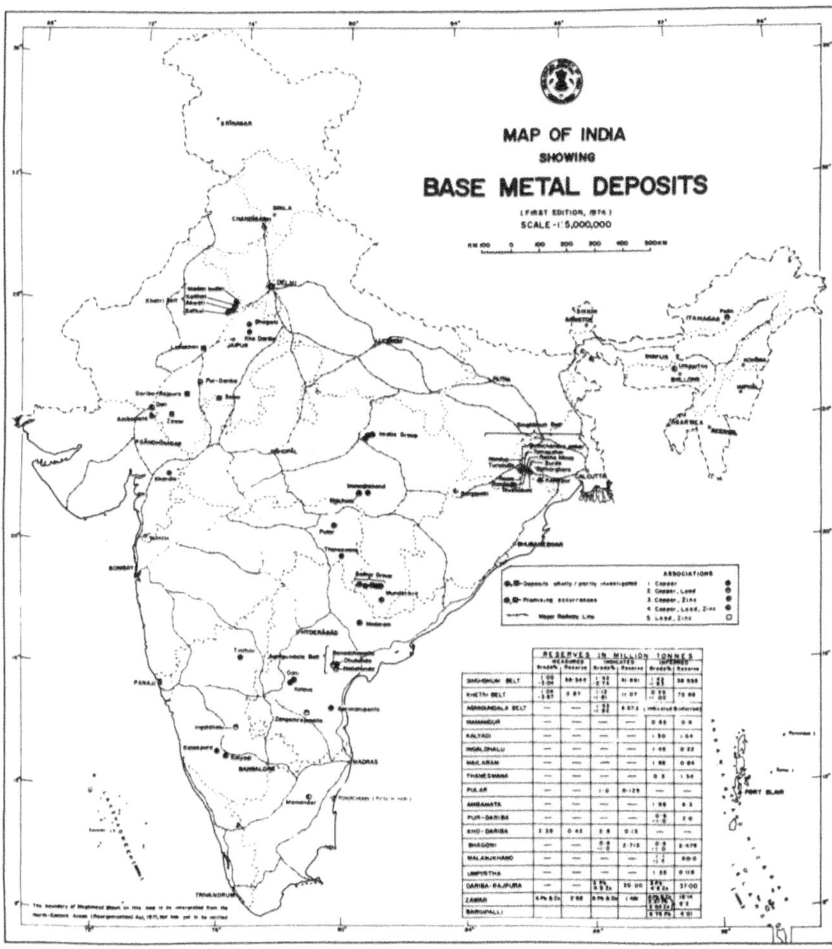

Figure 48 Base metal deposits of India (Courtesy Geological Survey of India)

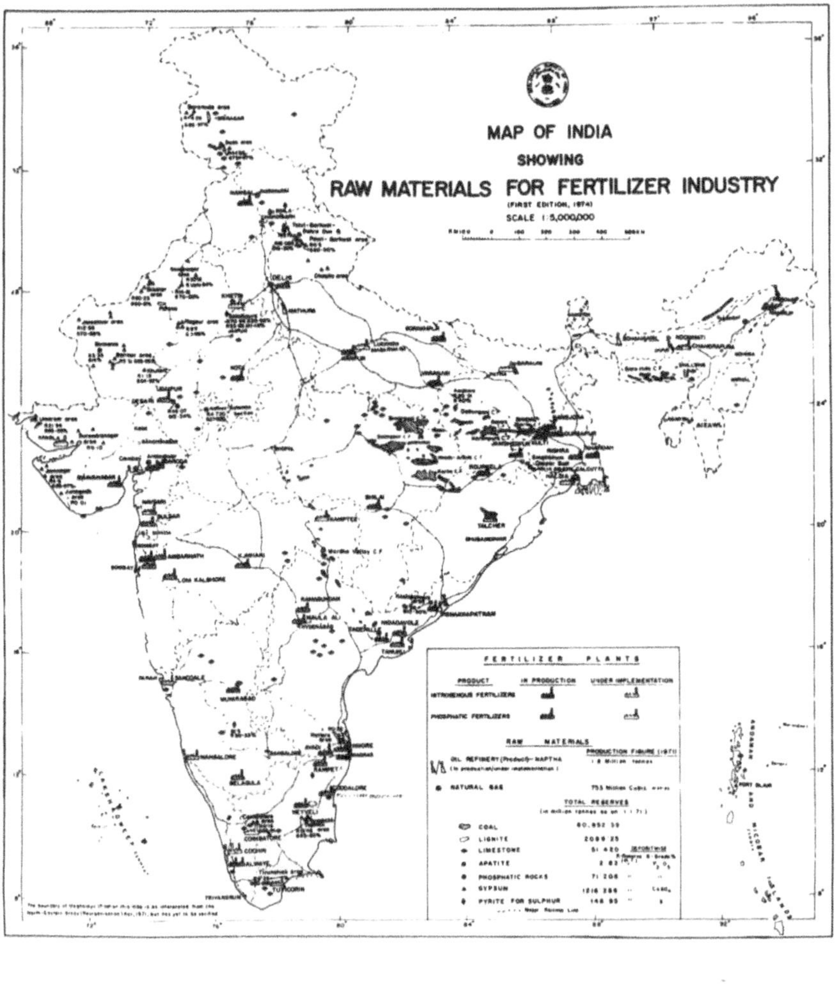

Figure 49 Fertilizers in India (Courtesy Geological Survey of India)

12
Indonesia

Indonesia is famous for low-sulfur oil, and output ranks about tenth in the world. Prospects for additional petroleum and natural gas are excellent, and a large coalfield has recently been found. The tin industry has long been one of the world's foremost producers. Laterite extraction is progressing, with aluminum still in the bauxite stage and nickel moving up to the metal stage. There is one large copper mine, and hope for finding others. The economy has been stimulated by petroleum. However, Indonesia is also well known for many agricultural commodities, such as palm oil, timber, coffee, tea, rice, rubber, and spices.

Petroleum is of such importance that it generates over half of the government's revenues and 60 percent of Indonesia's export earnings. During 1976, significant recovery was made from last year's financial crisis created by Pertamina, the state oil company. International monetary reserves, nearly depleted as a result of the crisis, were brought back to record levels in early 1977 on the strength of a good export performance and tighter financial controls on both Pertamina and the economy. Oil production established a record in 1976, but inflation was still about 20 percent for the year. Indonesia's first liquefied natural gas plant, located near Bontang in East Kalimantan and costing $700 million, was about to start production in the spring of 1977.

TABLE 9. INDONESIA: ROLE IN WORLD MINERAL SUPPLY
(Thousand metric tons, unless otherwise noted)

Major Commodities (Map Symbols)	Production 1976	Production 1975	Production 1974	World Output Share, 1975	Trade in 1975 Exports or Imports	Reserves (or Raw Materials)
Metals						
Aluminum, bauxite (Al)....	942	993	1,290	1.4%	Exports--973	Substantial
Copper, concentrate (Cu)..	220e	205	213	0.8%	Exports--175	New recent finds
Iron, sands (Fe)..........	315	353	365	Small	All exported	Moderate
Iron, steel (St)..........	Small	Small	Small	Minute	Imports--1,300	(Scrap)
Nickel, ore (Ni)..........	830	781	879	2 %	Exports--639	Substantial
Tin, mine (Sn, tons)......	23,340	25,346	25,630	8 %	Exports--7,400	2,500
Tin, refined (Sn, tons)...	23,322	17,826	15,065	8 %	Exports--14,400	(Domestic ores)
Nonmetals						
Cement (Cem)..............	NA	1,077	863	0.2%	Imports--1,609	(Adequate)
Granite (Gran)............	NA	635	424	Small	Some to Singapore	Moderate
Fuels						
Coal (C)..................	195	206	156	Minute	Neither	Up to 3,500,000
Oil, crude (Oil)..........	77,500	66,000	69,000	2.4%	Exports--54,000	1,500,000 "proven"
Oil, refined (Oil)........	13,000	12,000	12,000	0.5%	Neither	(Domestic crude)
Natural gas (Gas, 10^6 cu m)	8,500	6,300	5,700	0.7%	Neither as yet	700,000 "proven"

NA Not available   e Estimated

Significance of Minerals

1975 GNP was about $30 billion, and the gross value of oil output was about $7 billion. Exports totaled $7.1 billion in 1975, of which $5.31 billion was oil ($6.0 billion in 1976) and $0.26 billion was other minerals and metals. Imports totaled $4.8 billion in 1975, with metal imports contributing significantly.

Oil affects every aspect of the economy. Although by far the largest foreign exchange earner, the giant, state-owned Pertamina overspent in recent years and brought about a temporary balance-of-payments difficulty. However, oil money went into the building of many kinds of industrial plants. About a fifth of the oil is used internally, and this has meant better living standards and industrialization. One big nickel project will cost $840 million to complete. Large coal and aluminum projects are under way. The tin industry has helped to develop Bangka and Billiton islands, not to speak of the foreign exchange it has earned. Nickel, coal, and aluminum should be of increasing importance to the economy.

Mineral Supply Position

Indonesia exports most of its oil (production was about 1,560,000 barrels per day in 1976, or roughly 78 million metric tons) and almost all of its tin, copper, nickel, and bauxite. In 1975, tin exports were valued at $154 million, copper exports at $74 million, nickel exports at $21 million, bauxite exports at $6 million, and other mineral exports at $4 million. Japan has been by far the principal purchaser.

However, mineral consumption is increasing, as evidenced by oil. If coal is produced in large tonnages in a few years, a significant share will be locally consumed. Indonesia is using increasing quantities of cement, fertilizers, and metals. Only a small part of the cement and fertilizers is domestically produced and very little of the iron and steel. Indonesia is therefore thinking about building plants to alleviate the situation.

Nature of Mineral Enterprise

The government is trying to develop those industries in which private companies are not involved. The oil industry, headed by Caltex, is predominantly private international, except for a small part belonging to Pertamina. However, Pertamina is the government entity in all contractual arrangements. Pertamina has also been involved in steel, fertilizers, petrochemicals, and LNG. Indonesia's oil is widespread, much of it offshore. The Indonesians have not bothered with refineries except for refining the domestic consumption share. Petrochemical operations are still in the early stages.

Tin is also mainly a large-scale operation, and it is run by the government corporation P. N. Timah. The smelter belongs to the state, too. Billiton N.V. probably will participate in offshore tin operations, and its parent company, Royal Dutch Shell, is likely to get into the Indonesian coal business. The copper project in West Irian is worked by Freeport Mining under special contractual arrangements. One nickel project is under the Canadian company, INCO. Another nickel-producing operation is run by Aneka Tambang, which is Indonesia's nontin, nonoil government corporation. Most mining operations are fairly large, but manganese, sands, and gold are worked by small-scale operators.

The government's Second Five-Year Plan, covering fiscal 1974-1978, will stress infrastructure, basic industries, and fertilizers and petrochemicals, among other things. Foreign investments are welcome under a variety of contractual arrangements. Of late, oil contracts have been modified somewhat, but mining contracts have not.

Near the end of February 1977, Indonesia and Rio Tinto Zinc reached an understanding on a key mining contract covering copper and other minerals. If concluded, this contract should be the first nonoil mining deal since 1972 and the first agreement under Indonesia's so-called third-generation contracts. Foreign exchange revenues can be kept in special overseas accounts. There will be an export tax on unprocessed minerals, and a windfall-profit tax. Within a decade, 51 percent of Rio Tinto Indonesia's shares will be offered to Indonesian nationals. This was to be a model nonfuel contract of the future. However, in early March 1977, Broken Hill Pty of Australia was withdrawing its exploration activities in Indonesia, for reasons that are as yet unclear.

Principal Mineral Industries

More than half of the crude oil output is controlled by the Caltex subsidiary of Amoseas which owns the largest producing field in Indonesia, Minas in north-central Sumatra. However, about eight other companies are active in various parts of the country, primarily in the western half of the islands, both onshore and offshore. General exploration has given way to specific drilling in many instances, and various discoveries have been reported. If general conditions do not deteriorate, annual production can easily reach 100 million tons within five years. Some buildup of refineries and petrochemicals would be useful, although most oil will still be exported as crude. The higher oil price has presented operators with contract negotiation problems.

In 1976, the government of Indonesia reopened existing contracts with foreign oil companies and announced new profit-sharing and cost recovery terms for companies operating under both contract of work and production-sharing arrangements. The new terms, considerably less advantageous for the companies, feature an 85/15 split on equity earnings and a new, extended depreciation schedule for recovering operating costs. Meanwhile, oil exploration activities have declined significantly. The government has since sought to provide new oil exploration incentives: better pricing, allowing investment credits when start-up costs are high, and introducing quicker capital investment recovery schedules. Onshore oil fields reserved for Pertamina may also be opened up for international operations. Generally, foreign oil firms have expressed disappointment over recent developments.

Indonesia has the potential to increase tin production, but international quotas and stagnant prices during the early 1970s held up the investments necessary to expand output rapidly. However, tin prices rose sharply to more than $5 per pound in early 1977. P. N. Timah produced 17,181 metric tons of tin from Bangka in 1975, 5,209 tons from Belitung (Billiton), and 1,801 tons from Singkep. It has thirty dredges (from five to eighteen cubic feet) and ten additional smaller dredges that can be dismantled; it also has plans to acquire a new twenty-four-cubic-foot dredge. Billiton ordered a large dredge in late 1976 for its offshore project in the Pulau Tujuh area, and P. T. Koba Tin is already working gravel pump mines. The smelter at Muntok, called Peltin, has been expanded to 25,000-28,000 tons annually so as to take care of all of Indonesia's tin concentrate output.

The nickel business is only now coming into its own. The first stage of INCO's big nickel matte operation in Sulawesi came on-stream in late 1976 (37 million pounds of nickel per year, to be expanded eventually to 107 million). Aneka Tambang recently completed a $55-million, 20,000-tpy ferronickel smelter (4,200 tons of nickel) to utilize the low-grade ores of Pomalaa (it had been shipping high-grade ore to Japan). Another large nickel project—Pacific Nikkel on Gag Island, to employ the Sherritt Gordon Process—may come into being; tentative plans are to start a four-year construction program in mid-1977.

A vigorous expansion program is now under way to bring cement production up from 1 million tons per year to 6.3 million by 1978/79. For example, the Cibinong cement plant in West Java is being expanded to 1.1 million mtpy. The Indonesians are working on a complete self-supply structure in fertilizer by effectively utilizing natural gas. The country will eventually have a capacity of 3.4 million tpy in urea—15 percent is already in being, and an additional 50 percent is under construction. The coal program may take off if contractual concepts can be resolved; the long-term objective is to produce as much as 25 million tons a year from the Shell project. A one-million-ton, direct-reduction steel project is under way. Copper consists of one good mine (Ertsberg) in West Irian, whose further expansion underground hinges on workable contract arrangements. Freeport has also discovered another copper-gold prospect near Gunung Bijih and Ertsberg. Bauxite is being mined, but aluminum smelting and power at Asahan are for the future, to be developed jointly with Japanese companies.

Mine and Industry Workers

The Indonesians are learning about oil technology from actual operations. Those who have any geological and exploration training are often lured away from existing agencies, such as from the Geological Survey, to private industry. New workers have to be trained from the open-pits and processing plants. As yet, the Indonesians have not done much underground mining. Because tin production has already had a long history, the tin business has had suitable personnel and workers. There is a general shortage of all mining and industrial workers, as well as engineers and geologists, but more people are getting involved. The Indonesian Mining Association came into being recently. The country has had a good core of foreign-trained technologists in key government posts.

Mineral Transport

Interisland shipping is important for certain basic mineral products. For petroleum, the main domestic problem is to pipe the oil to Sumatra and then ship it to Java, where most of the Indonesians live. Port areas on the lesser islands are markets for mineral and metal products. For most large projects (such as nickel, coal, and bauxite), equipment must be flown in or roads built to send equipment in; then, in the case of low-unit-value materials, roads or railroads must be built to ship the material out. The existing infrastructure is generally weak. It is quite an undertaking to open a copper mine in mountainous jungles. Getting the oil out involves pipelines, relay stations, and suitable shipping facilities—all standard practice. For any of the ores or concentrates, conveyor belts, trucking, and roads are necessary. A high-unit-value commodity such as nickel might be flown out. Railroads are not a factor except in Sumatra; on the other hand, roads, ships, and ports are indispensable everywhere.

Energy and Power

Indonesia's electric power industry was not much more than a million kilowatts in early 1975. However, this sector will receive 7.5 percent of the budget during the Second Five-Year Plan. Most industrial plants have their own generating facilities, but the government power company serves most municipalities. The shortage of power prompted the Indonesians to insist on the Asahan power project (600,000 kilowatts). Some thought is being given to developing coal resources; this will conserve oil and thereby earn valuable foreign exchange. It is expected that energy production in Indonesia will be generated from the following sources by the year 2000 (in percent): hydro, 8; oil, 20; geothermal, 10; coal, 25; and nuclear, 37.

Summary Outlook

Indonesia must resolve the difficulties with Pertamina before moving ahead on the programs it envisages. The temporary tight financial situation may have influenced the attitude toward foreign investment; that is, it may have changed concepts as to what constitutes fair, workable deals. The Indonesians have been very successful in pioneering contractual arrangements, but recent developments have caused some concern. The planners have given increased attention to the overall energy policy, because alternatives exist, particularly in the light of newly found coal. Indonesia's future success in acquiring larger tin quotas will have a direct bearing on production. Stable commodity prices can be resolved only by supporting international organizations. The problem in base metals is to develop capability to promote more exploration and development. Better utilization of natural gas will mean expanded output of fertilizers, petrochemicals, construction materials, and perhaps the introduction of iron reduction. Nickel for export and aluminum smelting may have reached the pause stage. Indonesia needs to provide more and better-trained technicians and strengthen resource investigation and research support groups to help develop the mineral industries. How much the government should do and what kind of appropriations it should extend for mineral activities are significant issues.

Illustrations for Chapter 12

Figure 50 Map of Indonesia

Figure 51 Costumes of Indonesia (Courtesy Embassy of Indonesia)

Figure 52 Caltex oil operations in Central Sumatra, Indonesia (Courtesy American Overseas Petroleum)

Figure 53 Banka dredge operating offshore in Indonesia (Courtesy P. T. Tambang Tinah)

Outside view of plant

New reverberatory furnaces

Final casting of ingots

Discharging from reverberatories

Figure 54 Indonesia's 28,000-tpy Muntok (Peltim) tin smelter on Bangka Island (Courtesy Ir. M. Sîmatupang and Thomas Mackey)

Figure 55 INCO's 18,500-stpy (stage I) Soroaka nickel plant in Sulawesi, Indonesia (Courtesy International Nickel)

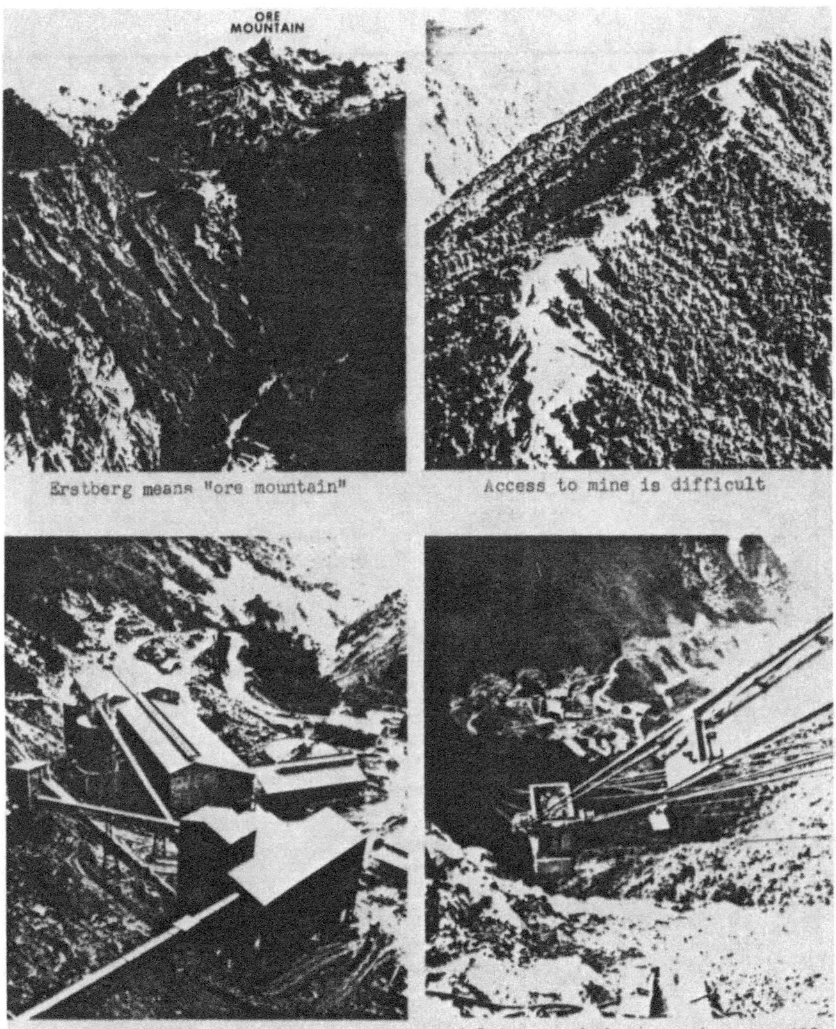

Figure 56 Freeport's 55,000-tpy Ertsberg copper operation in West Irian, Indonesia (Courtesy Freeport Minerals)

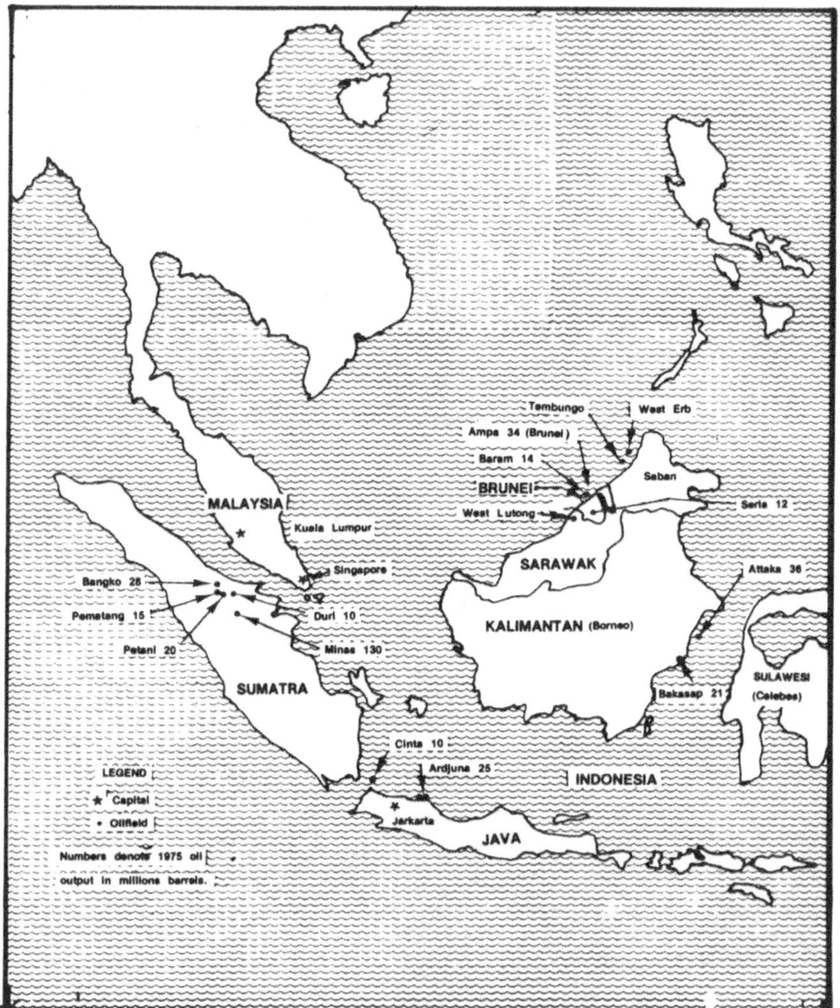

Figure 57 Oil fields in Indonesia, Malaysia, and Brunei

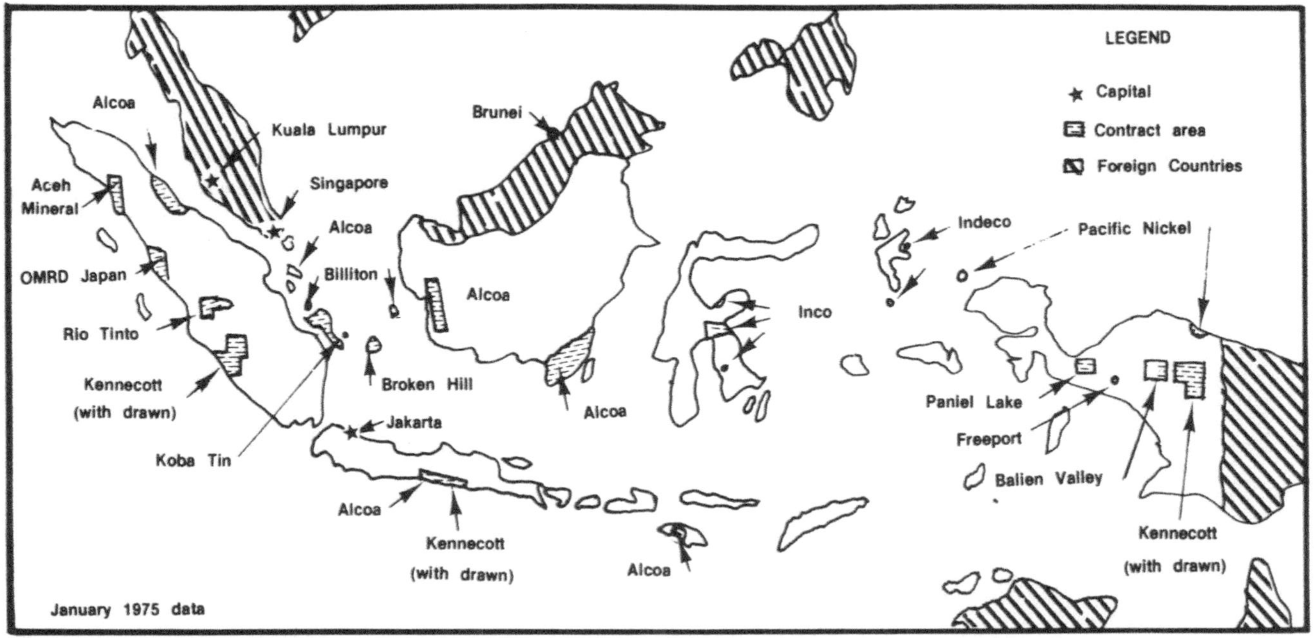

Figure 58 Mining contract areas of Indonesia (Courtesy Department Pertambangan R.I.)

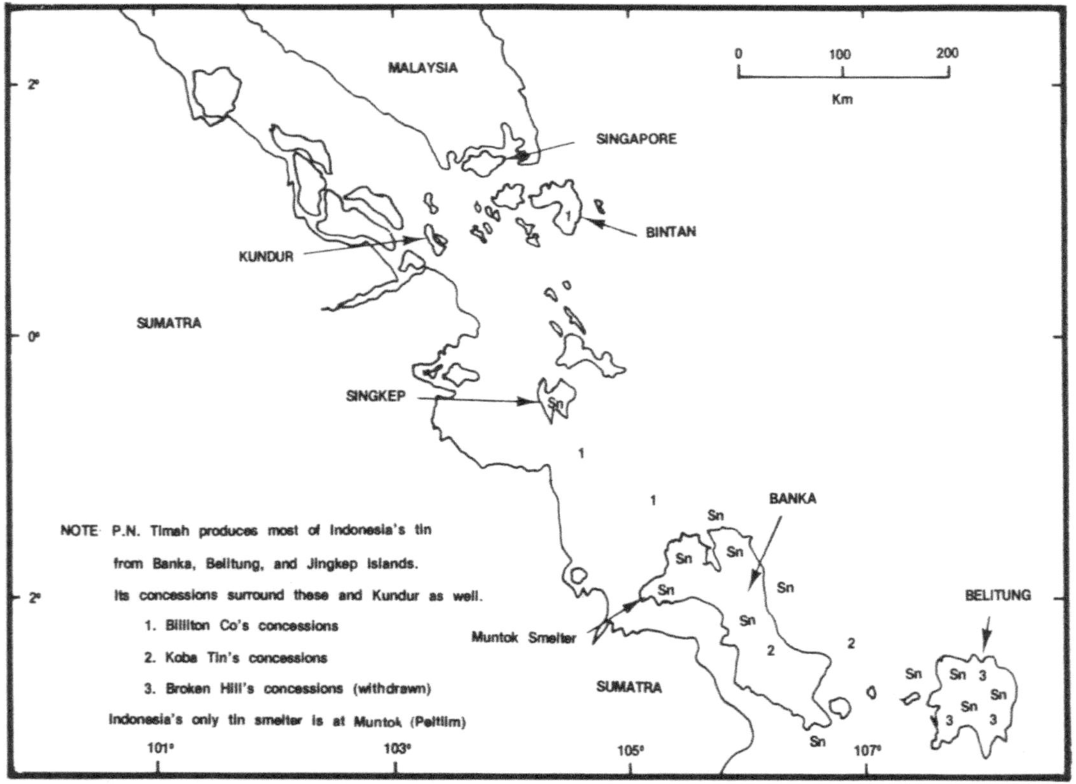

Figure 59 Tin fields of Indonesia (Courtesy P. T. Tambang Timah)

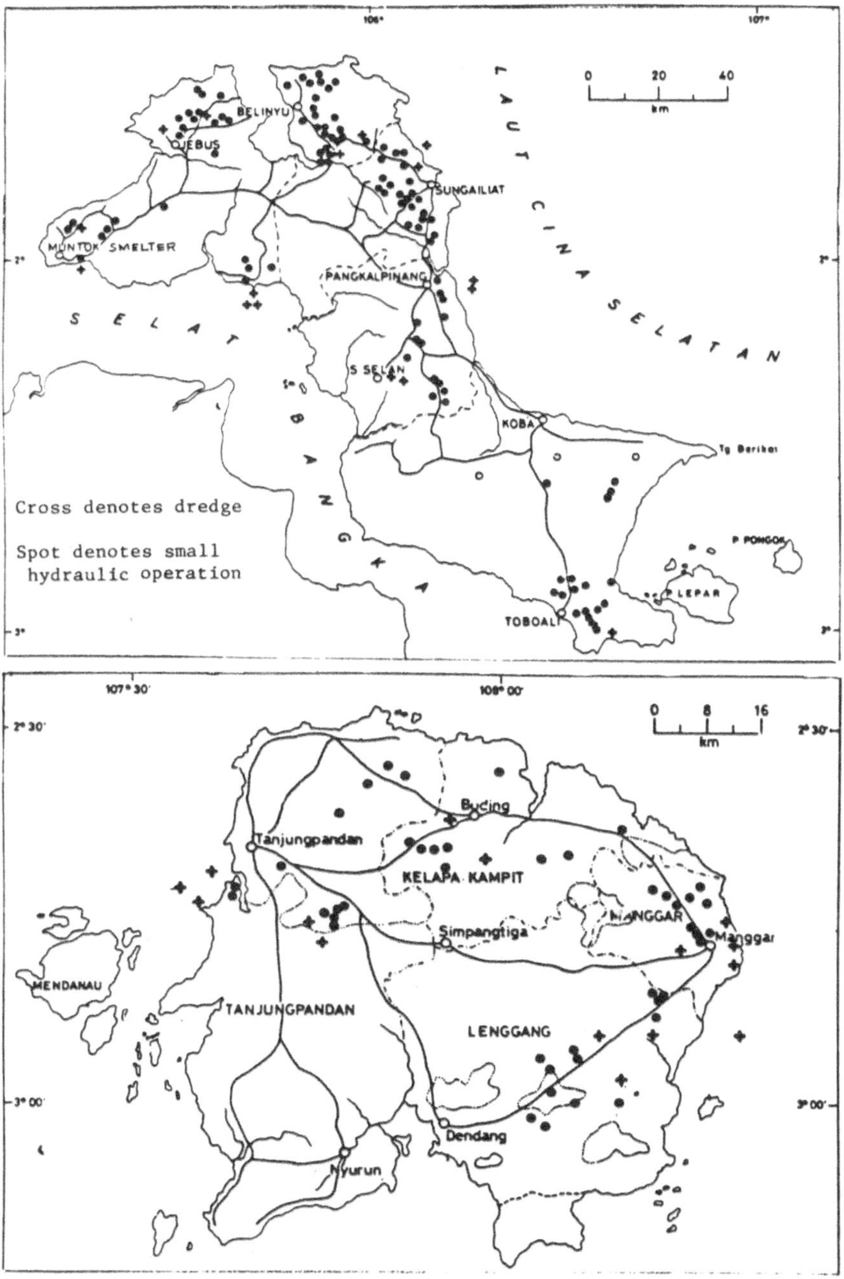

Figure 60 Tin mining on Bangka and Belitung islands (Courtesy P. T. Tambang Timah)

13
Japan

Japan has emerged as an influential factor in world mineral enterprise, even though it has relatively few indigenous raw materials. It is a world leader in mineral processing and the manufacture of many metals, for which it uses mainly imported raw materials. Japan is also a large consumer of minerals and metals, an important exporter of metal products, and of course one of the world's foremost exporters of industrial products. About half of its imports are mineral raw materials, and a quarter of all its exports are processed mineral and metal products. Japan is also noted for shipbuilding, and it transports much of the minerals it acquires in Japanese-made vessels.

Domestically, only seventeen kinds of metallic ores are produced from roughly 175 mines, and over twenty types of metallic ores are not produced at all. As for the major base metals, Japan produces more than a tenth of its requirements in only zinc and lead. However, it is more self-sufficient in nonmetallics. Japan is one of the world's top three producers of cement and limestone. About twenty-three nonmetallic minerals are produced from over 1,200 mines. However, an equal number of nonmetallics are not produced at all.

Japan's dependence on foreign minerals has steadily increased. Japan has therefore combed the world looking for

TABLE 10. JAPAN: ROLE IN WORLD MINERAL SUPPLY
(Thousand metric tons, unless otherwise noted)

Major Commodities (Map Symbols)	Production 1976	Production 1975	Production 1974	World Output Share, 1975	Trade in 1975 (1976) Exports or Imports	Reserves (or Raw Materials)
Metals						
Aluminum (Al)..........	919.4	1,013.3	1,118.4	7 %	Net imports--300 (285)	(Foreign bauxite & alumina)
Copper, mine (Cu)......	81.6	84.6	82.1	1 %	Imports--800 (650)	1,300
Copper, refined (Cu)...	864.4	818.9	996.0	10 %	Net imports--186 (210)	(Predominantly foreign ore)
Iron, mine (Fe)........		835	487	0.1%	Imports--83,000(84,000)	20,000
Iron, steel ingot (Fe).	107,400	102,300	117,000	15 %	Neither	(Mainly foreign ore)
Steel products.........	95,000	87,000	100,000	15 %	Exports--29,000 (37,040)	(Domestic steel ingot)
Lead, mine (Pb)........	51.7	50.6	44.2	1.5%	Imports--140 (100)	640
Lead, refined (Pb).....	219.1	194.2	228.0	5 %	Net exports--24 (imports)	(Mostly foreign ore)
Nickel (Ni)............	14.7	13.0	21.0	2 %	Imports--15.9 (12.0)	(Foreign ore and matte)
Ferronickel............		59.4	72.7	10 %	Imports--9.86 (14.3)	(Foreign primary materials)
Titanium (Ti, tons)....	6,346	7,582	8,913	Large	Exports--469 (1,632)	(Foreign rutile & ilmenite)
Tungsten, concentrate (W, tons)............	1,365	1,331	1,398	1 %	Imports--2,027 (2,605)	20
Zinc, mine (Zn)........	260.0	253.6	240.8	4 %	Imports--500 (520)	3,500
Zinc, refined (Zn).....	742.1	701.8	850.0	12 %	Net exports--222 (48)	(Mostly foreign ore)
Nonmetals						
Cement (Cem)...........	68,710	65,500	73,100	10+ %	Exports--4,098 (5,850)	(Abundant local limestone)
Limestone (Lime).......	147,500	144,000	160,800	10+ %	Neither	28,000,000
Pyrite (Pyr)...........	960	1,095	1,285	5 %	Neither	5,500
Pyrophyllite (Pyro)....	1,240	1,077	1,396	20+ %	Insignificant	145,000
Sulfur.................	NA	749	725	1.5%	Small	Oil refining byproduct
Talc...................	105	118	178	5+ %	Imports--170 (265)	Moderate
Fuels						
Coal...................	18,400	18,900	20,300	0.6%	Imports--64,000 (61,000)	1,000,000
Oil, crude (Oil, 10^3KL)	780	705	785	Minute	Imports--263,000(269,000)	Insignificant
Oil, refined (Oil, 10^3KL)..............	240,000*	225,000	235,000	7 %	Imports--11,000 (8,200)	(Imported crude oil)

NA Not available
* Japan's actual refinery crude runs in 1976 totalled 245,534 kiloliters.

raw materials. It has had a great influence on the development of mineral deposits around the world in the last decade—because of the demand for raw materials caused by the exponential growth in Japanese industrialization and the already established world supply-demand relationships among the known sources and markets. Japan has developed many supply sources itself, it has provided technical and financial assistance to initiate production, it has carefully learned about the development characteristics of individual countries, and it has exchanged finished goods and services in return for raw materials acquired. All of these have made it a successful competitor for the world's resources.

Japan's real economic growth rate has fallen from about 10 percent during 1960-1972 to 6 percent in 1973 and nearly to zero in 1974. A growth of 2.6 percent occurred in 1975, followed by an increase of 5.5 percent in 1976. The world oil crisis and the ensuing economic dislocations have been the basic cause of Japan's problems. Production cutbacks were carried out in all major industries during 1975; typical was steel output, which was 30 percent below capacity. Financially, the steel industry fared better than the nonferrous metals sector during the recession. It can be expected that Japan's mineral and metal output will move closer to installed capacity during 1977-1978.

Significance of Minerals

Japan's industrial and international trade structure is wholly integrated—from the search, extraction, acquisition, and transportation to the processing and conversion of mineral and energy raw materials into semimanufactured products and finished articles for domestic consumption and export. The astute Japanese businessman is highly skilled in negotiating for raw materials and in marketing industrial products and consumer goods throughout the world.

In 1974 Japan's rapid economic growth was slowed virtually to a standstill by the world oil crisis, but the situation improved in 1975 and 1976. The gross national product was about $452 billion in 1974, $488 billion in 1975, and $550 billion in 1976. In all cases, the value of mine output was at most 1 percent of the GNP and was headed by the cement and nonmetallics sectors, followed by coal, and then by nonferrous metal production. On the other hand, Japan's mineral output value, which includes the value added from processing imported materials, would be closer to 10 percent of the GNP. Steel, fuels, nonferrous metals, nonmetallics, and miscellaneous minerals and metals all contributed significantly to the total.

Transportation is an important aspect of the mineral situation in Japan. This is especially true of international shipping, but domestic land and coastal transport is also significant. The revenue derived from mineral transport is the most improtant aspect of the whole transportation business and far surpasses passenger revenues. Japan's total traffic, as measured by import shipments of minerals and export shipments of finished items, is large by world standards.

Mineral Supply Position

Japan's minerals, metals, and fuels industries are overwhelmingly the most important single factor in both overall trade and the country's economy. Data on industry production for 1974 are presented in addition to those of 1975 because the latter year was far from normal owing to the worldwide recession. Japan's total foreign trade in 1975 was about $113.6 billion—$57.9 billion in imports and $55.7 billion in exports. The values of the major mineral imports were crude oil, $19.6 billion; coal, $3.5 billion; iron ore, $2.2 billion; and nonferrous ores, $1.8 billion. Receipts of raw material supplies were sharply reduced during 1975 owing to soft export demand. The leading mineral export was iron and steel products, which accounted for about 75 percent of all mineral exports and nearly 20 percent of all 1975 exports.

Japan's total foreign trade in 1974 was about $117 billion (about one-fourth of GNP)—$62.0 billion in imports and $55.5 billion in exports. Mineral imports were about 55 percent of all imports, and mineral exports were 25 percent of all exports. By far the leading mineral export was again iron and steel, which accounted for $10.8 billion. The leading minerals imported in 1974 were crude oil, $18.8 billion; iron ore, $2.1 billion; coal and coke, $2.9 billion; nonferrous ores, $2.7 billion (copper alone, $1.6 billion); nonferrous metals, $2.0 billion (copper, $0.7 billion); refined oil, $2.2 billion; natural gas, $0.7 billion; and nonmetallics, $1.3 billion.

All imported minerals, and those produced locally, are consumed in Japan for the production of value added items, which in turn are exported or consumed domestically. Contrary to popular opinion, Japan itself is a very large consumer of mineral products. With regard to steel, however, it does export about a third of the products produced. Overall, Japan's per capita consumption of minerals, metals, and energy is on a par with the United States, and its per capita consumption of steel products is higher.

Nature of Mineral Enterprise

Japanese industry had its roots in its "mother" mines, as illustrated by great names such as Sumitomo, Mitsui, Mitsubishi, and Hitachi. The "Zaibaitsu" conglomerates were broken up during the U.S. occupation following World War II but have since been loosely reconstituted, even though independent firms retain their own identity. New companies were then developed for industries with little or no indigenous raw materials, as in the case of steel, aluminum, and oil firms. Both the old-time companies and the newer ones have established worldwide connections and have adopted a thoroughly integrated approach: they themselves contract for raw materials, supply assistance when necessary, arrange for shipment to Japan, convert the raw materials into finished products, and finally market these products locally and abroad. Even indigenous industries such as cement are internationally oriented with regard to technology transfer, interindustry connections, and sales.

Most Japanese industrial and mining companies are privately owned and fiercely competitive. On the other hand, they are often interrelated and often work together, particularly when developing new projects abroad. Company executives and government officials are often related through school ties. Japanese industry has close involvement with the government, which establishes policy guidelines, provides tax incentives and sometimes low-interest funds, assumes on occasion some exploration and development risks, regulates production and trade (albeit loosely), and recommends stockpiling objectives. Research and development on minerals and metals is emphasized by industry, government, and universities. Overall, the mineral industry is up to date by world standards, in terms of both basic technology and mechanization.

Japan's mineral and metal processing, refining, and fabrication industries are large and well planned. The country ranks in the world's first three in output of steel, aluminum, copper, zinc, cement, refined oil, fertilizers, pyrite, and a host of lesser minerals and metals. It is also in the first five in world output in industries such as coke, lead, and pyrophyllite. Limestone quarries are numerous and large. The biggest coal mine (Miike) produces only 4 million tons per year. The largest metal mine is Kamaiishi (iron), which produces just under 2 million tons of ore annually, followed closely by Kamioka (zinc). About six other mines produce above half a million tons per year.

Financially, Japanese industry is not overly strong. Proceeds are not always used for dividends, but rather for reinvestment capital for the expansion and modernization of facilities. During periods of prosperity production is quickly raised, and during periods of hardship the Japanese producers collectively tighten their belts. Keeping up with the best of technology is taken for granted, and shutting down older, but not necessarily obsolete, plants quickly is a way of life. The steel industry is healthy and prosperous because world demand is not slackening. The nonferrous base metal industries are technically strong but financially weak because of metal price fluctuations and inadequate diversification of the industry. The oil-refining industry has reached a plateau and is waiting for other industries to adjust to very high energy costs. The coal industry is doing better; the oil crunch has brought high prices, and the construction of nuclear power plants has slowed. The chemical and fertilizer industries are basically strong, but they, too, must adjust to higher costs and prices. As yet the very modern aluminum industry has not found a way to cope with excessive energy costs. Environment and pollution abatement expenditures are spiraling, although the best plants have already made provisions for pollution emission controls.

Among the most famous private mineral establishments are (1) nonferrous metals—Mitsubishi Metal, Mitsui Mining and Smelting, Sumitomo Smelting, Nippon Mining, Dowa Mining, and Nittetsu Mining; (2) steel—Nippon Steel (world's foremost steel company), Nippon Kokan, Kawasaki Steel, Sumitomo Metal, and Kobe Steel; (3) aluminum—Nippon Light Metal, Mitsui Aluminum, Mitsubishi Chemical, Showa Denko, and Sumitomo Chemical; (4) petroleum—Idemitsu Kosan, Maruzen Sekiyu, Mitsubishi Sekiyu, Nihon Kogyo, Nihon Sekiyu, Toa Nenryo, Showa Yokkaichi, and Kao Sekiyu; (5) coal—Mitsui Mining and Kokkaido Colliery and Steamship; (6) cement—Osaka Cement, Onoda Cement, Ube Industries, Chichibu Cement, Nihon Cement, and Sumitomo Cement, and (7) miscellaneous—Osaka Titanium, Toho Titanium, Ishihara Sangyo, Nippon Soda, Tekkosha Co., Awamura Metal, and Japan Molybdenum.

The Ministry of International Trade and Industry (MITI) plays a significant role vis-à-vis industry. The Energy and Resource agency is one of MITI's major arms. The Metal Mining Agency of Japan has been established to encourage mineral exploration at home and abroad. Similarly, a Japan Petroleum Development Corporation is in existence. There is a Metallic Mineral Stockpiling Association to regulate economic stockpiles and a Metal Mining Corporation to help finance the program.

Principal Mineral Industries

Japan's indigenous crude oil and natural gas industries are very small. The prospects for offshore oil are largely undetermined. Japan has part ownership of oil fields in the Kuwait–Saudi Arabia Neutral Zone. Imports of LNG should be important in the future. Currently, over 97 percent of the crude oil used is imported, of which three-quarters is from the Middle East. The crude is refined in Japan's large and modern refinery industry, which is owned by international consortiums and to a lesser extent by domestic firms (see map for details on capacities and ownership). Japan's consumption of oil is about half that of the United States or U.S.S.R. The recent oil crisis is forcing Japan to reexamine its economic and industrial objectives.

The output of the coal industry has dwindled to below 20 million tons per year, but this industry has connections with many coalfields abroad. The only large coal mine is Mitsui Mining's Miike mine in Kyushu. Coal imports have reached 60-65 million tons yearly and are used mainly for steelmaking. Prices for the coking coal imported have skyrocketed. Steam coal imports have attracted recent interest, partly because of the lag in nuclear energy development.

Japan's steel industry ranks third in world output and is still expanding. It produced an average of 110 million metric tons annually during 1972-1976 and depends overwhelmingly on imported raw materials. Per capita output is on a par with that of West Germany and much above levels in the United States and the U.S.S.R. Its coastal-based, ultramodern steel industry draws iron ores and coals from diverse sources, but primarily from Australia. These are brought in by mammoth carriers and charged into blast furnaces as large as 5,000 cubic meters (Japan has seven of the world's ten largest blast furnaces), which in turn feed large BOFs and up-to-date rolling mills. Despite the export of more than one-third of its steel products, Japan's home consumption of steel is very high. However, much steel goes into the industrial products that are exported. Japan's exports of steel products were 37 million tons in 1976, up 7 million tons over 1975. The major steelworks, headed by Nippon Kokan's Fukuyama Works, Nippon Steel's Yawata and Kimitsu works, and Kawasaki's Mitsushima Works, are shown in figure 74.

Outside of the "Kuroku" (or black ore) mines of the north and the world-famous Kamioka zinc mine, Japan's nonferrous metals industry is typified by a series of very modern smelters: Mitsubishi's Naoshima continuous copper smelter, Onahama's conventional copper smelter, Nippon Mining's flash smelters, Mitsui's Kamioka refinery and Miike vertical zinc retort plant, Akita Zinc's Iljima electrolytic plant, and the Hachinoe and Sumiko ISP plants. Dowa Mining is responsible for several of these projects. More than half the alumina and aluminum plants are very new. Many of the companies have good mines and additional projects abroad. Japan is the world's leading producer of refined zinc and third largest producer of refined copper and aluminum. As noted, the aluminum industry has the fundamental problem of energy cost, and the zinc refiners have some such difficulty, too. But the nonferrous base metals industry suffers mostly from price fluctuations; it is unable to spread out the price declines to the fabricating and consuming sectors, in which it has little control. When prices are high and demand brisk, the nonferrous industry does well.

The construction industry, headed by cement production and the mining of its principal raw material, limestone, generally does well. Cement production is close to the U.S. level, and limestone reserves are said to be over 100 billion tons. The biggest single limestone operation is about 20 million tons per year of $3 ore and employs medium large open-pit equipment. Japan has numerous large and modern cement plants, including many suspension-preheater kilns. Demand is steadily high because even during recession periods the government has pushed road projects and the like. However, the demand curve may be flattening out. Japanese cement companies, like other mineral and metal firms, are generally interested in overseas projects.

Mine and Industry Workers

Japan has outstanding workers and technologists with domestic and foreign experience to develop and operate mineral and metal projects both at home and abroad. The labor force is industrious, familiar with overcoming difficult conditions, and receptive to new ideas and methods. The Japanese technician is thorough, imaginative, and practical. High-level performance in Japanese industry is more the result of advanced technology than of relatively low salaries and wages (which no longer is the case, especially after the oil crisis and ensuing recession).

During 1975 as an average, there were only about 160,000 mine workers, compared with 4,730,000 in construction and 13,340,000 in manufacturing. The steel industry has about 250,000 workers; the coal industry 29,000; the oil industry 22,000; metal mining 17,000; nonferrous smelting 15,000; and nonmetallics 23,000.

Mineral Transport

Japan possesses a most advanced mineral transportation system, particularly ocean transport. Large oil tankers and ore carriers built by the Japanese dominate the world's seas, although they are often no longer owned by the Japanese. Other kinds of carriers, including Marcona System vessels, also carry mineral raw materials to Japan's smelters. Tankers usually carry only oil, although there are multipurpose oil-ore vessels and liquefied natural gas (LNG) vessels as well. One interesting feature of the mammoth tankers is that no oil vessel of more than 180,000 dwt can pass through the Malacca Straits between Malaysia and Sumatra, where the authorities are wary of oil spills. Large tankers sailing to Japan simply discharge at modern coastal refineries or ocean loading platforms, which then transfer the oil to pipelines or smaller vessels.

Ocean transportation of hard-rock minerals is even more interesting. Japan's large, integrated ironworks and steelworks are generally built right into the sea, with dredging and land reclamation creating enough fill for the initial section of the new works; expansion sections are built on top of land further reclaimed and supplemented with furnace wastes. The steelworks are, of course, capable of handling the largest carriers bringing in iron ore, sinter, pellets, coal, or scrap, and they feed these cargoes directly into mixing areas or furnaces. Nonferrous ores, concentrates, and scrap are brought in by smaller carriers to similar, smaller facilities.

Domestically, Japan has good coastal shipping ports,

which also accommodate smaller vessels to and from other places in the Orient. The country is famous for fast trains and a precision railroad system, which do a good job of transporting minerals and metals. The expanding highway system and truck fleets add a new dimension to short hauls, although the automobile traffic problem is becoming severe.

Energy and Power

Japan has traditionally provided enough energy and power for its needs from foreign and domestic sources. At one time it had access to the coal and shale oil of Manchuria and 50 million tons of indigenous coal a year. These sources are no longer important, leaving only the old standby of indigenous hydropower. As the country's energy requirements grew at exponential rates, Japan relied increasingly on imported crude oil while preparing the groundwork for nuclear power in the future. Expansion in local hydropower can no longer add much additional capacity, coal reserves are dwindling, and nuclear power development may not be able to move fast enough. The "oil shock" of 1973 came after Japan had converted most thermal power generators to fuel and diesel oil derived from foreign crude. Energy costs have since spiraled, with coal prices hitting a new high and with development and transport costs of LNG also much higher than originally planned. Regardless of these difficulties, Japan must still obtain an adequate supply of energy materials to run its industries.

Japan's electric power costs were high even before the oil crisis, and consuming industries often built their own power stations for specific projects in order to cut down on production costs. As of December 1976, Japan had a total installed capacity of 118 million kilowatts: 74 percent was thermal power, 20 percent hydropower, and 6 percent nuclear. Aggregate power output for 1976 was 505 billion kilowatt-hours. The country's total energy supply in the first quarter of 1975 was $91{,}000 \times 10^{10}$ kilocalories: 73 percent was petroleum, 17 percent coal, 6 percent hydropower, and 4 percent natural gas and atomic energy. Japanese power companies hope to have 27-30 million kilowatts of nuclear generating capacity by 1985—sharply revised downward from the original target. MITI forecasts that Japan will import 420-440 million kiloliters of crude oil and 24-30 million metric tons of LNG gas annually by 1985.

Summary Outlook

As a leading industrial and trading nation, Japan (and its economy) is very much affected by world developments, particularly those involving the United States, its principal trading partner. Since Japan trades and has economic relations with so many areas of the world, its economic stability in turn greatly affects other nations. The prosperity of the mineral economy is primarily related to industrial products, especially those that are made from metals (such as steel products per se, equipment and machinery, automobiles, and ships) and that are sold abroad. Although domestic consumption should not be belittled, much economic activity and often the final determinant of profits are derived from exports. In this regard, Japan's across-the-board efforts, based upon sound technology and good competitive position in making diverse products, should help it maintain, and perhaps improve, its lofty position in the future, despite interruptions created by the oil crisis.

Japan is also one of the world's major markets for industrial products, including minerals and metals. Some locally produced products are essentially consumed ultimately within the country, such as certain nonmetallics and construction raw materials (cement). However, other products derived from raw materials obtained elsewhere, after being converted to products of a specific level of manufacture, are not consumed domestically. In the case of steel, about one-third of the output is exported as such, and another significant portion is sold as industrial products, leaving less than half of the production for domestic consumption. Perhaps two-thirds of the nonferrous base metals are consumed within Japan. The country's consumption of conventional minerals and metals has probably reached a plateau, but demand should continue to grow for new products.

If combined foreign and domestic demand hold up, the steel industry should continue to expand somewhat while streamlining itself, mainly to satisfy a growing foreign market. Nonferrous base metals will have their ups and downs because of price, pollution, and energy cost problems. The Japanese are thinking more about producing abroad, since the strong demand for metals to make manufactured products rests primarily in foreign markets. The very modern Japanese aluminum industry is caught in the high-energy-cost squeeze and may have to invest more money in smelters abroad while retiring some capacity at home. Some smaller industries such as titanium and titania live on the foreign market. The construction raw materials industry should more than hold its own in the future. The local coal industry is dwindling, but its influence in developing mines abroad greatly helps in the purchase of foreign coal. The oil industry consists mainly of very modern refineries, and more capacity will be added. Production of petrochemicals should continue to grow. The chances that Japan will find large quantities of offshore oil are not particularly good. The nuclear energy industry is moving ahead more slowly than expected. Overall, high energy cost is forcing Japanese industry to make basic adjustments.

Japan has been obtaining raw materials from very diversified sources, and this trend will continue. Its worldwide impact has been so great that if problems arise, the economies of individual countries might be seriously affected. Supplying nations might even have to take remedial actions. During the world recession, cutbacks in Japanese output greatly reduced demand for foreign raw materials and resulted in renegotiation of contracts. Many supplying countries ran into additional trouble because of low prices in the face of spiraling energy costs. Even though iron ore suppliers could meet higher levels in deliveries and even though the price was still good, the demand was down. High-quality coking coal prices shot up to very high levels and of course caused the Japanese great concern. One redeeming feature for Japan was that shipping costs temporarily became low because of an oversupply of tankers. How much oil Japan will buy from China in the future is an intriguing question. With good planning and marketing practices, the Japanese should be able to obtain the necessary raw materials, despite the trend toward producer and export associations.

Illustrations for Chapter 13

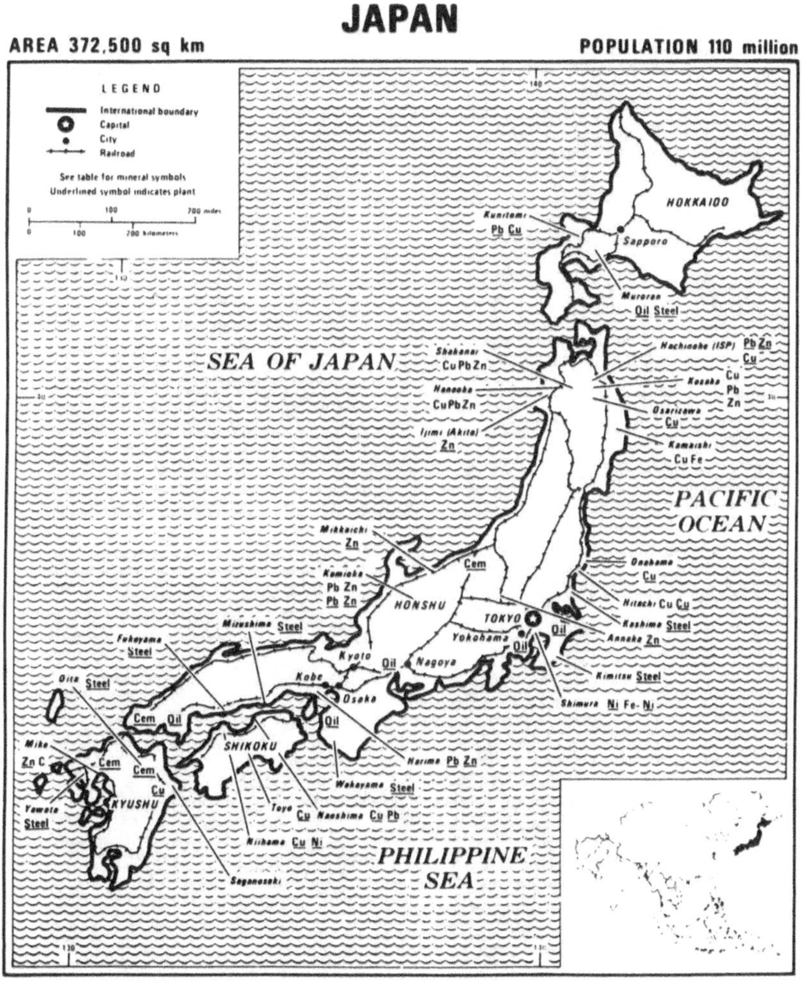

Figure 61 Map of Japan

Mt. Fuji

View near Hiroshima

Shrine in Kyoto

Stalls in Asakusa, Tokyo

Figure 62 Scenes in Japan

Figure 63 Mt. Fuji and cherry blossoms, the symbols of Japan, as viewed from Kawaguchi Lake

Figure 64 Main entrance to the Imperial Palace in Tokyo (Courtesy Embassy of Japan)

Figure 65 Sapporo's American Bicentennial ice carvings

A 483,000-dwt oil tanker, Nisei Maru (the world's largest ore carrier is about 200,000 dwt)

Raw material yards at Nippon Kokan's 16 million ton Fikuyama Works

Ore unloading and blast furnaces at Kimitsu Steelworks

Nippon Steel's 10 million ton Kimitsu Works

Nippon Kokan also builds offshore oil vessels and structures

Figure 66 Japan's integrated coastal steelworks have close tie-ups with shipping (Courtesy Nippon Steel and Nippon Kokan)

Kimitsu No. 4 -- 4,930m^3 -- world's largest blast furnace, in August 1976

300-ton No. 2 LD convertor

Wide flange bar mill

Figure 67 Nippon Steel's Kimitsu steelworks (Courtesy Nippon Steel)

▲ Saganoseki Smelter and Refinery

▲ Mikkaichi Smelter

◀ Hitachi Smelter and Refinery

Figure 68 Nippon Mining Co.'s smelters (Courtesy Nippon Mining)

The 50,000-ton continuous copper smelter
located next door to a larger conventional smelter

Converting furnace at right, smelting furnace in center,
and slag holding furnace at left

Figure 69 Mitsubishi Metal Corp.'s continuous copper smelter at Naoshima (Courtesy Takeshi Nagano, inventor of process)

The copper flash smelter at Toyo

The Imperial Smelting Process (ISP) plant at Harima

Control room for the Toyo flash smelter

Figure 70 Sumitomo Metal Mining's unique operations in Japan (Courtesy Sumitomo Metal Mining)

Electric precipitator facilities

Automatic controller

Suspension preheater

Figure 71 Japan's ultramodern cement industry (Courtesy Japan Cement Association)

Figure 72 Nuclear plant being built in Japan (Courtesy Ministry of Foreign Affairs)

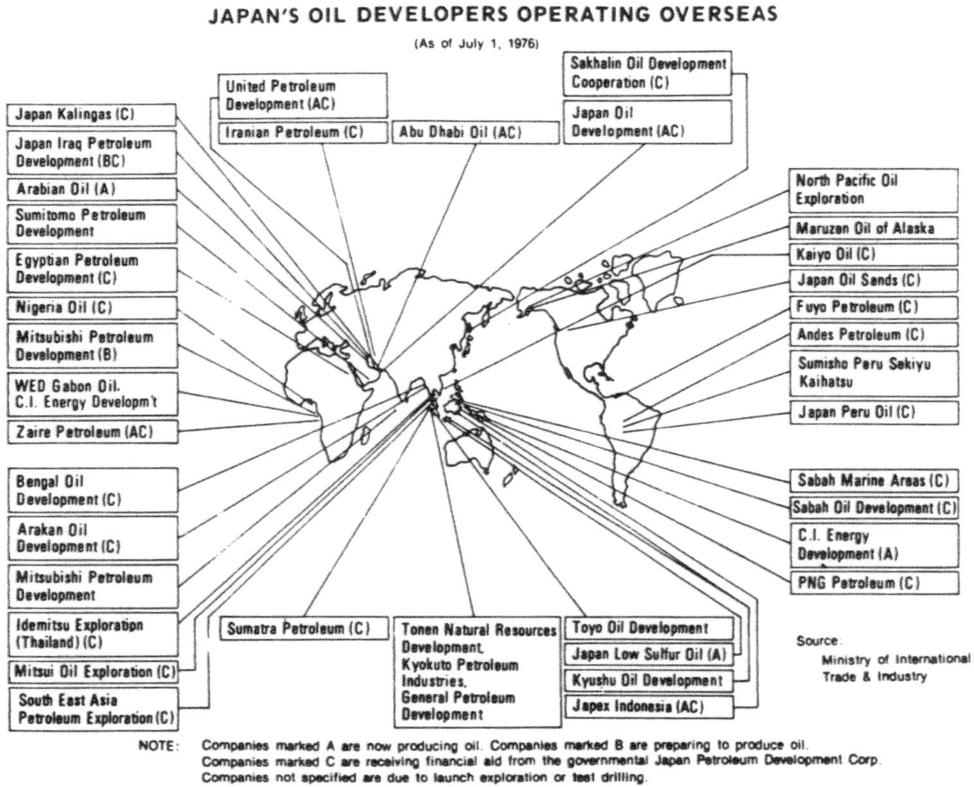

Figure 73 Japan's efforts to develop oil and gas overseas

	Works	Company	Annual Crude Steel Capacity(million tons)
1	*Muroran Works*	Nippon Steel	4.5
2	*Kamaishi Works*	Nippon Steel	1.4
3	*Kashima Works*	Sumitomo Metals	7.4
4	*Chiba Works*	Kawasaki Steel	6.5
5	*Kimitsu Works*	Nippon Steel	10.0
6	*Keihin Works*	Nippon Kokan	5.5
7	*Nagoya Works*	Nippon Steel	7.0
8	*Wakayama Works*	Sumitomo Metals	9.0
9	*Sakai Works*	Nippon Steel	5.0
10	*Funamachi Works*	Nakayama Steel	1.3
11	*Kobe Works*	Kobe Steel	3.0
12	*Kakogawa Works*	Kobe Steel	6.3
13	*Hirohata Works*	Nippon Steel	4.5
14	*Mizushima Works*	Kawasaki Steel	9.0
15	*Fukuyama Works*	Nippon Kokan	16.0
16	*Kure Works*	Nisshin Steel	2.7
17	*Kokura Works*	Sumitomo Metals	1.8
18	*Yawata Works*	Nippon Steel	9.0
19	*Oita Works*	Nippon Steel	3.6

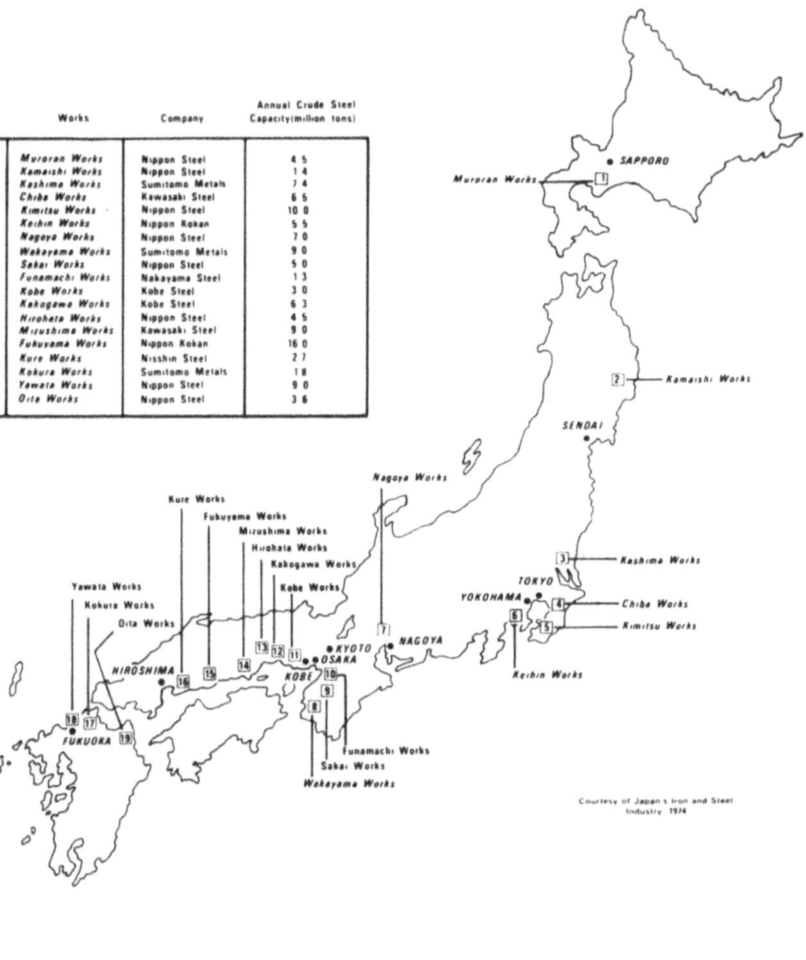

Figure 74 Integrated steelworks in Japan

Figure 75 Japan's leading nonferrous mines and smelters (Courtesy Japan Mining Industry Association)

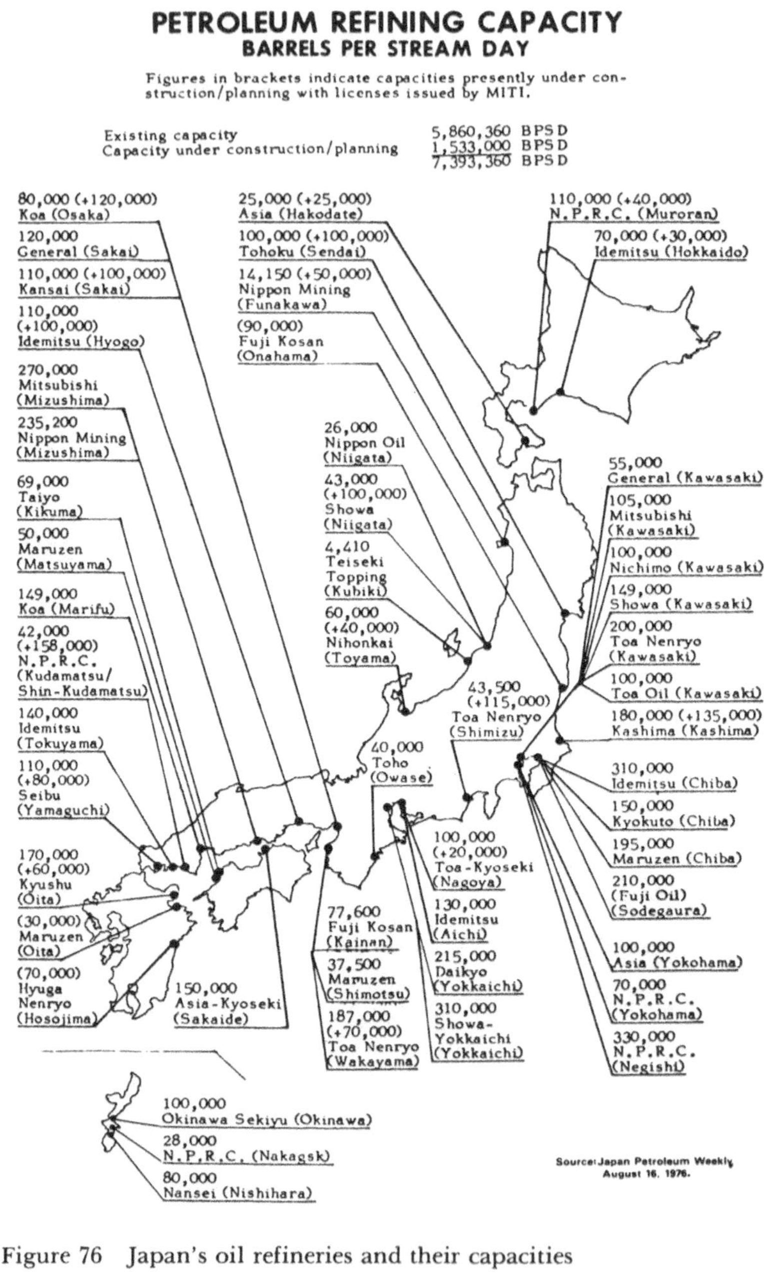

Figure 76 Japan's oil refineries and their capacities

No	Plant	Company	No	Plant	Company
1	Muroran	Nittetsu Cement	31	Akoo 1	Sumitomo
2	Kamiiso	Nihon Cement	32	Akoo 2	Sumitomo
3	Hachinohe	Sumitomo Cement	33	Niimi	Onoda
4	Ofunato	Onoda Cement	34	Itosaki	Nihon
5	Iwate	Tohoku Kaihatsu	35	Tokuyama	Tokuyama Soda
6	Yotsukura	Sumitomo	36	Nanyo	Toyo Soda
7	Tamura	Sumitomo	37	Ube	Ube Industries
8	Itoigawa	Myojo Cement	38	Isa	Ube
9	Omi	Chiyoda Cement	39	Onoda	Onoda
10	Omi	Denki Kagaku	40	Tosa	Nihon
11	Hitachi	Hitachi Cement	41	Kochi	Osaka
12	Tochigi	Sumitomo	42	Tenoura	Mitsubishi
13	Kumagaya	Chichibu Cement	43	Moji	Mitsui Mining
14	Chichibu 1	Chichibu Cement	44	Moji	Nihon
15	Chichibu 2	Chichibu Cement	45	Kita Kyushu 1	Onoda
16	Yokose	Mitsubishi Cement	46	Kita Kyushu 2	Onoda
17	Saitama	Nihon	47	Kanda	Mitsubishi
18	Ichikawa	Osaka Cement	48	Kanda	Kanda Cement
19	Nishitama	Nihon	49	Kanda	Ube
20	Kawasaki	Daiichi Cement	50	Tobata	Nippon Steel
21	Hamamatsu	Sumitomo	51	Kokura	Toyo Cement
22	Gifu	Sumitomo	52	Higashidani	Mitsubishi
23	Tamara	Onoda	53	Kurosaki	Mitsubishi
24	Fujiwara	Onoda	54	Kawara	Nihon
25	Tsuruga	Tsuruga Cement	55	Tagawa	Mitsui
26	Ibuki	Osaka	56	Tagawa	Aso Cement
27	Hikone	Sumitomo	57	Tsukumi 1	Onoda
28	Osaka	Nihon	58	Tsukumi 2	Onoda
29	Osaka	Osaka	59	Saeki	Nihon
30	Sakai	Osaka	60	Yatsushiro	Nihon

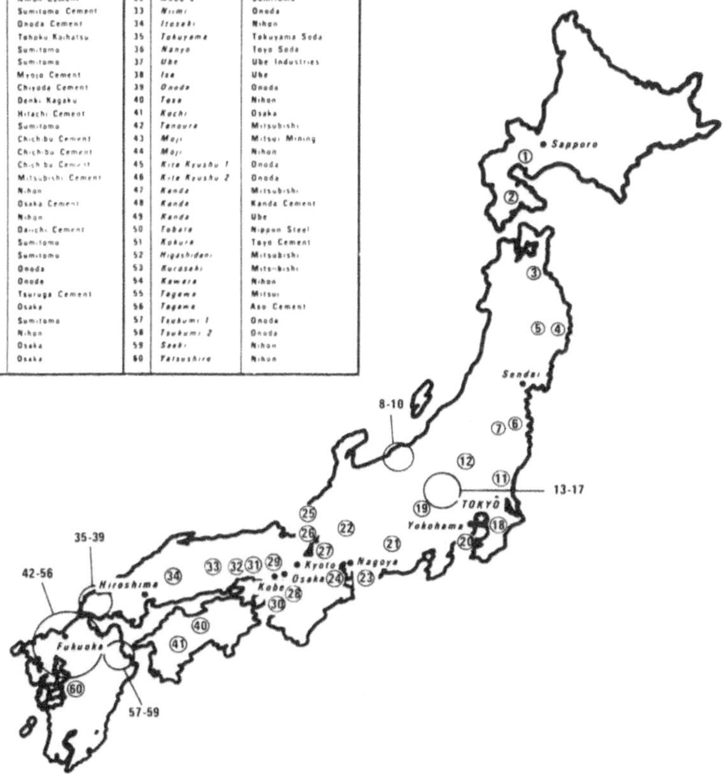

Figure 77 Cement plants in Japan

14
Laos

This landlocked country in the heart of old Indochina has a communications problem, for it has no railroads and only about 4,000 kilometers of all-weather roads. War ravages were great, inflation remains troublesome, and the population growth rate is still high. Agriculture (primarily rice) provides a livelihood for 80 percent of Laos's 3.2 million people, who live mainly in the Mekong Valley and southern Laos. What little industry the country has is concentrated in Vientiane, the capital. The principal mineral now produced is tin, although there is fair potential for other minerals. Various foreign countries and international agencies are trying to help the economy.

Significance of Minerals

The mine tin output of 500 to 800 tons per year (522 tons in 1975 and 748 tons in 1973) is worth $4-6 million of foreign exchange. There is potential for other minerals, such as potash on the Vientiane Plain.

Mineral Supply Position

Laos sells all its tin and consumes nominal quantities of minerals (mainly construction raw materials). It is considered the least-developed country in old Indochina.

Nature of Mineral Enterprise

Apart from tin, which will be described below, Laos has deposits of lead-zinc, coal, iron ore, and sylvite-potash. Lead-zinc with precious metal values has been discovered in the Capaban, Chepon, and Vientiane regions. Deposits in Chepon have been confirmed. Coal occurs near Saravane and north of Vientiane. Alluvial gold was found years ago in the Toraminh region of Kuing Khong and iron ore near Xien Khouang. Potash deposits and rock salt have been found near the Thai border, and foreigners have been asked to help. U.S. aid has been made available through the Mekong Program.

Principal Mineral Industries

Laos's estimated tin reserves may be on the order of 65,000 tons in 0.5-1 percent ore, and actual reserves may be much larger. Some feel that an annual output of 2,000 to 3,000 metric tons of mine tin can be probably sustained, compared with the 500-700 tons now produced. The main producer is Phon Tiou, about 80 kilometers north of Thakhek. managed by the French Société d'Etudes d'Exploitations Minières de l'Indochine. Annual capacity at Phon Tiou is 1,800 tons of 60 percent tin concentrates. Tin is also mined at Nongsun in the Boneng district, which produces perhaps 100 tons of concentrates yearly. A Japanese concern, Mitsubishi Metal, at one time showed some interest in building a tin smelter.

Mine and Industry Workers

Laos has a small number of workers experienced in tin mining. New workers must be trained for any other industries, and training may be a difficult problem.

Mineral Transport

Shipping tin for export is not too troublesome because of its high unit value. Developing any other mineral industries would pose extremely difficult problems. Even now, sending in supplies and machinery to new areas is expensive and hazardous.

Energy and Power

Laos's production and consumption of energy are now small. However, coal has possibilities in the future. Meanwhile, the Asian Development Bank is helping to build (through financing and management) the second phase of the Nam Ngun hydroelectric project, which might cost about $25 million.

Summary Outlook

Because of economic geography, mineral and industrial development in Laos is basically difficult. However, high-intrinsic-value export items and some construction materials that can be used in the local economy can be produced successfully. The key to mineral and industrial development in Laos is political stability and international assistance.

Illustrations for Chapter 14

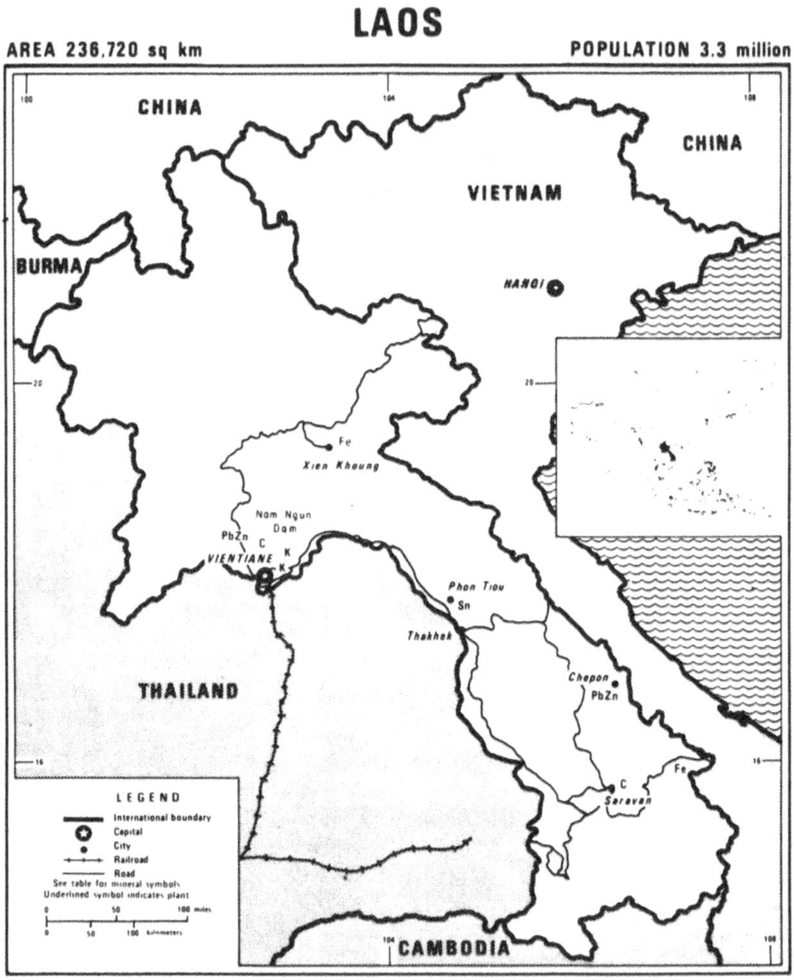

Figure 78 Map of Laos

Figure 79 Hmong women and children of Laos

15
Macao

Macao, a mortmain of China, has been administered by the Portuguese since 1887. It still relies on Portugal for some financial assistance. Macao is located about forty miles west of Hong Kong and comprises an area of sixteen square kilometers. It is best known for the tourism its casinos attract, for the production of fireworks, and for textile and knitted goods. Macao has no mining industry and is dependent on imported fuel and construction materials. Two new 23,000-kw thermal-powered generators add significantly to the electric power supply of Macao. Two additional reservoirs are being built, and several others are on the drawing boards to make Macao eventually self-sufficient in drinking water.

Illustrations for Chapter 15

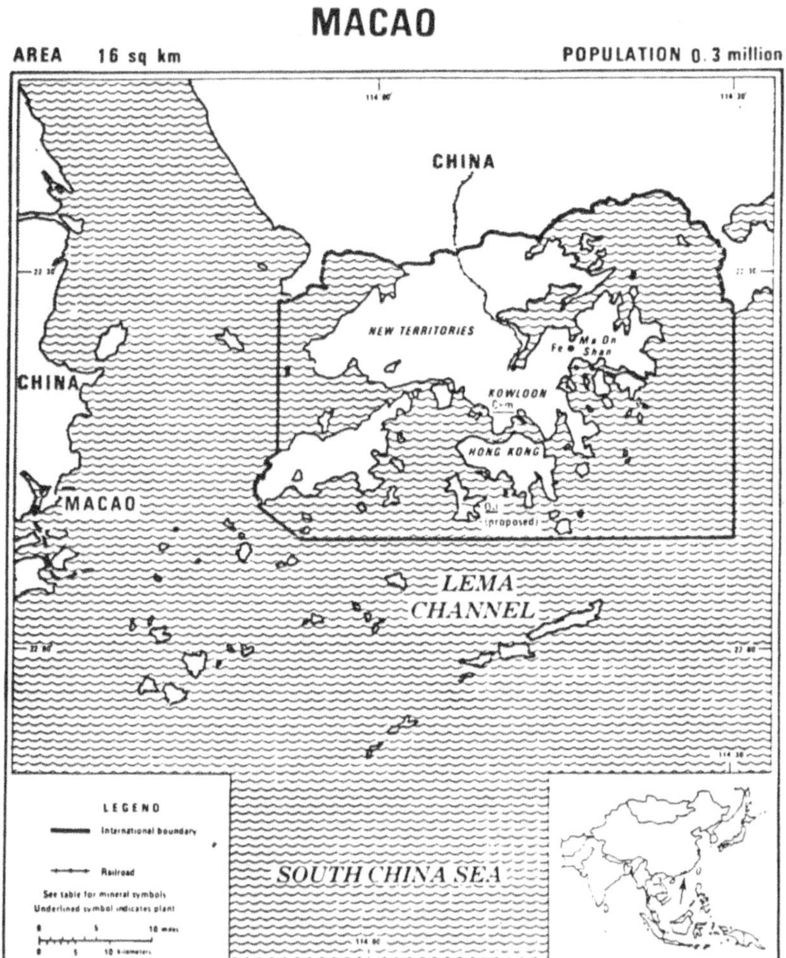

Figure 80 Map of Macao

China coastline as seen from Penha Hill

Staircase to St. Paul's Church

Figure 81 Macao away from the gambling casinos

16
Malaysia

Malaysia has long been famous as a tin exporter. For a short time, it was also a significant iron ore producer—a position it has since totally relinquished. The country is making significant progress in oil and gas but is losing prominence as a bauxite producer. A new copper mine came on-stream recently.

Exports are basic to the economy, which supports a relatively high living standard for the city population. Minerals are important, but agriculture and forestry outrank minerals. Malaysia is starting to manufacture various industrial products for export. In minerals, the high oil price is favorable, but tin prices fluctuate a great deal, causing small mines to sprout up and then close down.

During the Second Five-Year Plan (1971-1975), real output grew at an annual average of 7.5 percent, although it was only 3.5 percent in 1975. The Third Five-Year Plan (1976-1980) had a slow start, partly because of the sudden death of Prime Minister Tun Abdul Razak. But the economy recovered smartly in 1976, and prospects for a planned GNP growth of 8.2 percent during the third plan are good. In this plan, the mineral sector is expected to become more important, reflecting the anticipated growth of the oil, copper, and construction materials industries. The Third Five-Year Plan will also stress private investment. Malaysia's estimated

GNP growth in 1976 was about 25 percent over that of 1975, but inflation was only 3 percent. Malaysia's 1976 trade surplus was $1.48 billion, compared with only $280 million in 1975.

Significance of Minerals

Malaysia's 1975 GNP was $8.1 billion. Gross exports were $3.565 billion for the year, headed by rubber at $724 million, palm oil at $560 million, tin at $426 million, logs and timber at $397 million, and petroleum at $294 million. Mineral exports are basic to the economy, and copper will soon join the ranks, although it is potentially less important than oil and tin. Malaysia is by far the world's leading producer and exporter of tin. It has emerged as an oil producer of some consequence, and output by 1980 could easily be twice the 1975 level. Malaysia's gross exports rose by nearly a third in 1976 (over 1975).

Despite export earnings, some of Malaysia's oil is saved for local consumption, and additional supplies of low-grade crude are imported. Malaysia has a high standard of living and many cars. Cement output is small but important to the economy. The growing demand for metals has prompted several feasibility studies on building an integrated steel plant. Mineral markets are not particularly large, which is understandable in view of the relatively small population of 11 million.

Mineral Supply Position

Malaysia exports almost all the tin it produces. Formerly, it also smelted large tonnages of Indonesian tin concentrates. Malaysia's refined tin exports totaled 77,635 tons in 1975, including 23,790 tons to the Netherlands, 22,916 tons to the United States, 10,183 tons to Japan, and 4,667 tons to the U.S.S.R.

Malaysia's surplus of oil for exports is already very important to the economy. If production increases as significantly as hoped for, then exports can be substantially increased. Actually, crude output rose by more than 50 percent in 1976.

TABLE 11. MALAYSIA: ROLE IN WORLD MINERAL SUPPLY
(Thousand metric tons, unless otherwise noted)

Major Commodities (Map Symbols)	Production 1976	Production 1975	Production 1974	World Output Share, 1975	Trade in 1975 Exports or Imports	Reserves (or Raw Materials
Metals						
Aluminum, bauxite (Al)....	660	704	947	1 %	All exported	Moderate, offgrade
Copper, concentrate (Cu)..	80	21	0	0.1%	Exported to Japan	Can support capacity
Ilmenite (Ti)............	160	112	149	3 %	Bulk exported	Sizable, tin byproduct
Iron, ore (Fe)...........	308	348	481	Minute	Mostly exported	Limited
Monazite (M, tons)........	2,000	3,300	1,700	10 %	Exports--3,300	Sizable
Tin, mine (Sn, tons)......	62,480	64,364	68,122	37 %	Imports--18,400	1,000
Tin, refined (Sn, tons)...	78,017	83,070	84,394	40 %	Exports--77,635 (82,162 in 1976)	(Bulk local)
Zircon (Zr)...............	3	10	3	Small	All exported	Moderate, tin byproduct
Nonmetals						
Cement (Cem).............	1,700e	1,428	1,368	0.2%	Small exports	(Adequate)
Fuels						
Oil, crude (Oil)..........	8,028	4,680	3,880	0.2%	Exports--3,139 Imports--2,720	Moderate potential
Oil, refined (Oil).......	NA	4,700	4,600	0.2%	Small trade so far	(Local and imports)

NOTE: Monazite, zircon and copper concentrate output are estimated.
NA Not available e Estimated

The first shipment of copper concentrate from Sabah took place in January 1976—7,000 tons. Malaysia's production of bauxite declined from 1,143,000 tons in 1973 to 704,000 tons in 1975; all of this has been exported.

Nature of Mineral Enterprise

Tin is basic to West Malaysia's economy. Tin technology is outstanding—from exploration to dredges, gravel pump operations, and smelting. Dredging and smelting operations are primarily run by Caucasians, and gravel pump operations by Malaysians of Chinese descent. Most of the mineral industry has been private until recently.

The Malay Peninsula has promising base metal mineralization, particularly in the central granite range. However, the general conditions in individual states are not particularly attractive to the foreign investment needed for exploration and development. Iron mining from two good deposits and many small deposits near limestone knolls has dwindled to nominal levels. Bauxite comes from the laterites, and high-grade reserves are being depleted. Other minerals of some importance include tin-related materials—ilmenite, monazite, zircon, and columbite—and limestone, stone and gravel, and clays. There is a synthetic rutile plant in Lahat near Ipoh. The Mamut porphyry copper project is located in Sabah on the north side of Borneo, where the geology is quite different. In Sabah and offshore Sarawak, the oil and gas fields are worked by foreigners.

The Malaysian government is becoming more involved in mineral activities. Petronas, the state oil firm, successfully negotiated production-sharing agreements with Esso and Shell in early 1977 for a 83.5/16.5 split in favor of Malaysia. Pernas, the government mining arm, is involved in offshore tin. It recently bought over 51 percent of the stocks of Anglo-Oriental and now controls forty-three of Malaysia's fifty-five dredges. One objective of Pernas is to ensure Malay national participation in the Malaysian economy.

Principal Mineral Industries

The Kinta Valley around Ipoh is the world's foremost tin-producing district. Secondary areas are Kuala Lumpur (the capital) and a new area to the south called Kuala Langat. However, workable tin ground is getting scarce, signaling the decline of an industry of 60,000 to 70,000 tons per year. Output by Western dredges has already been surpassed by small Chinese gravel pump operations (about 750 in the spring of 1976). Anglo-Oriental, formerly controlled by London Tin, dominates dredging, although the Chinese-owned firm of Petaling Tin operates the largest dredge. Sungei Besi has the country's only open-pit tin mine. There are two good smelters—Butterworth and Penang—which are smelting less tin than previously because Indonesia has started to smelt its own tin. But tin price is the key. Low prices in early 1975 forced many gravel pump operations to shut down, and record prices of over $5 a pound in early 1977 have brought new prosperity to the tin industry. The Fifth Tin Agreement was recently implemented. The tin quota is not a great problem for Malaysia.

Royal Dutch Shell and Esso are the two principal production-sharing contractors with Petronas. Shell has four fields in offshore Sarawak and the new Samarang and West Erb fields in offshore Sabah. Sarawak already produces 100,000 bpd, and Shell's two Sabah fields may eventually produce 150,000 bpd each. Shell also has significant gas reserves in Bintual on the Sarawak coast. It has a 60,000-bpd refinery at Lutong, Sarawak, and a 31,000-bpd refinery at Port Dickson near Kuala Lumpur. Esso's Tembungo field sixty miles north of Kota Kinabalu, Sabah, may eventually produce 100,000 bpd if contractual arrangements are settled. Esso has a 33,000-bpd refinery at Port Dickson. Malaysia ranks about thirtieth among the petroleum-producing countries, and its proven oil reserves are said to be as high as 2.5 billion barrels, or 350 million metric tons. Natural gas reserves may be 15 trillion cubic feet, or 425 billion cubic meters.

The Mamut joint venture in a mountain area in Sabah is a Japanese subsidiary of Mitsubishi Metal Corporation. This medium-sized, $100-million porphyry copper mine was built for 126,000 tons of concentrates (32,000 tons of copper)

per year and is capable of earning $50 million of foreign exchange annually.

Mine and Industry Workers

Malaysians are well versed in the techniques of tin exploration, dredging, and gravel pump operations and have a fair knowledge of smelting. The tin industry employs about 38,000 workers. Skilled workers in dredging and smelting are mainly Malays or Chinese, and gravel pump operators and workmen are primarily reasonably well educated Chinese. An increasing number of Malays have left the countryside and joined the technical and labor force in mining and industry. There is no problem finding experienced workers for the tin business.

Malaysians also have a fair knowledge of open-pit operations; they have worked on surface iron mines, tin mines, and many kinds of quarries. They are also very good at maintaining engines, motors, pumps, and vehicles. However, only a handful of people know about underground, hard-rock mining, simply because few such operations exist; when the need arises, suitable underground workers can be trained. There is now a core of manufacturing and high-technology workers, and more can be trained. Malaysia has many university-educated engineers and accountants, including a growing number of technicians trained abroad.

Mineral Transport

Malaysia's transport facilities meet only the immediate needs of the western and central parts of the Malay Peninsula, with most of the railroads and roads extending north and south. The economy has been centered in a few big cities, the rubber plantations, and the tin fields, which are located in the west. The central sections of the country are rather wooded, and the Malaysian government is trying to develop the east coast. An east-west highway is being built between Penang and Kota Baru under heavy security guard.

The tin industry has no problem shipping the valuable concentrate on paved and unpaved roads. However, mining equipment has to be moved on trucks or in any other manner feasible. Relocating tin dredges is a difficult task, but the Malaysians are experienced in this respect. The railroads were basic for iron ore shipments, since this industry was prominent at one time. Road building and construction materials rely on roads and highways for their development. New mining areas require the construction of special shipping outlets.

Most oil in Sarawak and Sabah is near the coast or offshore; thus, ships, platforms, and pipelines are fundamental. Consideration is being given to ship repair and construction facilities for oil transport. The Mamut copper mine is in a mountainous area of Sabah and requires special roads, aerial tramways, and air transport.

Energy and Power

Malaysia does not produce or consume much coal, and hydropower development has been limited. The country's industry and services are run mainly on oil. Surplus oil is obviously most meaningful to the economy. Although the oil crisis pushed world prices up sharply, Malaysia was less affected—thanks to its domestic oil production.

Malaysia's installed power capacity is about a million kilowatts (two-thirds thermal and the rest mostly hydro), with the government owning over 90 percent of the capacity. National power output was about 5 billion kilowatt-hours in 1975, with approximately three-quarters generated by thermal plants. Electric power costs rose about 55 percent in March 1975. For areas served by hydropower, there is the usual load shedding when rainfall is low and when generator breakdown occurs. A $120-million, 350,000-kilowatt hydroelectric and dam-lake project is being developed in the Temenggor area of Perak.

Summary Outlook

In tin mining, extraction will become increasingly difficult as workable reserves and virgin areas become scarcer. Total output probably will decline in the long range, and dredging will continue to give ground to small gravel pump operations, which are going deeper and using larger pumps.

Offshore tin shows some promise. The smelters will not be able to operate at full capacity because of reduction of imports of tin concentrates. The tin industry should experience a temporary upsurge, if the record high prices in early 1977 are any indication.

If hard-rock metal mining is to be established on the Malay Peninsula, certain traditional difficulties, problems related to states' rights, and the lack of incentive for foreign investment need to be overcome. There is local money for tin but not for base metals so far. Mamut established a mining precedent in Sabah and Sarawak. But contracts are getting harder to negotiate, with Pernas taking positions not always attractive to private investors. Overall, there seem to be good untapped resources in hard-rock minerals. The Malaysians are capable of developing nonmetallics as the need arises.

Malaysia is already producing close to 10 million tons of crude oil per year and could eventually produce at twice this rate with the known fields alone. According to Petronas, Malaysia will spend $600 million on oil and gas exploration and development in 1977-1978. The company may also seek to establish additional oil refining, fertilizer, petrochemical, and energy-intensive industries to take advantage of Malaysia's petroleum resources. At the end of 1976, Petronas was preparing to reopen negotiations with Royal Dutch Shell and the Mitsubishi Corp. on developing a very large liquefied natural gas project in Sarawak.

Malaysia has a basic problem of poverty in the countryside and is trying to improve the education and living standards of the Malays. Recently, there has been some guerrilla disturbance, but this problem has been successfully dealt with before. The government has done good work in overall planning, building up infrastructure and developing new dimensions of the economy, such as opening up the east coast, Sarawak, and Sabah.

Illustrations for Chapter 16

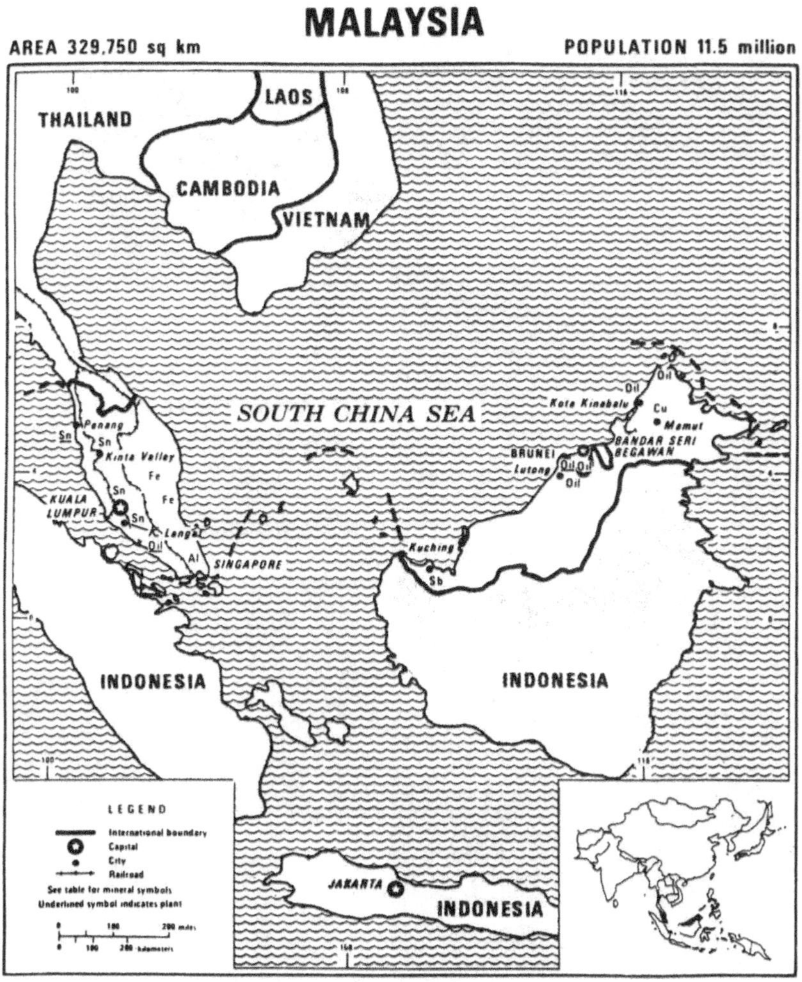

Figure 82 Map of Malaysia

Figure 83 Malaysia's capital Kuala Lumpur

Secretariat Building--
a landmark in Kuala Lumpur

National University in Kuala Lumpur

World's number 1 in palm oil

World's number 1 in rubber

Butterworth and Penang, where the world's premier tin smelters are located

Malayawata's steelworks at Prai

Figure 84 Cities and industries of Malaysia (Courtesy Embassy of Malaysia)

Selangor No. 2 near KL--
largest dredge in Malaysia

Front view of Selangor No. 2
showing buckets

"Palong" of gravel pump
operation in Kinta Valley

Cleaning "palong" which recovers
crude tin concentrates

Hydraulic monitor at work

Monitor operator of gravel
pump operation

Figure 85 Tin operations in Malaysia (Courtesy Malayan Tin Bureau)

Figure 86 Author with world's largest tin dredge—Selangor No. 2 near Kuala Lumpur—in background

General view of concentrator

View of west side of pit

Figure 87 Sabah's 32,000-ton Mamut copper mine, Malaysia

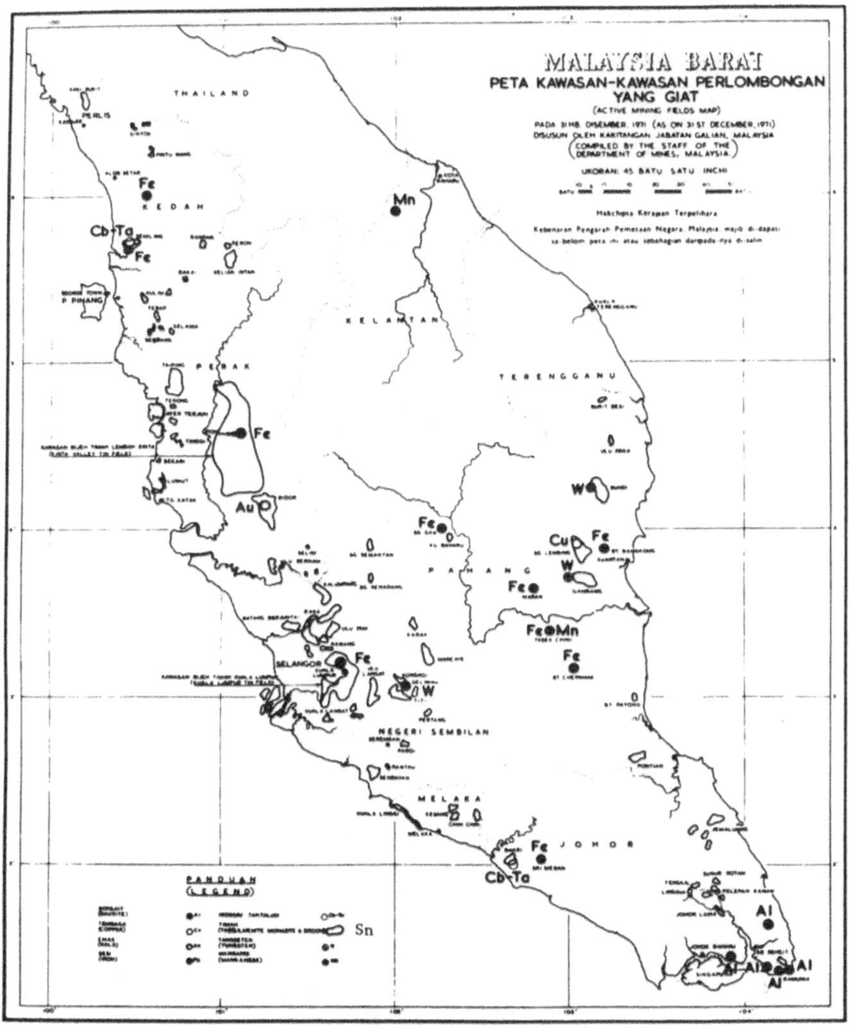

Figure 88 Mining areas of West Malaysia (Courtesy Malaysia Department of Mines)

AREA 329,750 sq. km

MALAYSIA

POPULATION 11.5 million

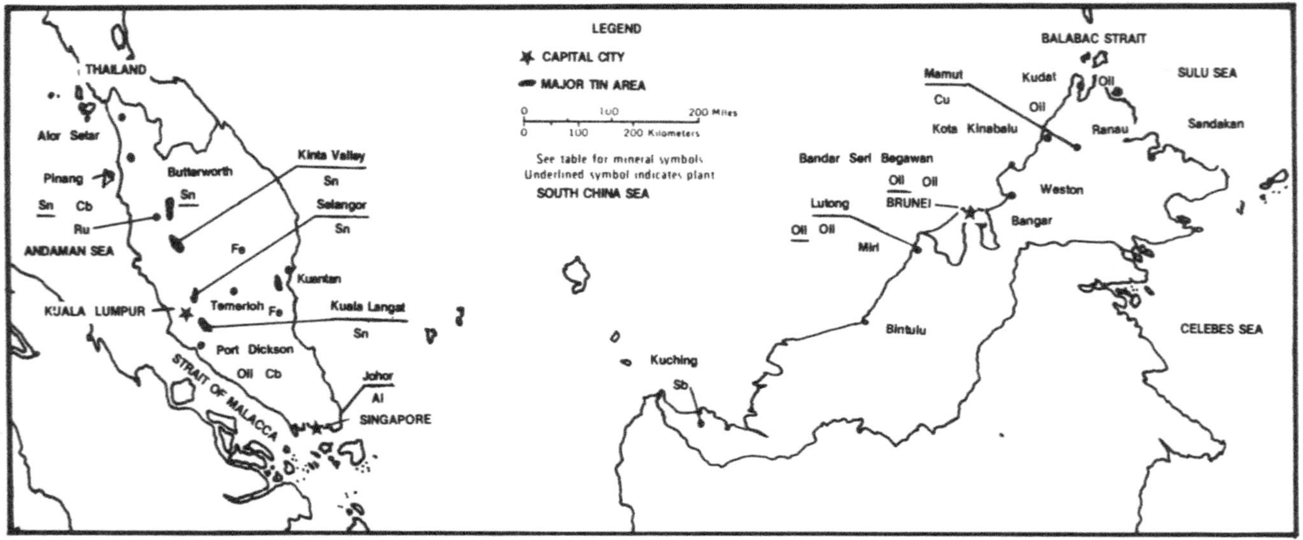

Figure 89 Mineral facilities of Malaysia

17
Mongolia

Mongolia is a large, landlocked "buffer state" of only 1.4 million people between China and the U.S.S.R. Its terrain ranges from the Gobi Desert to the Altai Mountains. Historically a pastoral country, Mongolia is entering an era of mineral, industrial, and agricultural development. Most minerals will be exported, however, since domestic use is nominal except for coal. Fluorspar output is large by world standards. Development of the Erdenet copper-molybdenum deposit in Bulgan Province has begun, and it should become an important mineral supplier to the U.S.S.R. by 1982.

Mongolia's Sixth Five-Year Plan covers 1976-1980. During this period, the announced plan is to more than double capital investment in industry over the previous five years and to increase gross industrial output by 63 percent. In 1976, overall capital investments amounted to about $740 million, and the plan for 1977 is about $930 million. Most of these investments will be directed toward industry, especially minerals. Gross industrial output has been increasing at 5-7 percent annually, and targets have generally been fulfilled.

Significance of Minerals

Government revenue in 1975 was about $815 million, most of which derived from livestock and agriculture.

Mineral output value may have been $65 million in 1975. The mining industry is given high priority in new economic plans, and geological prospecting will be intensified, stressing coal, copper, gold, zinc, and fluorspar.

Mineral Supply Position

Mongolia's trade is mostly with the U.S.S.R. Mineral imports include petroleum (about 370,000 tons from the U.S.S.R. in 1975), coal and coke, semimanufactured steel products for structural applications, and steel pipes. Metallurgical-grade fluorspar and tungsten concentrates were the major minerals exported. All of the estimated 2.5 million tons of coal, 150,000 tons of cement, 40,000 tons of lime, 25,000 tons of gypsum, and 10,000 tons of salt produced in 1975 were apparently consumed in Mongolia.

Nature of Mineral Enterprise

All mining enterprises are state-run, and the U.S.S.R. (principally) and the East European countries provide Mongolia with financial and technical aid. Aside from fluorspar and coal, Mongolia's mineral industry is in its infancy. By the early 1980s, Mongolia should have fully developed the Erdenet project and have explored for additional copper and molybdenum reserves in South Gobi Province and for gold in the northern regions. Other new mining ventures will be made in fluorspar, tin, and tungsten. There are a small cement plant at Darhan and a small oil refinery at Dzunn Bayan.

Principal Mineral Industries

Coal mining is Mongolia's foremost mineral industry, and output from about fourteen open-pit mines totals 2.5 to 3 million tons yearly. The major coal mines are Nalayha, Sharyn Gol, and Chuluun (Aduunchuluun); all three will be "reconstructed" and expanded in the next few years. A plan is under way to develop the new Baganuur deposit into a two-million-ton mine by about 1980.

Mongolia's output of fluorspar, from a fairly large mine at Berh (Berhin) is about 7 percent of the world's total and is important to the East European countries. Already producing at 300,000 metric tons annually, Berh will be greatly expanded in the future. Other fluorspar mines might also be developed. Tungsten comes from the Burentsogt mine and a scheelite deposit in Hayrhan Mountains, and the combined annual output may be 100-200 tons of concentrates.

Stripping has already begun at Erdenet, where eventually 12 million cubic meters of earth will be removed annually to clear the way for producing 15-20 million tpy of copper-molybdenum ore by 1982. In that year, Erdenet is expected to provide a production value equivalent to 40 percent of Mongolia's 1975 gross industrial output. Approximately $120 million were spent on Erdenet in 1975. The Erdenet complex will have about twenty-four "enterprises and shops" and will start producing 4 million tons of ore per year by 1979, at which time there will be housing for 15,000 people. The reserves may be as much as a billion metric tons of 0.9 percent Cu ore. The ore belt is said to be 25 kilometers long, 2.7 kilometers wide, and more than 500 meters deep.

Mine and Industry Workers

The work force in mining may total 2,500, compared with 20,000 in construction and 45,000 in other industries. Technical aid and worker training are provided by the U.S.S.R. and through the programs of the Council for Mutual Economic Assistance (CMEA).

Mineral Transport

Northeast Mongolia is serviced by the Choybalsan-Borzya railroad. The longest railroad extends north-south from Siihbaatar to Dzamin Uud, passing through the capital, Ulaanbaatar (Ulan Bator), and connecting with the Soviet Union and China. A railway has already been built between the Erdenet project and Darhan, and another railway will shortly be commissioned between Erdenet and Salhit. Hard-surface roads link provincial capitals and provinces. During 1976-1980, Mongolia expects that overall cargo traffic will be increased by about 40 percent.

Energy and Power

Electricity output was 818 million kwh in 1975, and installed capacity (all thermal) was about 270,000 kilowatts. The power for Erdenet will come from the U.S.S.R. Plans have reportedly been made to build hydroplants on the Silenge River for the Darhan-Selenge industrial region and on the Hovd River for western Mongolia. Most energy is derived from the burning of coal. Mongolia has about 1,000 electric power stations and 2,000 kilometers of transmission lines.

Summary Outlook

The CMEA provides Mongolia with aid in science and technology and will probably help develop such minerals as nonferrous metals, coking coal, and phosphate rock. Soviet geologists have reportedly already helped discover 150 mineral deposits. By the time the Sixth Five-Year Plan ends in 1980, Mongolia intends to have raised coal production to about 5 million tons and electric power to nearly 1.5 billion kwh. If plans for Erdenet are fulfilled, this complex should eventually be producing 100,000 to 150,000 tons of mine copper annually, along with several thousand tons of mine molybdenum.

Illustrations for Chapter 17

Figure 90 Map of Mongolia

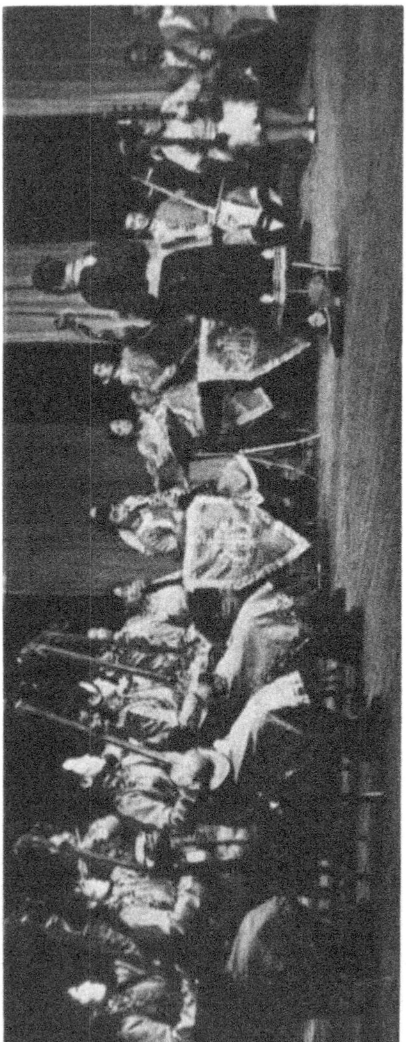

Figure 91 Mongolian musicians and costumes

Figure 92 Ulan Bator and its sports festival

Trucking at Bayantee

Dragline at Bayantee

Trucking at Sharon Gol

Shovel at Sharon Gol

Figure 93 Two open-pit coal mines in Mongolia

IN THE CONSTRUCTION OF THIS MAJOR INDUSTRIAL PROJECT AND ITS CENTRE — THE TOWN OF ERDENET—OUR WORKERS ARE WORKING SHOULDER TO SHOULDER WITH THEIR SOVIET FRIENDS, BORROW THEIR RICH EXPERIENCE, RAISE THEIR OWN SKILLS AND ARE CONSOLIDATING STILL MORE THE TRADITIONAL BROTHERLY FRIENDSHIP OF THE SOVIET AND MONGOLIAN PEOPLES. IT MAY BE SAID WITHOUT FEAR OF EXAGGERATION THAT ERDENET IS NOT ONLY A GREAT CONSTRUCTION SITE BUT A GIGANTIC CENTRE FOR TRAINING HIGHLY-SKILLED WORKERS AND ENGINEERING AND TECHNICAL PERSONNEL. THE BUILDING OF THE NEW INDUSTRIAL COMPLEX IS OF IMMENSE IMPORTANCE IN A FURTHER BUILD-UP OF THE COUNTRY'S INDUSTRIAL POTENTIAL, IN INCREASING THE REPUBLIC'S EXPORT POTENTIAL. IT OPENS UP FINE PROSPECTS FOR DEVELOPING THE RICH NATURAL RESOURCES OF THE REGION AND CREATES THE POSSIBILITY OF AN INTEGRATED DEVELOPMENT OF THE NEIGHBOURING REGIONS.

Yu. TSEDENBAL,
First Secretary of the MPRP Central Committee
(from the Report to the 17th Congress of the MPRP)

CITY AT A COPPER MOUNTAIN

by Ts. DORJSUREN

Legends about the incalculable wealth of Mt. Erdenetiin-obo have been known in our country since time immemorial. It was called "Treasure Mountain", for "erdenet" means "precious". According to the legend, Erdenet kept hidden in its bowels a unique topaz the size of a horse. Greedy merchants tried to dig up the treasure, but a torrent of water suddenly gushed forth from the mountain. The water spread over the valley, forming a beautiful lake and sealing off the underground riches completely... ▶

Figure 94 Mongolia's most important economic project—Erdenet

Figure 95 Additional views of the Erdenet project

18
Nepal

The landlocked Kingdom of Nepal, bounded on the north by Tibet and the south by India, is best known for Mt. Everest and the other high peaks of the Himalayas. Less than half the total land area is cultivated or forested. Agriculture accounts for about 70 percent of the gross domestic product and employs over 90 percent of the labor force. Minerals play a very minor role in the economy. During fiscal year 1974-1975, mineral production was valued at approximately $1.2 million out of a GNP of $1,201 million.

There are many copper, lead, and zinc showings in the central and eastern parts of Nepal. However, few of the mineral occurrences are commercially exploitable. There are tentative plans to develop a lead-zinc deposit at Lari, thirty-five miles northwest of Katmandu. A 12 percent combined lead-zinc ore has been reported, but detailed drilling for reserves will be necessary before mining begins. Because of the extremely rugged terrain, a considerable tonnage of ore must be confirmed in order to assure commercial viability of the operation.

Nepal's first cement plant (Himal) began operating in 1975 and should supply 25 percent of the country's needs. The government plans to build a plant of 200,000-250,000 tons per year at Hetaunda, south of Katmandu. Completion of this second plant, planned for 1980, would make Nepal self-sufficient in cement, a commodity that was totally imported before 1975. In Katmandu there is also a small steel products plant operated by Himal Iron and Steel, Ltd.

Illustration for Chapter 18

Figure 96 Map of Nepal

19
North Korea

The Korean peninsula was once referred to as the embroidered land of 3,000 ri, full of treasures from its fertile soil and rich natural resources. The Democratic People's Republic of Korea is contiguous with China in the north and is separated from its southern neighbor by the 1953 demarcation line. The Six-Year Plan initiated in 1971 gave high priority to the development of basic industries and minerals to complement agriculture. Indigenous minerals are abundant and multifarious; important minerals extracted are anthracite, bituminous coal, lead-zinc, magnetite, cement, and magnesite. However, no oil has been found.

Significance of Minerals

North Korea's GNP in 1975 was estimated at about $10 billion. Agriculture accounted for possibly a third of this. The value of mineral output in 1975 may have been $1.9 billion: coal accounted for $1.1 billion, nonmetallic minerals (including cement) for $0.4 billion, and metal ores for $0.4 billion. GNP growth in 1976 was possibly 7 percent, with industry and mining reportedly contributing 70 percent of the 1976 GNP.

Since 1971, North Korea has promoted a program of basic construction, with emphasis on mining, metals, and chemicals. Major production targets for 1976 are reportedly as follows (in million tons): steel, 3.8 to 4.0; nonferrous metals,

TABLE 12. NORTH KOREA: ROLE IN WORLD MINERAL ECONOMY
(Thousand metric tons, unless otherwise noted)

Major Commodities (Map Symbols)	Production 1976	1975	1974	World Output Share, 1975	Trade in 1975 Exports or Imports	Reserves (or Raw Materials)
Metals						
Copper, refined (Cu)......	15	15	15	Minute	Neither	(Scrap and imports)
Iron, ore (Fe)...........	10,000	9,500	9,000	1 %	Exports--200	Moderate
Iron, pig (Fe)...........	3,500	3,000	2,800	0.6%	Exports--minor	(Local ore)
Iron, steel ingot (St)....	3,900	3,500	3,200	0.5%	Minor both ways	(Local materials)
Lead, mine (Pb)..........	100	95	90	3 %	Exports--some	Moderate
Lead, refined (Pb)........	80	70	70	2 %	Exports--13	(Local ore)
Tungsten, mine (W, tons)..	2,200	2,200	2,100	6 %	Exports--sizable	Sizable
Zinc, mine (Zn)..........	170	160	160	2.5%	Exports--some	Moderate
Zinc, refined (Zn)........	140	140	130	3 %	Exports--40	(Local ore)
Nonmetals						
Apatite (P)...............	400	400	400	0.4%	Neither	Small to medium
Barite (Ba)...............	120	120	120	3 %	Exports--100	Moderate
Cement (Cem)..............	7,000	6,500	6,000	1 %	Exports--500	(Adequate)
Graphite (Gra)............	80	75	75	20 %	Exports--sizable	Sizable
Magnesite (Mg)............	2,000	2,000	1,800	20 %	Exports (clinker)-- 1,000	Extensive
Pyrite (Py)...............	500	500	500	2 %	Neither	Small
Salt......................	500	500	500	0.2%	Neither	Small, plus seawater
Talc......................	100	100	80	Small	Exports--50	Small
Fuels						
Anthracite, coal (C)......	40,000	37,000	32,500	17 %	Exports--small	Large
Bituminous coal (C).......	10,000	8,000	7,500	0.3%	Imports--moderate	Small
Coke......................	2,500	2,200	2,000	0.6%	Imports--moderate	(Mainly local)

NOTE: All data estimated.

0.45; coal, 50 to 53; cement, 7.5 to 8.0; and chemical fertilizers, 2.8 to 3.0. The North Koreans claimed complete fulfillment of the six-year-plan ending in 1976.

Mineral Supply Position

North Korea's principal trading partners are the People's Republic of China, France, Hong Kong, Japan, Romania, and the U.S.S.R. Mineral exports in 1975 totaled possibly $600 million, and the major items were iron concentrate, steel, lead-zinc, barite, cement, refractory clays, magnesia, and coal. Mineral imports were estimated at $400 million, primarily aluminum, chromite, manganese ore, steel products, ferroalloys, coke, coal, petroleum, asbestos, and sulfur. Large purchases of capital goods and machinery were made to help implement economic development plans, and this caused a trade gap of perhaps $400 million with the Western countries in 1975 and of perhaps another $700 million with Eastern Europe and China together. In 1976 the trade gap was reduced to about $250 million, with imports of $850 million and exports of $600 million.

The bulk of steel and cement produced is consumed domestically because of the government's drive for industrial expansion. There are no petroleum resources, and sizable quantities have had to be imported, mainly from the U.S.S.R. and China. Coal has been used as an industrial fuel as well as in space heating. Chemical fertilizers are indispensable to agriculture. Refractory products such as clay and magnesite are both consumed and exported.

Nature of Mineral Enterprise

North Korea's industries are all state-owned enterprises, and each plant is responsible to the State Planning Bureau for meeting production targets and standards. Under the Ch'ollima Movement, all work teams are exhorted to excel, so as to accelerate output, increase productivity, and improve morale. Incentives and awards are given to teams that surpass targets.

North Korea is the world's second largest producer of anthracite. Its cement capacity is on a par with that of

Taiwan and less than that of South Korea. In the Orient, only Japan, China, and India surpass North Korea in iron and steel production. The country is also a medium-sized producer of lead and zinc, and output is being raised to provide larger surpluses for export. North Korea leads the world in magnesite production.

Aside from coal, steel, and cement, which will be described later, many other minerals of consequence are being produced. There are old, but fair-sized, lead-zinc smelters at Munpyong and Nampo processing domestic concentrates from the Komdok, Kapsan, and other mines (a part of the concentrate is also exported). A new ore-dressing plant, a long-distance conveyor belt, and high-speed mining equipment were recently put into operation at the Komdok mine. Peru furnished 50,000 tons of copper concentrates to the Hungnam smelter in 1975. Three small aluminum reduction plants have been reported, and a new 20,000-ton plant is being completed. North Korea converts most of the magnesite to magnesia before export. Nickel, precious metals, and mercury are also extracted. Sizable quantities of barite are being supplied to the Soviet Union under a long-term barter deal. Phosphate ores are produced at the Unsan mine. An oil pipeline connecting with China's Taching field has recently been completed.

Principal Mineral Industries

Plans call for the doubling of coal production to about 100 million tons by the end of the next economic plan (begins 1977). The coalfields in North Hamgyong Province, close to the Kim Chaek ironworks, will be expanded. Kukdong and Yangjong are two new coking coal mines that together furnish a million tons annually. The Aoji and Kogonwan mines are already producing large quantities of coking coal. South Pyongyang and Kangwon are other provinces supplying coal to the steel industry. Major anthracite mines are Sinchang and Anju in South Pyongyang Province, Sudang in South Hamgyong Province, and Chaeryong, Tokchon, Kangdong, and Kangso. Relatively new hard-coal mines that have reportedly done well recently include Hukryong,

Chonsong, Hyonkum, Kowon, Namjon, Sinwon, Taegum, and Yongjin.

Most iron ore production comes from Musan, Chaeryong, Unyul, Hasong, Kwangchon, and Tokchon, and new mines have been opened at Tokonsong and Sohaeri. Musan, with more than a billion tons of low-grade, taconite-type ores, is being expanded to over 6.5 million tons of iron concentrate yearly. Ores and concentrates from Musan and elsewhere are sent to iron and steel complexes at Hwanghai, Kangson, and Kim Chaek. These plants have recently been modernized, raising North Korea's steel capacity to 4 million tons per year. A new rolling mill was recently installed at the Kim Chaek Steelworks, and additional projects were also built at the Kangson Steelworks.

The drive for basic development has called for the expansion of existing cement facilities and the building of new plants. The 3-million-tpy Sunchon Cement Works has been undergoing expansion to double capacity. A 5-million-tpy cement plant being built in the Chonnae-ri area was scheduled for completion in 1976. Other cement plants are at Pongsan, Komusan, Majong, Haeju, Sunghori, and Kusong. At the end of 1976, North Korea's cement capacity was about 8 million tpy; the target for the last year of the next economic plan is 20 million tpy.

Mine and Industry Workers

The North Korean labor force consists of 7.5 to 8 million people, about half of whom are in industry and the rest in agriculture, animal husbandry, fisheries, and related fields. Approximately 175,000 are employed in the mining sector. In its attempt to create a highly industrialized state, North Korea has been hampered by an acute shortage of skilled labor. Efforts to augment labor resources included combined work-study programs for students and the use of volunteer labor.

Mineral Transport

A ninety-eight-kilometer pipeline is being used to transport slurried iron concentrate from Musan to the Kimchaek

Iron and Steel Works in Chongjin. A ten-kilometer cableway was installed to transport coal from the Kangso Colliery to the Kangson iron and steel complex near Pyongyang. An oil pipeline has been built on the China side of the frontier, although how this connects within North Korea is not known. The country has a relatively good transport system.

The railroads provide the principal means of transportation, hauling about 90 percent of all freight and about 70 percent of all passenger traffic. The rail density is highest in the southwest, with Pyongyang the country's rail center. About 900 kilometers, or one-fourth, of the rail network have been electrified, including the Chongjin-Rijin line. Electric traction has been introduced on all trunk lines between Pyongyang and Sinuiju and between Pyongyang and Rajin. Electrification of the Pyongyang-Sariwon line is being completed. Diesel traction is being introduced on the nonelectrified railways. The Ichon-Sepo railway links the east and the west, and the Sinchon-Unyul railway services the west coast. The Kanggye-Musan railway, now being constructed, will run through the northern inland districts.

Energy and Power

The bulk of North Korea's fuel requirement is based upon domestic coal, and special demand for refined petroleum has so far been met by imports (about a million tons from the U.S.S.R. in 1974 and 1975). However, a petroleum refinery is being constructed to process Chinese crude oil from northwest of Harbin; the Chinese may supply as much as 1.5 million tons of crude annually. Energy available from hydropower is estimated at 10 million kilowatts, principally from the Amnokgang and Tumangan rivers. Hydropower overshadows thermal power (from coal). The recently commissioned 1,600,000-kw plant at Pukchang, the old 500,000-kw plant at Pyongyang, and the Chongchon-gang steam plant appear to be North Korea's only important thermal stations. The North Koreans hope to generate 50 billion kwh of electricity per year by the end of the next economic plan, compared with possibly 30 billion kwh in 1976.

Summary Outlook

The objective of the 1971-1976 economic plan was to attain two-thirds self-sufficiency in the raw materials required by domestic industry. Moreover, high priority was given to mining and metallurgy in order to expand the country's industrial base. The next economic plan, scheduled to go into effect in 1977, calls for doubling the output of steel, nonferrous metals, coal, cement, and chemical fertilizers by 1980.

Illustrations for Chapter 19

Figure 97 Map of North Korea

Figure 98 North Korea's Komdok nonferrous mine

Model workers at the Samsin colliery

Coal loading at Samsin

Coal drilling

Coal loading at Sinchang

Figure 99 Two of North Korea's collieries—Samsin and Sinchang

98-km iron slurry pipeline from Musan to Kimchaek steelworks

Top: Mining and loading at the Musan openpit iron mine

Bottom: Long conveyor system feeding Musan concentrate into sintering furnaces of Kimchaek steelworks

Downstream section of the 98-km pipeline

Figure 100 Musan iron mine and shipment of concentrates to steelworks

Hwanghae Steelworks

Kimchaek (Chongjin) Steelworks

Figure 101 Two major steelworks in North Korea—Hwanghae and Kimchaek

Figure 102 New cement works at Sunchon—first-stage capacity will be 3 million tpy

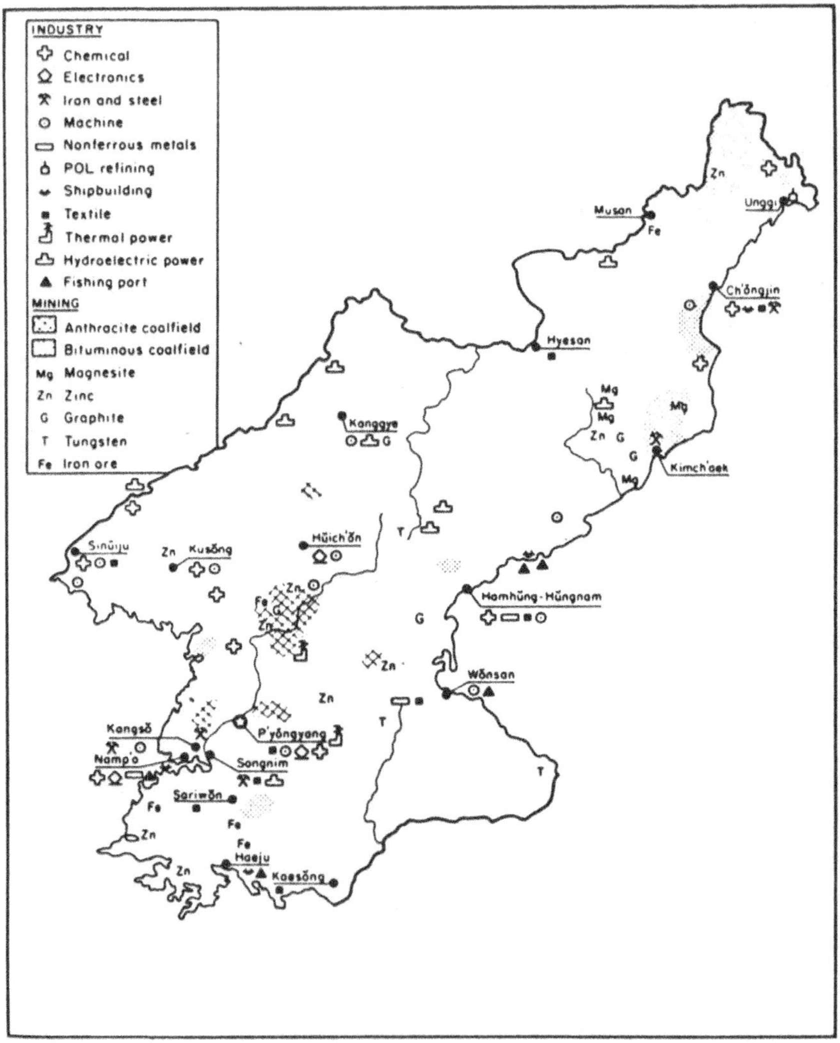

Figure 103 The basic industries of North Korea

20
Pakistan

Pakistan's mineral industry has not had much of an impact on its economy. Its importance is expected to grow, however, as the country attempts to substitute domestic fuels and materials for increasingly costly imports. Oil-poor and coal-poor Pakistan plans to develop local uranium to replace much of the energy now supplied by imported petroleum. The construction of new fertilizer, cement, and steel plants is aimed at cutting down foreign exchange requirements. The government favors a mixed economy of public and private ownership and has done little to encourage domestic private investment. However, foreign private investment is welcome in most fields. The real GNP growth rate was about 5 percent in 1976 and may reach 8 percent in 1977. There was a trade deficit of approximately $1 billion, which was made up by remittances and aid disbursements. Pakistan is currently placing special emphasis on the development of infrastructure, including ports, water supply, drainage systems, gas pipelines, oil refining, electric power, and cement plants.

Significance of Minerals

In 1975 Pakistan's mineral production value was estimated at approximately $70 million (excluding cement, which probably had a value of over $60 million). GNP in the

TABLE 13. PAKISTAN: ROLE IN WORLD MINERAL SUPPLY
(Thousand metric tons, unless otherwise noted)

Major Commodities (Map Symbols)	Production 1976	1975	1974	World Output Share, 1975	Trade in 1975 Exports or Imports	Reserves (or Raw Materials)
Metals						
Chromite (Cr)..........	8	11	12	0.1%	Exports--------e/18	2,000
Copper, ore (Cu).......	---	---	---	---	Neither	200,000
Nonmetals						
Aragonite..............	26	27	22	Small	Exported	Small
Cement (Cem)...........	e/3,100	3,200	3,500	0.5%	Exports------1,370	(Adequate)
Fertilizers, N. (Fert).	3,160	2,960	NA	Small	Little trade	(Natural gas)
Gypsum (Gyp)...........	422	298	215	0.5%	Surplus	67,000
Phosphate rock (P).....	---	---	---	---	Imports---------460	2,500
Salt, rock.............	420	404	368	Minute	Exports----------11	85,000
Fuels						
Coal (C)...............	1,080	1,300	1,100	Minute	Small imports	450,000
Oil, crude (Oil).......	280	290	340	Minute	Imports------3,100	30,000
Oil, refined (Oil).....	e/3,700	e/3,500	3,300	0.1%	Imports------1,100	(Mostly imported)
Natural gas (Gas, $10^6 M^3$).........	5,000	5,000	4,450	0.3%	Neither	400,000

e/ Estimated.

fiscal year ending June 30, 1975, was $10 billion. Thus, the mineral industry contributed a very small share of the total. Natural gas, valued at about $40 million, was the leading natural mineral product. Other minerals of consequence were limestone (the main raw material for cement), coal, crude oil, salt, and chromite. In 1975, Pakistan produced about 3.2 million tons of cement, 1.3 million tons of coal, 630,000 tons of salt, and 11,000 tons of chromite (reserves may be 2 million tons).

Mineral Supply Position

Most mineral output was for domestic consumption, with only a small portion exported. In fiscal 1975, exports of minerals and mineral-related commodities were valued at $47 million, or 4 percent of total exports ($1,057 million). Cement exports were valued at $28 million, and incidental exports of crude petroleum and refinery products at $14 million. Mineral imports were larger than mineral exports because Pakistan lacks many resources. The mineral import bill in fiscal 1975 totaled $728 million, or 35 percent of all imports ($2,088 million). Expenditures of $337 million for crude petroleum and refinery products and $269 million for crude and semifinished metals represented 83 percent of all mineral imports.

Nature of Mineral Enterprise

The government maintains control of industries considered essential to the economy. In the mineral field, these include cement, salt, nuclear power, and energy distribution. Most major new mineral enterprises will be publicly owned, including copper, steel, and phosphate rock operations. The government has noncontrolling investments in various other mineral fields, including fertilizers, coal, natural gas, crude petroleum, and oil refining.

Most private investment in minerals is of foreign origin and concentrated in the petroleum and natural gas industries. Pakistan Petroleum Ltd. (a subsidiary of Burmah Oil Co.) and Esso Petroleum Co. own the two major gas fields. American Oil Co., Continental Oil Co., Marathon Oil Co.,

Pakistan Oilfields, Ltd. (a subsidiary of Attock Oil Co., Ltd.), Texasgulf Inc., Total Pakistan (Cie. Française des Pétroles S.A.), Trend Exploration, Ltd., El Paso Natural Gas, Broken Hill Pty., Ltd., and Wintershall A.G. are active in petroleum exploration. Two of the country's three oil refineries (Pakistan's total refining capacity is about 74,000 bpd) are also controlled by international oil companies.

Public financing has accounted for an increasing share of mineral capital in recent years. Pakistan government funds, along with loans from the World Bank, Asian Development Bank, and the Middle East oil-producing countries, have provided the bulk of capital inputs for mineral development. Foreign private investment has been a minor factor in fields other than petroleum and natural gas. The contribution of domestic private capital is small, and its growth has been discouraged by the nationalization of local firms. The largest domestic investor is the Fancy Group, the owner of the major chromite mines.

Principal Mineral Industries

Natural gas is Pakistan's leading mineral produced and the only relatively abundant fossil fuel. The Sui and Mari gas fields account for more than 90 percent of the national production (approximately 5 billion cubic meters annually). There are also nine small and little-developed fields. The gas pipelines serving most of the larger urban centers are being expanded to handle increased demand. The estimated total reserves of 400 billion cubic meters (including about 200 billion from Sui and 100 billion from Mari) constitute roughly a hundred-year supply at current output rates. However, demand is steadily increasing. For this reason, the government is looking into alternative energy sources. Declining domestic petroleum production met less than one-tenth of Pakistan's requirements in 1975. The government's Oil and Gas Development Corp. and various foreign companies recently discovered an oil and gas deposit at Dhodak with oil reserves of about 200 million barrels. A $42-million, 40,000-bpd oil refinery is being built at Multan in central Pakistan in a joint venture between the governments of Pakistan and Abu Dhabi.

Pakistan has large deposits of lignite-to-subbituminous coals that are high in moisture and impurities. The government has initiated two coal development projects: the construction of a coal-fired power plant at Lakhra, and the upgrading of coal at Sharigh for use in the steel mill under construction near Karachi.

The agricultural economy of Pakistan needs more fertilizer than is currently produced. To cut down on the rising cost of fertilizer imports, the government and private industry are building four new fertilizer plants, three based on natural gas and the fourth on a 2.5-million-ton deposit of marketable phosphate rock. A proposed fertilizer complex, which will include ammonia and urea plants, is expected to produce 700,000 tons of various fertilizer compounds annually.

Other mineral-related developments currently under way include construction of the country's first integrated steel mill near Karachi (two 1,750-mtpd blast furnaces scheduled for completion before 1980) and investigation of a 200-million-ton, low-grade porphyry copper deposit at Saindak, in the Baluchistan desert of far western Pakistan. The Saindak deposit was drilled again in early 1976 with UNDP help, but the remote location, lack of water supply, and inadequate transport facilities have so far delayed mine development. A new barite industry of 20,000 mtpy is being developed.

In 1975, Pakistan exported more than two-fifths of its cement output, or 1.37 million tons (mainly to nearby Middle East countries). Rising demand has prompted plans to raise output and cut down on exports. The State Cement Corporation plans to increase Pakistan's cement production by 1.5 million tons by about 1979. Plants at Karachi, Javedan, and Mustehkam will be expanded by about 300,000 mtpy each. New plants may be built at Spintungi near Sibi in Baluchistan, at Gadani in Lasbela, and at Kohat in northwest Pakistan.

Mine and Industry Workers

Less than half a percent of the labor force (or at most 100,000 workers) is directly employed in minerals. However, some of the country's 3.3 million manufacturing workers are also engaged in such mineral-related activities as cement and fertilizers. Additional labor is available and can be trained. Professional and technical skills are in short supply.

Mineral Transport

Transport facilities are uneven in Pakistan. Facilities are adequate along the valley of the Indus River and its tributaries, where most of the country's 5,400 miles of railroads and 21,000 miles of roads (11,000 miles of all-weather roads) are located. In much of the desert regions to the east and west of the rivers and in the mountain region to the north, surface transportation is poor to nonexistent. Adequate road or railroad access routes are available to serve the principal existing mineral production sites, and the natural gas pipeline system is being expanded to new areas. However, mineral development in remote locations, notably the copper deposit at Saindak, is difficult since new transport facilities must be built.

Energy and Power

Pakistan has few fossil fuel resources, except for natural gas. Approximately 15 percent of the total import expenditures in 1975 were for petroleum, the most widely used fuel. Declining production and unsuccessful exploration activity offer little current prospect of an adequate domestic oil supply. Natural gas supplies about one-fourth of the energy demand. Little use has been made of the extensive low-grade coal resources, although the government is developing the Lakhra and Sharigh projects in order to expand coal utilization. Construction of the Tarbela and Kalabagh dams will more fully utilize the country's hydropower potential. The government plans to build a series of nuclear power plants to be fueled by uranium resources in the Dera Ghazi Khan area. However, the financing for these nuclear plants is still uncertain. During 1977-1978, Pakistan plans to commission a 125,000-kw steam plant and nine 25,000-kw gas turbines.

Summary Outlook

The principal economic issues include the energy problem, the balance of payments, and the role of private investment. Efforts to deal with energy involve the substitution of indigenous fuels for petroleum, mainly natural gas, coal, and uranium. Efforts to cut down the balance-of-payments deficit involve building up domestic fertilizer, cement, and iron and steel production capacity. Domestic private investment in minerals and industry has not made much headway, but the government is trying to attract foreign investors, particularly those who can provide advanced technology, large capital inputs, and new export markets.

In early 1977 it was announced that oil and gas in considerable quantities had been found at Dhadak in the Dera Ghazi Khan District of Punjab. According to preliminary indications, oil reserves could amount to 200 million barrels, and gas reserves could be equivalent to half those of the Sui gas field.

Illustrations for Chapter 20

Figure 104 Map of Pakistan

Figure 105 Pakistan's scenes—old and new

Flaring at the Sui gas field

Surfuric acid plant at Lyallpur

Coal desulfurization pilot plant

Gas installation at Sui

Figure 106 Natural gas and industrial plants in Pakistan (Courtesy Embassy of Pakistan)

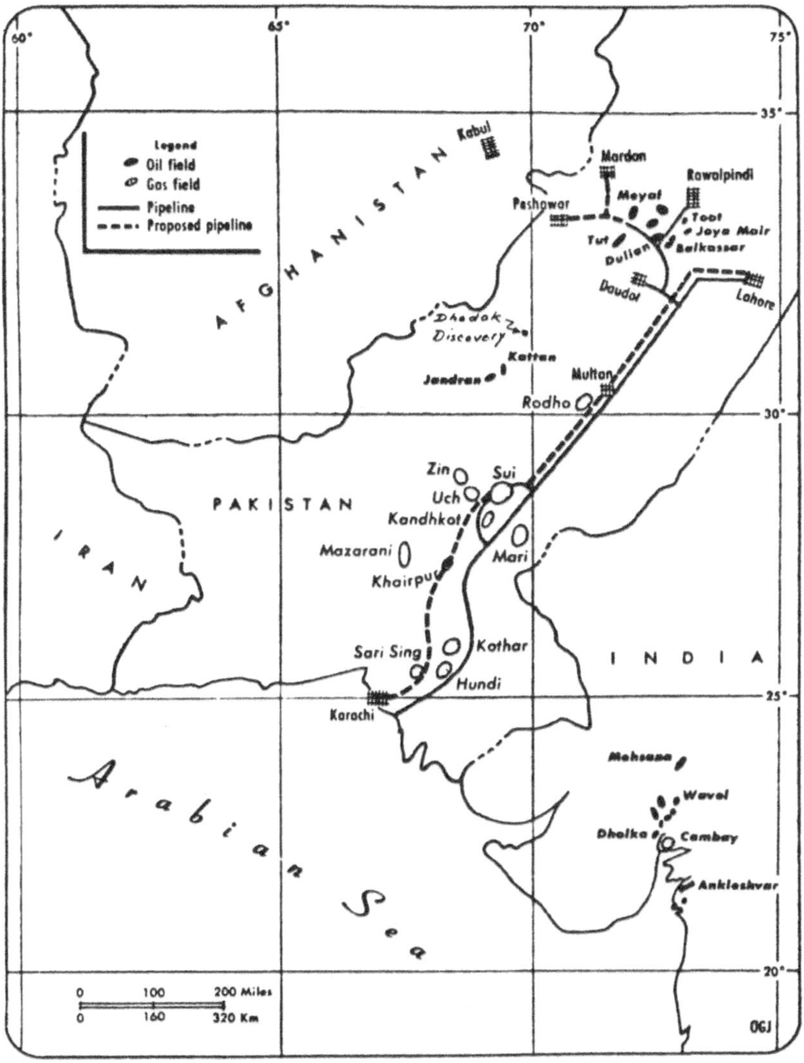

Figure 107 Planned gas expansion in Pakistan

21
Papua New Guinea

The Territory of Papua New Guinea, comprising the Trust Territory of New Guinea and the Territory of Papua, was administered by Australia from 1949 to 1973 and was granted self-government on December 1, 1973. On September 16, 1975, it became an independent nation, and the newly formed political entity was renamed Papua New Guinea. Its capital is Port Moresby. Most of the country's land area is on the eastern half of New Guinea Island, and the rest is on five main island groups: Bismarck Archipelago, Solomon Islands, Trobriand Islands, D'Entrecasteaux Islands, and the Louisiade Archipelago. Papua New Guinea is rich in resources but is largely undeveloped. The economy has traditionally been based on rubber, cocoa, tea, coffee, and copra plantations and more recently on the mining and sale of copper, gold, and silver.

Significance of Minerals

The country's GNP was estimated at about $1.2 billion in 1975. The mining sector accounted for $230 million from the sales of concentrates containing copper, gold, and silver; plantation crops (copra, cocoa, coffee, timber, and other agricultural products) accounted for about $175 million; manufacturing for $84 million; and services and other inputs for the remainder.

Mineral Supply Position

Since it has no smelter and refinery facilities, Papua New Guinea exports copper concentrates containing gold and silver for processing abroad, principally to Japan. There has as yet been no commercial discovery of oil and gas in the country. Sales of copper ores and concentrates and plantation crops such as coffee, tea, cocoa, timber, and other agricultural products provide foreign exchange for the purchase of petroleum and petroleum products, machinery, transport equipment, foodstuffs, and other items. The local market for metals and construction materials is limited by the small population and lack of industries.

The little exploration that has been done has been by Japanese, Australian, and South African firms and by the government-owned OK Tedi Development Co. for mineralization of other copper and gold occurrences and for nickel, bauxite, and titanium. Other mineral deposits that potentially may be developed include copper occurrences in the Star Mountains in northwest Papua New Guinea, porphyry copper at the Frieda River prospect and the nearby Yandira copper prospect, and gold on Misima Island in Milne Bay.

A Mineral Resources Stabilization Fund receives all income accruing to the government from major natural resource processing. This fund acts to insure an even flow of revenue and attempts to insulate the economy from fluctuations in world metal prices.

Nature of Mineral Enterprise

Bougainville Copper is the only large-scale mining operation in Papua New Guinea. The Department of Natural Resources, however, states that many gold and silver prospectors are working in Morobe, Eastern Highlands, Enga, Western Highlands, and West Sepik and Madang provinces. Total earnings for these small prospectors were only about $2.2 million in 1976, or a fraction of Bougainville's output value.

Principal Mineral Industries

Bougainville Copper Pty., Ltd. began copper mine production in 1972 from the Panguna copper porphyry deposit in the Kawerong Valley on the western slope of the Crown Prince Range on south-central Bougainville Island. Reserves were estimated at 870 million tons averaging 0.47 percent copper and 0.62 grams of gold per ton. The owners of Bougainville Copper are Conzinc Riotinto (53.6 percent), the government of Papua New Guinea (20 percent), and public shareholders, who include around 9,000 Papua New Guineans (26.4 percent). In 1975, production of ores and concentrates totaled 595,946 tons containing 172,477 metric tons of copper, 445,110 troy ounces of gold, and 981,416 troy ounces of silver.

Mine and Industry Workers

Not until the 1930s were the people of Papua New Guinea introduced to the basic aspects of the modern world. Traditionally, the key sector of the economy was agricultural plantations, which were largely owned by foreign nationals and operated with local labor. At present, up to 70 percent of the population is dependent on agriculture for a livelihood. There is a lack of skilled workers and professional staff, and the labor force must be trained to utilize present-day technology. The only mine is operated by an Australian company and employs 3,500 workers. The company has a personnel development program, which includes a mine training center and offers scholarships at various schools and universities.

Mineral Transport

Papua New Guinea is mountainous, and its mineral resources are located in remote, relatively inaccessible areas. The cost of setting up a mining industry and transporting the materials extracted may be the chief deterrent to future mineral resource projects. The cost of providing infrastructure and roads is largely left to the individual mining company. Bougainville Copper Pty. has developed housing and other amenities at the coastal town of Arawa to support its mining operation at Panguna.

Energy and Power

All principal cities in the country have some electricity and water supply, although electricity generation is restricted in the more remote areas. The Electricity Commission has continued to develop the Ramu hydroelectric project, which includes three fifteen-megawatt generators. Initial power generation would benefit Lae and a number of places in the highland areas. A feasibility study is being completed on the country's largest potential hydroelectric project, Purari, and the commission is investigating the possibilities of small hydroelectric projects for rural electrification.

Summary Outlook

The country's mineral potential seems promising, even aside from copper. The development of other minerals could earn much-needed additional foreign exchange for Papua New Guinea and thereby raise its standard of living. The Purari River basin, which has an area of 73,000 square kilometers and drains into the Gulf of Papua, may offer as much as 10,000 megawatts of reasonably priced hydroelectric power. Energy-intensive industries, such as metal smelters and refineries, may be prospective users of this power. Because of the occurrence of fossil fuels in various areas of Australasia, oil and natural gas exploration has continued to attract foreign investment. A natural gas deposit has been found in the Gulf of Papua, with reserves estimated at 1,000 billion cubic feet.

Illustration for Chapter 21

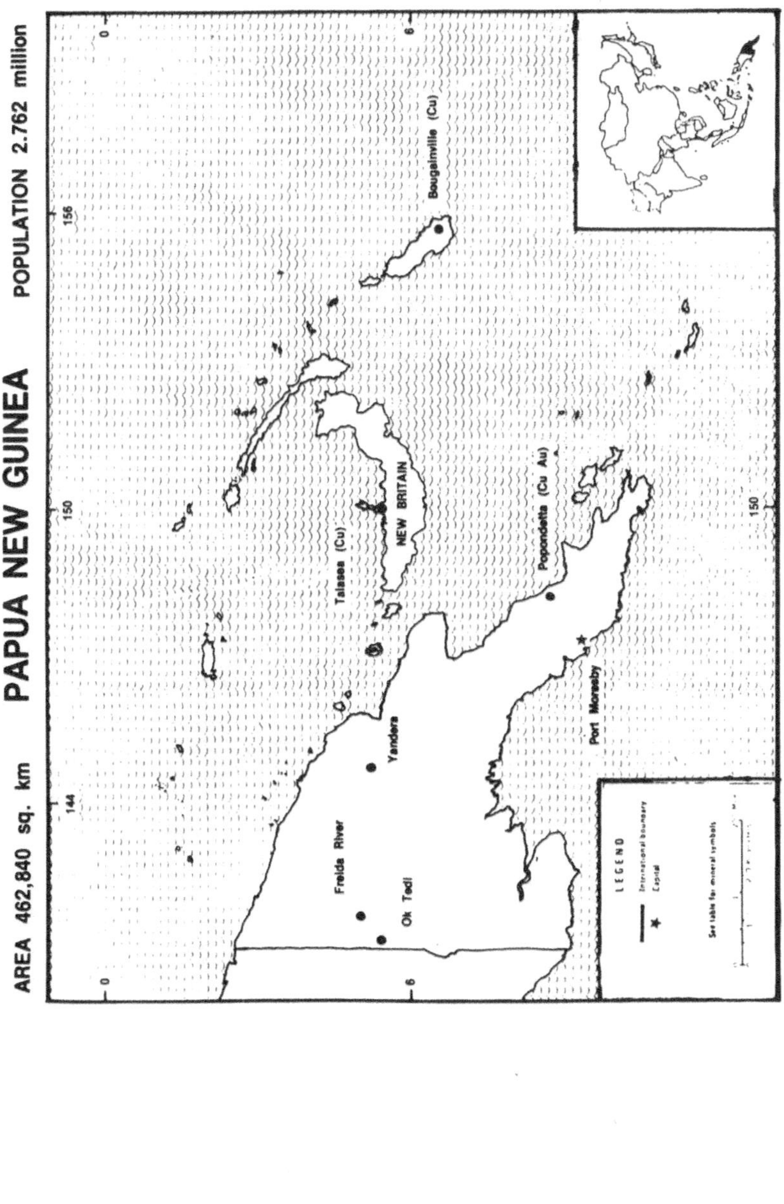

Figure 108 Map of Papua New Guinea

22
Philippines

Although famous for its minerals, the Philippines has various other well-known exports, such as sugar, coconut oil, lumber, and copra. The Philippines is part of the Pacific fire belt with its own brand of porphyries. It has become a major copper producer over and above its significant gold production. In fact, it is a medium-sized world producer of both metals. Nickeliferous laterites and basic mafic rocks bearing chromites are also present. There are the volcanics that helped form the "black ores," complex nonferrous metal ores, and perlites. Geologic diversity is further exemplified by deposits of zinc, mercury, manganese, and iron sands. The Philippines is not just a mineral exporter but is also a fuel and metal consumer of some consequence. Cement is produced, and additional mineral processing facilities will be built in order to cut down on imports. But the fuel base is extremely weak, and the 1976 fuel import bill of about $1 billion was more than twice the value of mineral exports. The Philippine balance of payments, although slightly improved, still showed a deficit of about $1 billion in 1976.

The Philippine economy did not have a good year in 1976, but it was better than in 1975. Real economic growth at 6 percent was higher than in the previous year, and inflation at 7 percent was lower. GNP in 1976 was about $17.5 billion.

TABLE 14. PHILIPPINES: ROLE IN WORLD MINERAL SUPPLY
(Thousand metric tons, unless otherwise noted)

Major Commodities (Map Symbols)	Production			World Output Share, 1975	Trade in 1975 Exports or Imports	Reserves (or Raw Materials)
	1976	1975	1974			
Metals						
Chromite, met. (Cr)......	84.7	99.0	100.4	2 %	All exported	2,000
Chromite, ref. (Cr)......	314.5	421.1	429.1	Large	All exported	10,000
Copper, mine (Cu)........	238.1	228.4	225.5	3 %	All exported	10,000
Gold (Au, 10^3 oz.).......	501.0	501.8	437.6	1.3%	Unknown	Moderate
Iron, concentrate (Fe)...	571	1,351	1,608	0.2%	All exported	100,000
Lead, mine (Pb)..........	4.6	3.4	1.3	0.1%	Mostly exported	Small
Nickel, refined (Ni).....	17.8	9.5	0.3	1.2%	All exported	("Billions of tons" laterites)
Silver, (Ag, 10^3 oz.)....	1,513	1,620	1,718	0.5%	Unknown	Moderate
Zinc, mine (Zn)..........	11.4	10.5	7.7	0.2%	All exported	Unknown
Nonmetals						
Cement (Cem).............	4,500[e]	4,263	3,562	0.6%	Small surplus	(Limestone sizable)
Gypsum (Gyp).............	62	118	126	0.2%	Neither	Synthetic
Fuels						
Oil, crude (Oil).........	--	--	--	--	Imports--9,136	None so far
Oil, refined (Oil).......	[e]9,500	8,400	9,100	0.3%	Imports--500 (1974)	(Imported crude)

[e] Estimated.

Commodity prices improved somewhat, including copper prices. However, copper output was slightly lower in 1976 because of sluggish demand by Japan and because of a down time at one of the leading producers. The gold industry was in great difficulty because of rising costs and low prices. This prompted the government to give thought to gold subsidies again.

Significance of Minerals

GNP was about $15.5 billion in 1975. To this the mineral industry contributed $660 million, or 4 percent. Despite the global recession and low metal prices abroad, Philippine mineral exports in 1975 were valued at $387 million, or 15 percent of all exports. Petroleum imports alone were equivalent to roughly one-fourth of all 1975 imports, and metal imports were of secondary importance. The Philippines is the leading producer of copper, gold, and chromite in Asia. Copper output is about 3 percent of the world's share, and gold is nearly 1.3 percent. The country is the world's foremost producer of refractory chromite.

The widespread occurrence and distribution of minerals have meant a great deal to economic development in the Philippines in terms of communities, roads, interisland shipping, engineering, training, and progress in industrialization. The mineral industry is moving forward from merely handling raw materials to basic development, processing, smelting, and fabrication.

Mineral Supply Position

The Philippines is best known for exports of metal concentrates, mainly to Japan. Almost all the leading minerals are mined for export, except for gold, which has a special relationship with the Government Central Bank, and items such as cement, which mainly go into the domestic market. Mine copper production showed little change in 1973-1975, but exports in 1975 were down somewhat in tonnage (762,428 tons of concentrates in 1975 and 830,454 tons in 1974) and considerably down in value owing to low prices. Refractory chromite has a special market in the

United States because of the demand by the U.S. steel industry. One Philippine producer hopes eventually to produce and export over 30,000 tons of nickel annually, although start-up difficulties have restricted production to about half of this in 1975. Philippine iron sands are shipped to Japanese blast furnaces for slagging purposes and stabilizing refractories. All the metallurgical chromite and iron ore hitherto mined have also gone to Japan.

Alongside exports of raw minerals, the Philippines has been importing increasing quantities of metals and fuels for domestic consumption, further processing, and even fabrication. As a result, Philippine planners have begun to think about building smelters to refine part of the ores that are exported. The need for nonferrous metals, especially copper and aluminum, is getting close to 50,000 tons per year. The annual demand for steel products is moving toward one million tpy. Most industries are run by imported petroleum, which has become very costly. The country hopes to find more local fuels and power but may have to resort to more efficient utilization, expansion of exports to pay for the fuel bill, and eventual introduction of nuclear power. The need for cement will continue to grow, and additional facilities will be built to satisfy demand.

Nature of Mineral Enterprise

All the big mining companies are private. Although many have foreign connections (mainly North American and Japanese), Philippine domestic capital is strong in mining. A number of mining firms are predominantly Philippine, and most others have substantial Philippine equity. U.S. involvement in mining began in pre–World War II days, but U.S. companies have shown little interest since that time. Many Americans have made their home in the Philippines, and Arizona miners have played a significant role in the development of the copper industry. More recently, the Japanese have contributed heavily to mining and metallurgy in the Philippines—through technical and financial aid and advance purchase of output. The Canadians are partners in some companies. Because of foreign involvement, the mining industry is technically fairly advanced by world standards, except that the shovels and trucks are a little smaller than those employed in the newest open-pits in Minnesota and Utah. The largest open-pit in the Philippines compares favorably with those in Arizona, and the country even has block-caving mines. Owing to the nature of the ore bodies, various mines do not lend themselves to very large scale operations.

The most famous Philippine mining company is Atlas Consolidated, a subsidiary of A. Soriano Corp., with principal operations on Cebu Island. In 1976, its gross was $157.7 million (net profit of $25.4 million), output was 103,053 metric tons of mine copper, and reserves were 881 million tons of ore averaging 0.46 percent copper. Atlas was hoping to build a copper smelter in Bataan, but the Philippine government has advised a delay in favor of another smeltér sponsored originally by Lepanto Consolidated and Marinduque Mining—a $250-million, 84,000-tpy Outokumpo flash smelter, to be located possibly in Batangas. Lepanto, with primarily American capital and mines in Luzon, has a high-grade gold-energite ore body; it has traditionally shipped to the Asarco smelter in Tacoma, Washington. The high arsenic content of the ore caused a temporary suspension of mining operations for most of 1976. Marinduque did well in producing 32,656 tons of mine copper in 1976, but it had severe trouble with the Sherritt-Gordon process in its nickel refinery (75 million pounds per year) on Nonoc Island. With a profit of $3.7 million in 1975, Marinduque suffered a loss of $11.1 million in 1976. Lepanto lost $0.23 million in 1975 but had a net income of $1.8 million in 1976. Marinduque's Sipalay and Bagacay mines were discovered by Mitsui Mining and Smelting geologists. Philex Mining, with a 30,000-tpy copper, block-caving mine in Baguio and with a gross of $60 million and profit of $20 million in 1976, is connected with Nippon Mining of Japan. Benguet Consolidated, the country's oldest mining company, is heavily invested with U.S. money and is the country's leading gold producer. Benguet Consolidated, which has many mining properties and owns various nonmining firms, grossed $39.8 million in 1975 but suffered a loss of $1.7 million in 1976. This company also operates Consolidated Mines' famous Masinloc refractory chromite mines, which grossed $12.7 million in 1976. Marcopper, a new firm, produced 47,534 tons of mine copper, grossed $50 million, and had a net income of $8.5 million in 1976. New mineral discoveries are steadily being made.

Currently under martial law, the Philippines mining industry has attained greater stability than in the past. While there are more controls, there is also more legal flexibility when industries are in trouble. Taxation is currently a percentage of the gross rather than profit. The industry tax holiday provision has been revoked. Foreign participation in joint ventures is encouraged, with equity share allowable at no more than 40 percent and no less than 25 percent. There is a 30 percent export duty on copper when the price tops 90 U.S. cents per pound, but this is now academic. The gold industry is being assisted in various ways. Savings in corporate taxes are possible by declaring stock dividends. During 1975, percentage depletion was phased out and cost depletion introduced. The government is considering reduction of allowable exploration and development costs. Various tax incentives under the Investment Incentive Act and Exports Incentives Act have created a better mining investment climate.

Principal Mineral Industries

The copper industry is the prime force in the country's mineral development. There are five major companies and a similar number of smaller companies. Many prospects are either being developed or considered for future development under high price conditions. Atlas Consolidated, the leading producer, will add a milling capacity of 32,000 tons of ore per day by 1978. In all, the Philippines is likely to push annual production to more than 300,000 metric tons of mine copper within the next five years. One smelter is already in the works, to be designed and built by Arthur G. Mackee and Parson Jergens. This $200-million, 84,000-tpy copper smelter will be owned by the Philippine government, five

Philippine copper producers, and foreign companies in roughly equal proportions.

The gold industry is second only to copper in gross output value. Occurrences are widespread, either alone as precious metals or associated with copper. However, gold production and trading always have price and control problems. For monetary reasons, the government usually helps the industry when it is in trouble. It is difficult to make money in gold alone; hence, output from purely gold operations is hardly likely to increase. In late 1976, Benguet Consolidated threatened to shut down operations because of financial difficulties. By-product gold is associated primarily with copper. In all, Philippine gold output has been about 500,000 to 600,000 ounces annually.

The famous refractory chrome industry in Zambales is the only one of its kind in the world. Deposits are sizable, but the grade is uneven. The lump ore is much desired for refractories, but the fines are little in demand. Continuing sales to the U.S. market and specifications of the product are the keys to this industry ($12 million gross, half million tons per year). The Philippines has extensive laterites, and there is now a large nickel project under the management of Marinduque Mining at Nonoc. Atlas at one time was considering another nickel project on Palawan. Acoje, the producer of metallurgical chrome, also produces a little nickel.

Iron and steel illustrate the stage of development of all metal industries. The Philippines is making headway in ore extraction and metal fabrication and is trying to close the gap in between. There is a small electric smelting iron and steel enterprise in Iligan, Mindanao, based upon scrap iron, to meet the mounting demand for steel products. The government intends to promote the development of an integrated steelworks, utilizing conventional techniques or direct reduction; in either case, most of the raw materials will have to be imported. Kawasaki Steel is building a 5-million-tpy plant in the Philippines to supply its blast furnaces in Japan with iron sinter.

The cement industry is already close to 5 million tons per

year in capacity and $100 million in annual gross sales. There are seventeen companies, each with a plant operating around the islands of the Philippines. National capacity can be increased as warranted, and recently there has been a small surplus of cement for export.

Except for lubricants, gas oil, and diesel, by far the bulk of the oil is imported as crude and refined by three refineries with a combined capacity of 274,000 barrels per day. Philippine oil consumption is expected to rise to 360,000 bpd, or about 18 million metric tons per year, by 1980. The three refineries have to be modified to accommodate the large quantities of high-wax, high-salts crude oil imported from the People's Republic of China. Philippine annual oil requirements are already close to 10 million tons. Of late, the search for petroleum has become more intensive, with some showings of unproven potential. Among the foreign companies involved in joint-venture oil search are Cities Service, Husky Oil of Canada, Salem Energy of Sweden, and China Petroleum of Taiwan. The Philippine National Oil Commission has extended a package of incentives to stimulate oil exploration. Meanwhile, oil is a hot item in the Philippine stock exchange.

Mine and Industry Workers

Because the Philippines has a long tradition in both surface and underground mining, there is no special problem finding suitable workers to run the mines and mills. Although additional people have to be trained for new projects, help is available from experienced workers from existing facilities. The smelters, refineries, and fabricators face a more acute problem, since there is little background experience to draw upon. However, the native work force can be trained in reasonably short time, particularly since the general level of education is good. There has been a shortage of technical personnel, and private industry frequently entices able and trained workers away from the Philippine Bureau of Mines or other such government agencies.

Mineral Transport

Interisland shipping and access roads are difficult problems in Philippines mineral transport. More major highways and a few railroads can be used, particularly in Luzon, but mining can presently be sustained as is—as long as the mines are accessible to small ports. These ports need wharfs, conveyors, and transshipment facilities for loading onto large ships. So far, the mines are adequately serviced by building roads and shipping facilities to accommodate their products. Of course, air transport is often indispensable in bringing in supplies and transporting personnel. Enlarging and deepening major ports on Luzon helps bring in equipment, metal products, and fuels. At the new smelting centers, ore delivery ports need to be built, especially to accommodate vessels for coal and iron of at least 50,000 dwt. Ships used for copper concentrates and bauxite can be much smaller. Some industrial areas need to build facilities for unloading medium-sized oil tankers.

Energy and Power

The energy requirements of the Philippines are steadily expanding. The need for oil is basic—from interisland ships to cars in metropolitan Manila, to industrial plants and power plants, and to all the surface and underground equipment in the mining centers. Most of the power is thermal, fired by diesel oil. Coal production is nominal, and hydropower development has been well below the country's potential. In 1975, the Philippines' installed power capacity was about 3.2 million kilowatts—two-thirds thermal and one-third hydro (two-thirds public and one-third industrial). Overall electricity output for 1975 was approximately 14 billion kilowatt-hours. The existing electric plants are generally near the big cities, and there is a significant concentration around greater Manila. Most industries and mines have their own power plants. Power is costly, unsteady, and increasingly in demand. The problem is to build enough facilities to meet specific needs. In the future, nuclear power will be significant.

Summary Outlook

How long the present stability will last and under whose auspices are basic questions for investors. The resource potential is promising (particularly for copper), and development capability and capital exist within the country for joint ventures. However, nailing down exploration and exploitation rights is often difficult, since concessions can easily pass into the hands of applicants not serious about mining. Government regulations are getting complicated, as in many other countries. The energy problem will be increasingly acute, and contracting steady supplies is basic. Independent policies and friendly relations with all countries seem to be a trend for the Philippines. The trade of domestic raw materials for Chinese oil has been a recent development. The Philippines is basically a private enterprise country, although the government has been playing a larger role in the economy. Generally, mining can be expected to move forward, with improving sophistication in metallurgy, processing, and fabrication in the years ahead.

Illustrations for Chapter 22

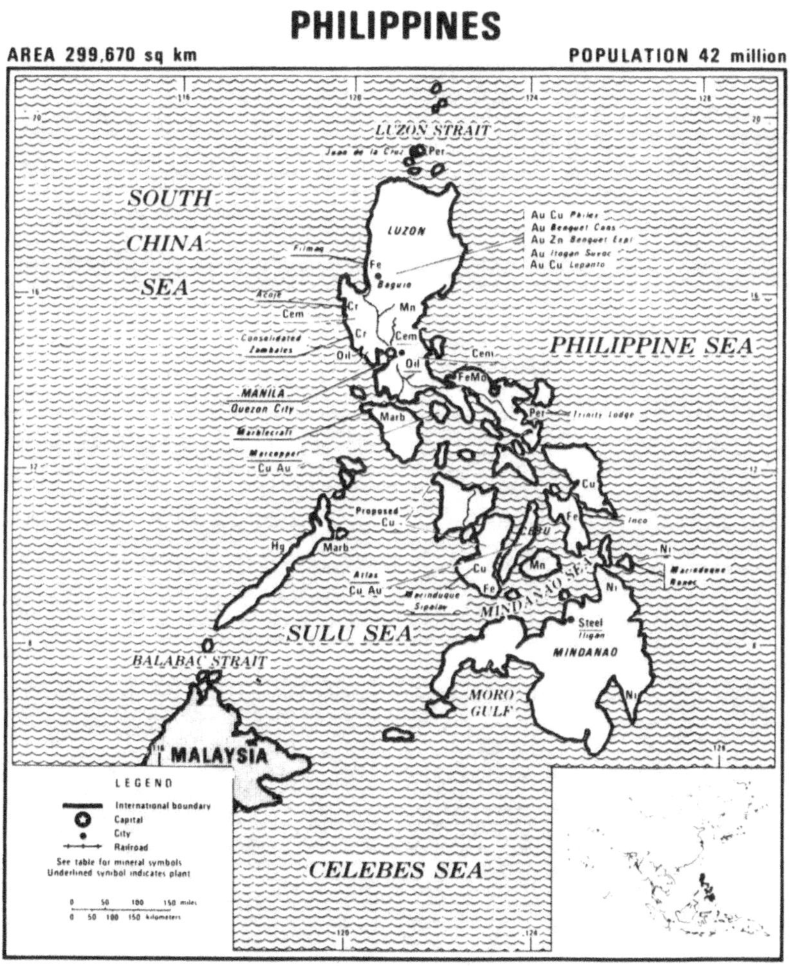

Figure 109 Map of the Philippines

Figure 110 General scenes in the Philippines (Courtesy Embassy of Philippines)

Figure 111 Banyanihan dancers of the Philippines (Courtesy Embassy of Philippines)

1 Underground operations in the Tubo Shaft. 2 Development heading work at the 900m Level. 3 The day's first shift ends as workers leave mine adit. 4 The LEPANTO community has allocated land in support of the First Lady's Green Revolution program. 5 Surface construction activity at the Tubo Shaft. 6 The first raise boring machine in operation in the entire Southeast Asian region.

Figure 112 Gold-copper mine of Lepanto Consolidated (Courtesy Lepanto Consolidated)

THE ATLAS COMPLEX SHOWING FRANK, CARMEN AND BIGA OPEN PIT MINES, MALUBOG AND SIGPIT WATER RESERVOIRS AND THE COMMUNITY AREA.

Figure 113 Panoramic view of Atlas Consolidated's copper operation at Cebu (Courtesy Atlas Consolidated)

1 of 3 23-yard electric shovels at Carman Pit

2 of 3 new electric drills at Carman Pit

Frank Pit ore goes to underground crusher

Biga Pit operation

Figure 114 Equipment used at Cebu for mining copper (Courtesy Atlas Consolidated)

Figure 115 Marinduque Mining's nickel plant on Nonoc Island

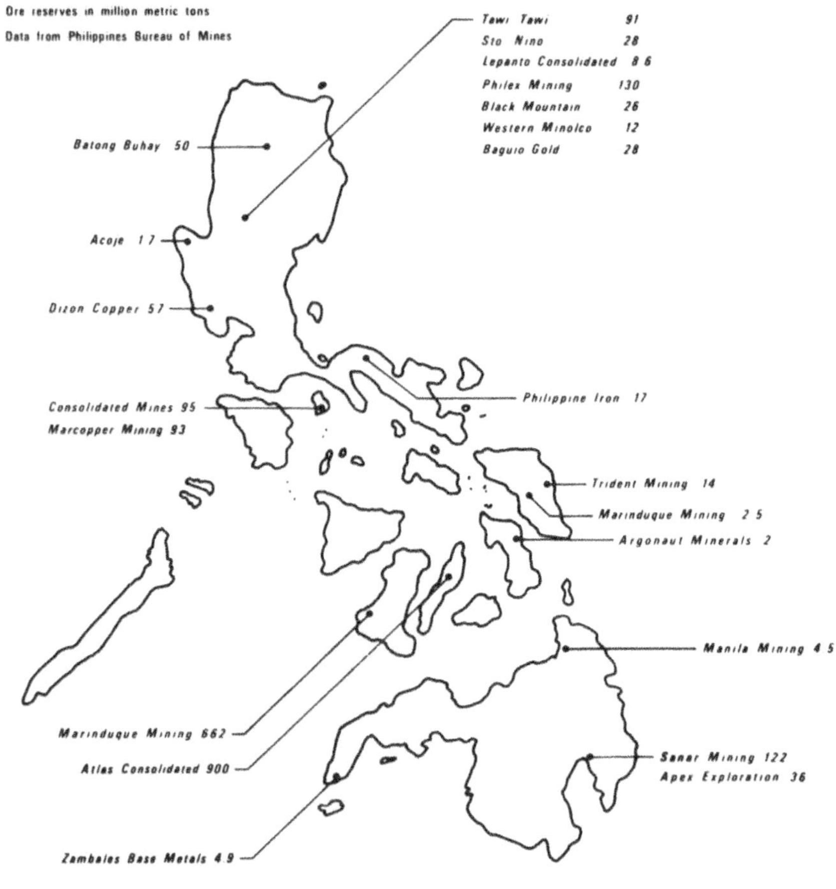

Figure 116 Major copper deposits in the Philippines, 1975

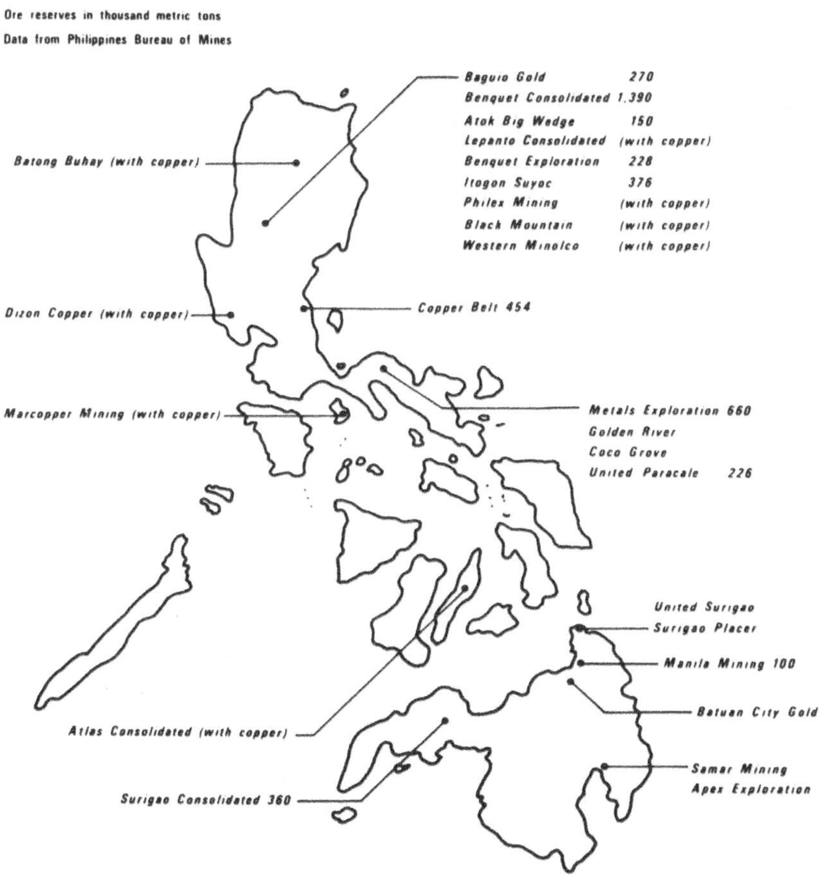

Figure 117 Major gold deposits in the Philippines, 1975

23
Singapore

This island republic of only 586 square kilometers (225 square miles) and 2.3 million highly educated inhabitants (1977) lives on trade, shipping, tourism, manufacturing, and oil-related activities. Singapore is the world's fourth largest port and may become the third largest. Large quantities of oil are imported, refined and sold for bunkering, exported, or locally consumed. The island has the world's third largest petroleum refining complex (after Rotterdam and Houston) and the world's second largest single refinery (owned by Shell). Southeast Asia's oil exploration activities are headquartered here. There is some local dredging, land reclamation, and quarrying, but no underground mining. Singapore's economy was booming until the recent oil crisis hit the republic's best customers—the United States, Japan, and Indonesia. Modest growth was made despite the difficulties, and the economic situation started to look better at the end of 1976. Forecasted real growth in 1977 is 6 percent to 8 percent, compared with 7 percent for 1975 (after adjusting for inflation).

Significance of Minerals

Singapore's GNP in 1975 was about $5.8 billion, up by 4 percent over 1974. This compares with an annual growth of over 10 percent in the early 1970s. Mineral-related activities contribute significantly to the GNP, and this primarily means elusive oil with its many ramifications—value added from refining, shipping benefits, marketing gain in bunkering and sales, construction of vessels and rigs for offshore work, and oil exploration support. A rough guess would be that oil-related activities contributed possibly 10 percent to GNP during 1974-1976. Singapore's oil import bill was $2.04 billion in 1974 and $2.55 billion in 1976.

Mineral Supply Position

Singapore is an entrepôt trading port and a country with few raw materials of its own. It imports large quantities of oil but retains only a small part for consumption. In 1974 (a better year than 1975), Singapore imported about 23 million metric tons of crude and 4.3 million tons of oil products, exported about 16.2 million tons of products, and consumed about 4 million tons of products. The bunkering figure is unknown but must be several million tons yearly. In 1975, crude oil imports were only 18 million tons, and refined oil exports were 11.9 million tons (refined oil imports were 4.8 million tons); but trade started to pick up in late 1975 and early 1976. In fact, crude oil imports had risen to 21.3 million tons in 1976; refined oil imports, to 6.2 million tons; and refined oil exports, to 13.0 million tons.

The republic also imports up to 1.5 million tons of steel products annually and produces roughly 200,000 tons locally from scrap. Most of this is used internally, although a part goes into ship construction and repairs. Singapore produces (from imported clinker) and consumes just over a million tons of cement annually. About 2 million cubic meters of "broken granite" are produced and consumed annually.

Nature of Mineral Enterprise

Singapore has very little mineral industry apart from its very important oil-refining industry. However, it is the headquarters of Southeast Asia's oil exploration and offshore-vessel-support activities.

Principal Mineral Industries

Singapore's refineries have a combined capacity of about 1 million barrels per day, headed by Shell Eastern with 530,000 bpd, Esso Singapore with 231,000 bpd, Mobile Singapore with 175,000 bpd, Singapore Petroleum with 65,000 bpd, and BP Singapore with a very small capacity. Shell is looking for a partner to build a petrochemical complex. The industry was working at much below capacity during most of 1975, particularly Shell, whose naphtha is no longer quite so welcome in Japan. The end of the war in Vietnam also called for adjustments. The refining situation improved in 1976, with refinery capacity utilization increasing to 55 percent from 40 percent in 1975.

Oil exploration, where Americans are prominent, was also having difficulty. By mid-1976, about one-fourth of the 3,500 Americans in the oil community had left Singapore. Bethlehem Singapore, the leading offshore rig producer, cut back its work force sharply because of the slowdown in exploration in Southeast Asia. Work contracts in Indonesia and Malaysia have become harder to live with, and U.S. congressional activities are worrying oil companies. The reduction of petroleum exploration budgets in Southeast Asia is hurting Singapore.

Mine and Industry Workers

Singapore has about 3,200 workers in "mining and quarrying," 25,000 workers in fuels and chemicals (including 3,400 in oil refining), 4,000 workers each in metal industries and nonmetallic products, 9,000 workers in utilities, and 40,000 workers in construction.

Mineral Transport

Singapore has good wharfs and roads for ship landings and truck transport of bulk materials. Some items come from the Malay Peninsula by highways. A large floating oil storage terminal serves several refineries. Singapore can handle the largest of tankers, although the nearby Malacca Straits is limited to about 180,000 dwt.

Energy and Power

Singapore operates on a liquid-fuel energy economy. Because of its large refineries, it has no problem acquiring oil. It produced 4.6 billion kwh of electricity in 1976 from perhaps 1 million kilowatts of thermal generating capacity. New major industrial projects will require the construction of auxiliary power facilities.

Summary Outlook

Singapore's economy will make out nicely with entrepôt trade and tourism alone, but manufacturing and oil activities add to its prosperity. Manufacturing will continue to progress, and growing metal use may someday justify the construction of an integrated steelworks. Oil exploration in Indonesia has declined, and work in the other countries of Southeast Asia is rather uncertain. Oil refining may not be able to operate at full capacity unless existing facilities are modified or new facilities are built to accommodate special crudes and markets. Singapore may well approach the People's Republic of China with an offer to supply oil exploration vessels and erect facilities to refine the high-wax, low-sulfur Chinese crude. The construction of the long-delayed "Sumitomo" petrochemical complex in Singapore was expected to get the go-ahead by mid-1977, and this should give a major boost to the economy.

Illustrations for Chapter 23

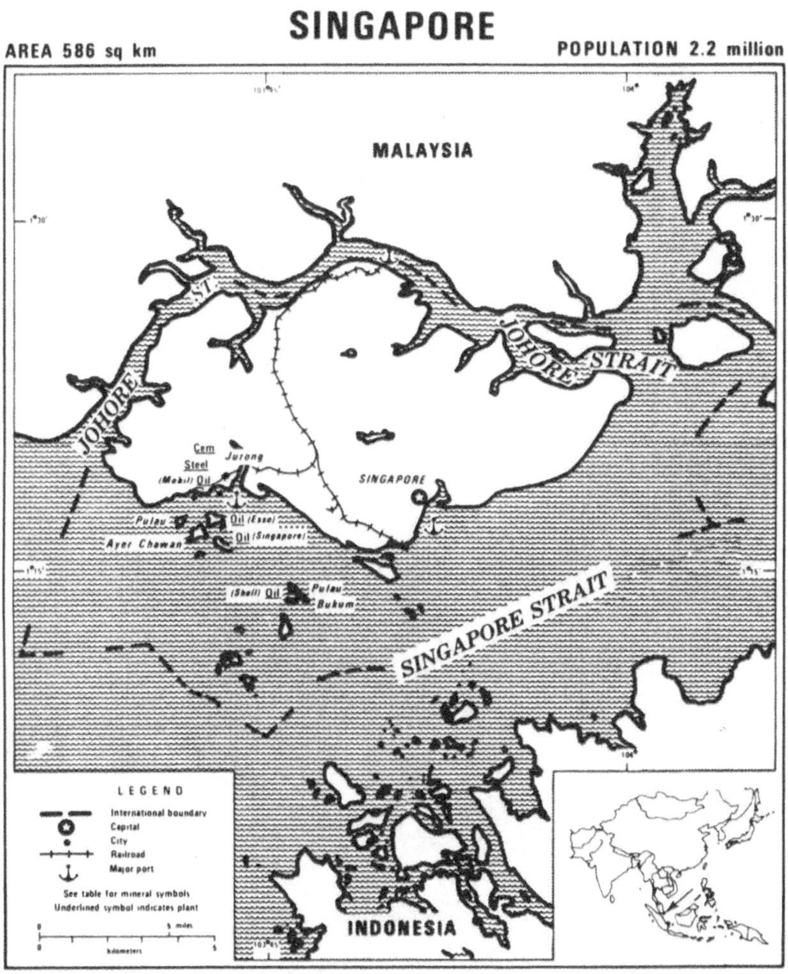

Figure 118 Map of Singapore

Figure 119 The quiet side of the world's fourth largest port—Singapore's native junks and high rises

Figure 120 Housing and land reclamation in Singapore

Figure 121 Singapore has world's third largest oil-refining complex on Pulao Bukum (Courtesy Asiatic Petroleum Corp.)

24
South Korea

South Korea is increasingly being regarded as a mineral-producing country of some consequence. Its mineral economy shows considerable diversity in product type and extraction level, and its output of anthracite, graphite, and tungsten ranks it among the world's largest producers of each. The cement industry is being expanded significantly to meet road and construction needs. Large oil refineries and fertilizer plants are in existence, and a major integrated steelworks is already well beyond the first stage of completion. Firm plans are being made to build large nonferrous smelters and petrochemical plants. South Korea has become a medium-sized industrial and trading nation and is also well known for tourism, textiles, electronics, and shipbuilding. It is making a strong effort to leapfrog in technology and thereby catch up with the established industrialized countries by the end of the century. South Korea has made good economic and industrial progress, despite large military expenditures. It is launching its Fourth Five-Year Plan, which will cover the period 1977 to 1981.

Significance of Minerals

In 1975 GNP was about $18.7 billion (1976 GNP was about $21.5 billion), and mineral production (excluding

TABLE 15. SOUTH KOREA: ROLE IN WORLD MINERAL SUPPLY
(Thousand metric tons, unless otherwise noted)

Major Commodities (Map Symbols)	Production 1976	Production 1975	Production 1974	World Output Share, 1975	Trade in 1975 Exports or Imports	Reserves (or Raw Materials)
Metals						
Aluminum (Al, tons).....	17,600	18,000	17,671	0.1%	Imports--22,161	(Mainly imported)
Bismuth, (Bi, tons).....	174	113	131	3 %	Some exported	Tungsten byproduct
Copper, refined (Cu, tons)	29,737	20,928	12,399	0.2%	Imports--10,373	(Mainly imported scrap)
Iron, ore (Fe, 56% Fe)..	621	644	625	0.1%	Imports--1,494	120,000
Iron, steel ingot (St)..	2,698	2,010	1,935	0.3%	Neither	(Local pig, scrap)
Steel products..........	3,407	2,184	1,933	0.4%	Imports--1,368	(Local steel ingot)
Lead, mine (Pb, tons)...	11,500	12,200	10,500	0.3%	Exports--3,400	10^7 Pb-Zn ore
Lead, refined (Pb, tons)	7,762	5,739	4,606	0.2%	Neither	(Mainly domestic ore)
Tungsten, concentrate (W, 70% WO_3, tons)....	4,660	4,403	4,193	8 %	Exports--3,278	$13x10^6$ 0.5+ WO_3 ore
Zinc, mine, (Zn, 50% Zn, tons)................	56,200	45,700	42,300	0.8%	Exports--23,800	10^7 Pb-Zn ore
Zinc, refined (Zn)......	27,222	20,922	11,548	0.4%	Imports--3,500	(Domestic ore)
Nonmetals						
Asbestos (Asb, tons)....	4,800	3,700	5,700	0.1%	Imports--57,000	Small
Cement (Cem)............	11,873	10,129	8,842	1.4%	Exports--2,439	Limestone, adequate
Fertilizer (Fert, Urea).	848	925	812	1 %	Neither	(Nitrogen fixation)
Fluorspar (F, tons).....	20,200	28,300	33,000	0.6%	Exports--10,700	1,000,000 ore
Graphite (Gr, tons).....	47,700	47,200	104.9	12 %	Exports--36.0	38,000,000
Kaolin (Kao)............	470	513	484	Small	Some exported	10,000
Phosphate rock (P)......	--	--	--	--	Imports--706	None known
Pyrophyllite (Pyro).....	349	323	329	10 %	Some exported	10,000
Salt....................	694	665	574	0.3%	Imports--312	Seawater
Talc....................	140	94	114	10 %	Exports--8.6	10,000
Fuels						
Anthracite (C)..........	16,400	17,600	15,300	8 %	Neither	550,000
Oil, crude..............	--	--	--	--	Imports--15,395*	None to date
Oil, refined (Oil)......	17,500	15,500	14,000	0.5%	Imports--955	(Imported crude)

* Crude oil imports in 1976 was about 18.5 million tons and projected imports in 1977, 20.8 million tons.

value added on raw materials, which were primarily imported) totaled about $500 million. Thus, the mineral share of GNP was roughly 3 percent. Actually, the value added from mineral processing and smelting would be considerably greater than the value of the indigenous mining output. The mining of anthracite coal dominates South Korea's mineral economy, providing about $300 million in 1975. This output was also important by world standards—it was about 8-9 percent of total world production. In terms of value, limestone and its derivative, cement, are next in importance, furnishing roughly $50 million and $150 million (over half of the cement output is value added) in 1975, respectively. Although South Korea produces some 8 percent of the world's tungsten, its annual value to the country is only about $30 million, or 0.6 percent of all exports ($5.08 billion in 1975).

South Korea's value added for the mineral industry sector has a great deal to do with its efforts to industrialize. Almost every new or planned plant is large by world standards. Thus, South Korea is becoming a smaller model of Japan in its mineral and industrial activities. It is also making a serious effort to mine as many indigenous resources as possible. South Korea's oil import bill in 1975 was $1.339 billion, and its steel import bill was $345 million—compared with total imports of $7.27 billion.

Mineral Supply Position

South Korea is self-sufficient in some minerals, has surpluses of others, and is greatly deficient in still others that are fundamentally important to industrialization. All the anthracite is consumed locally, mainly for space heating. After domestic needs are met, there is a surplus of cement and certain ceramic raw materials available for export. Some exotic metals and nonmetallics are mainly produced for export, such as tungsten, bismuth, graphite, fluorspar, talc, and pyrophyllite. As South Korea develops its industries, more of the exports will be needed for local use. Some base metal ores are currently exported, simply because there are no facilities to process them into usable form.

Meanwhile, mineral and metal imports have been substantial and costly. In 1975 petroleum imports were 18.4 percent of all imports; chemicals, 5.4 percent; fertilizers, 1.9 percent; nonferrous metals, 0.9 percent; and other crude minerals and fertilizers, 1.3 percent. Crude oil imports were 135 million barrels (valued at $1.6 billion) in 1976 and may reach 152 million barrels in 1977. The country has little bituminous coal and will have to import substantial quantities once the integrated steelworks begins production. Much more iron ore than is now used will also have to be imported. Of course, as the steelmaking raw material imports increase, the demand for iron and steel product imports might be lower. The large nonferrous smelters being built or planned will require mainly imported ores. Unless substantial quantities of oil and gas are found, there is no recourse but to import. Nuclear energy will also require imports of fissionable materials in the future.

According to the Ministry of Commerce and Industry, South Korea plans to import 3,872,000 tons of iron ore in 1977 (domestic demand was estimated at 4,722,00 tons), 148,000 tons of copper concentrates (domestic demand, 172,000 tons), 6,700 kilograms of gold, and 64,000 tons of asbestos. South Korea also plans to export 18.5 tons of silver, 20,000 tons of lead concentrates, 86,000 tons of zinc concentrates, 3,630 tons of equivalent tungsten concentrates, 177,000 tons of kaolin, 49,000 tons of talc, 300,000 tons of limestone, 58,000 tons of amorphous graphite, 1,400 tons of crystalline graphite, 6,000 tons of fluorspar, 4,000 tons of feldspar, 244,000 tons of agalmatolite (pyrophyllite), 190,000 tons of silica stone, 10,000 tons of silica sand, and 3,000 tons of diatomaceous earth.

Nature of Mineral Enterprise

South Korea has a fair-sized indigenous mineral resource base, one that is strong in anthracite, tungsten, limestone, and a few special nonmetallics. Placer gold mining is no longer attractive because of high land values. Various workable, but relatively small, base metal deposits have been recently uncovered through good geological prospecting.

There is hope of finding oil, particularly offshore, and foreign investments are invited in this respect. But South Korea's prominence in basic industries lies in mineral processing, smelting, and fabrication rather than in the mining of indigenous resources. There are four large industrial complexes already in existence—Busan (Pusan), Ulsan, Pohang, and Inchon. Two others are being built—Onsan and Pukpyong in the east.

Quite a number of large mineral-oriented and metal-oriented industrial plants already exist. The Kyungin Energy Co.'s 60,000-bpd Inchon refinery will be expanded by another 60,000 bpd. Sunkyung Co. will build a new 150,000-bpd refinery at Ulsan. Namhae Chemical Co. is putting up a large multiproduct fertilizer plant at Yosu. Dow Chemical Co. is working on a $30-million soda-chlorine plant. The big new 2.6-million-tpy (eventually 8.5 million) Pohang steelworks will be complemented by a second integrated steelworks by 1983. Large copper and zinc smelters are nearing completion, and the construction of a new aluminum reduction plant has begun.

Yeoung Poong Mining Co. is prominent in nonferrous metals, and Dae Han Iron Mining Co. runs the iron business. Both are private Korean companies. The government-owned Dae Han Coal Corp. produces about one-third of the country's anthracite, and many smaller private companies produce the rest. The Korean Tungsten Mining Co. is down from full government ownership to 8.7 percent. The privately owned Ssangyong Cement Industries Co. is expanding its Donghai plant to become one of the largest in the world.

All of South Korea's 1,000 mines are small to medium in size. Mining itself is not attractive to foreigners because the deposits are small. The government can waive the 50 percent participation limitation provision if foreigners are interested. Larger projects are started by the government, often with foreign aid, but most smaller projects are private with state assistance. The government returns them to private auspices when feasible. There is a Korea Mining Promotion Corp., which draws on the Korean Institute of Geoscience and Mineral Resource for help. The Korea Institute of Science and Technology aids private industry in resource development. Mineral resources and basic industries are very important in the country's economic development program.

Principal Mineral Industries

The anthracite industry has done very well under difficult mining conditions: steep, broken, and relatively thin coal seams. Prices affect the industry's well-being, but these are controlled by the government. Coal is no longer fundamentally used for electric power generation, but for space heating, and private output is now twice as much as government production. South Korea's recoverable reserves of coal are good for perhaps twenty-five years at a mining rate of 20 million tons annually. Dae Han's biggest mine is Chang Song, 600 meters deep. The leading private company is Sam Chang, whose Samchuk mine has good reserves. Because of high oil prices, coal production is being pushed.

The cement industry is expanding rapidly, with capacity expected to reach 23 million tons by the end of 1977. In a few years South Korea expects to consume 13 million mtpy and export 7 million tons. Ssangyong Cement recently awarded a European consortium a contract to expand company capacity by 5.6 million tons. Tongyang Cement Co. is sharply expanding capacity in its Samchuk plant with a Fuller Co.–designed suspension preheater system (S.F. Process of Ishikawajima-Harima). Seven companies with nine plants were operating in late 1976; the largest plant was Donhae of Ssangyong Cement rated at nearly 3 million tons.

South Korea's tungsten industry ranks fourth in the world and is centered on the Sangdong scheelite operation, which belongs to the Korea Tungsten Mining Co. Sangdong, the largest single tungsten mine in the world, is being worked deeper and with leaner ore at about 0.7 percent WO_3. Korea Tungsten has had a synthetic scheelite plant for some time and has recently added an ammonium paratungstate (APT) plant. Sangdong produces various products totaling over 2,000 metric tons in tungsten content per year, including 650 tons of paratungstate. A tungsten powder and carbide plant has been built at Taegu.

Yeoung Poong Mining, which dominates the nonferrous metals sector, operates three medium small mines (including Yeonhua in the east near Sangdong) and has found a few others for ready development. This company produces virtually all of the country's mine lead, zinc, and silver and is responsible for the 80,000-ton Bonghwa zinc smelter now being completed and a 50,000-ton lead smelter to be built near Onsan in a few years. The new copper smelter and the aluminum smelter now being constructed, both 100,000 tpy, are also in the smelter complex in the Onsan industrial area; however, two other companies will run these plants.

South Korea's refining situation tells the oil story. Combined capacity has reached 435,000 bpd, which is about a third more than the crude oil imported in 1975. The government has joined hands with three foreign companies to build three refineries. Korea Oil Corp., with a plant at Ulsan rated at 215,000 bpd, is a joint enterprise with Gulf Oil Corp. Honan Oil Refinery Co., with a plant at Yeosu rated at 160,000 bpd, is a joint enterprise with Caltex Co. Kyungin Energy Co., with a plant at Inchon rated at 60,000 bpd, is a joint enterprise with Union Oil Co. Korea Oil is greatly expanding naphtha cracking facilities at Ulsan. Many other downstream petrochemical plants are being built by individual companies in connection with the two other refineries. The two large fertilizer companies are Chung-ju and Honam, both of which are connected with oil and gas complexes. Korean oil exploration has been offshore, with no promising results except near Pohang. The Koreans plan to raise oil-refining capacity sharply to 670,000 bpd by 1981, mainly through the construction of two new refineries in joint ventures with Middle East countries.

Mine and Industry Workers

In 1975, there were about 70,000 mining and quarrying workers, or approximately 5 percent of all the workers in manufacturing. South Korea has several decades of mining experience and has now built up knowledge in construction, smelting, refining, and processing. The work force is highly educated and is capable of learning new industrial techniques fairly quickly, especially if technical aid is provided by foreign concerns (either associated with joint venture projects or as consultants). Korea Kaiser Engineering Co. was recently established. A large work force is now building many new projects. The availability and quality of South Korea's mine and industry workers are edging up toward Japanese standards, although on a less sophisticated scale.

Mineral Transport

Rapid progress has been made in transportation, with U.S. contribution particularly noteworthy in regard to highways. There are now about 9,000 kilometers of highways, about half of which are paved, including some very good truck roads. The long-term plan is to triple the highway mileage. Existing railroad mileage is about 3,150 kilometers, about 100 kilometers of which are electrified. The government has expanded and modernized the harbor facilities at Pusan and Inchon to accommodate 50,000-dwt ships and has further developed industrial ports at Ulsan, Pohang, Yeosu, and Masan. South Korea will have adequate large ports to accommodate imports of mineral raw materials and exports of industrial products. Land transport should be generally adequate, particularly for trucks. Access roads to mines and smaller industrial facilities must be constructed as needed. Coal is usually railed to markets.

Energy and Power

South Korea has the facilities to provide more than adequate power for its present needs. Thermal capacity was rated at about 4.40 million kilowatts in 1976 and hydropower capacity at about 170,000 kilowatts. In addition, the Gori nuclear power plant of 490,000 kilowatts is nearing completion. Almost all thermal plants are powered by liquid fuel: anthracite could be better used in other ways, it was felt, and it is expensive to construct hydroplants. The sharp rise in oil price has made the country's energy planners give more consideration to the use of atomic energy in the future and possibly to the use of anthracite again. There is a

125,000-kilowatt, anthracite-fired plant at Yeoundong, and a second section is under construction.

Approximately 23.1 billion kilowatt-hours of electricity (over 90 percent thermal) were generated in 1976, up 16.5 percent from 1975. The major mineral and metal consumers in 1976 were metals and products, 22 percent; chemicals, 15 percent; nonmetallics, 10 percent; and mining and quarrying, 3-4 percent. Thus, about half of the electricity was used by mineral-related industries. Power costs are relatively high, but industrial demand will be provided for as needed, and electrical transmission is good.

South Korea is looking to double its power generation capacity (1976 output) by the end of the Fourth Five-Year Plan (1981) and to triple it by 1986. In the decade ahead, the hope is to raise hydropower by nearly 100 percent, thermal power by 50 percent, and nuclear power roughly to a par with thermal power. The country has two experimental nuclear reactors owned by the Korean Atomic Energy Institute and another owned by the Kyonghui University of Seoul. South Korea plans to complete five nuclear power stations by 1985, and its Korea Nuclear Fuel Development Corp. will help to implement this program.

Summary Outlook

Korean industrial undertakings are large and modern by world standards. There has been economic stability, despite intense differences in regional ideology. The government has implemented farsighted plans and created a sound infrastructure; no longer underdeveloped, South Korea is ready to take off industrially. Foreign companies have found South Korea a good place to invest, and domestic capital and know-how are also building up steadily.

Most mineral deposits are small and difficult to work, but the Koreans have done well under these circumstances. In fact, the recent geologic reconnaissance effort has uncovered better mineral potential than was expected. Nonetheless, the future of the country's industrial base will lie in the completion of new projects, which are large design by world standards. South Korea has grown from a minimal industrial base to a rather sophisticated base, which allows it to use the most advanced technology in new plants (often with foreign partners). The country is moving toward high-level technology, as seen from the advanced concepts it employs, especially in electronics and computers. Meanwhile, increasing quantities of minerals, metals, and fuels must be imported to support growing industrial activities. South Korea has done well in improving its economy despite large defense expenditures. Its economic thrust is in exports of goods and services. Exports by 1980 are expected to double the $10 billion in 1977. Korean construction companies, which have won $2.5 billion worth of contracts in the Middle East alone, were negotiating for a further $4 billion worth there.

Illustrations for Chapter 24

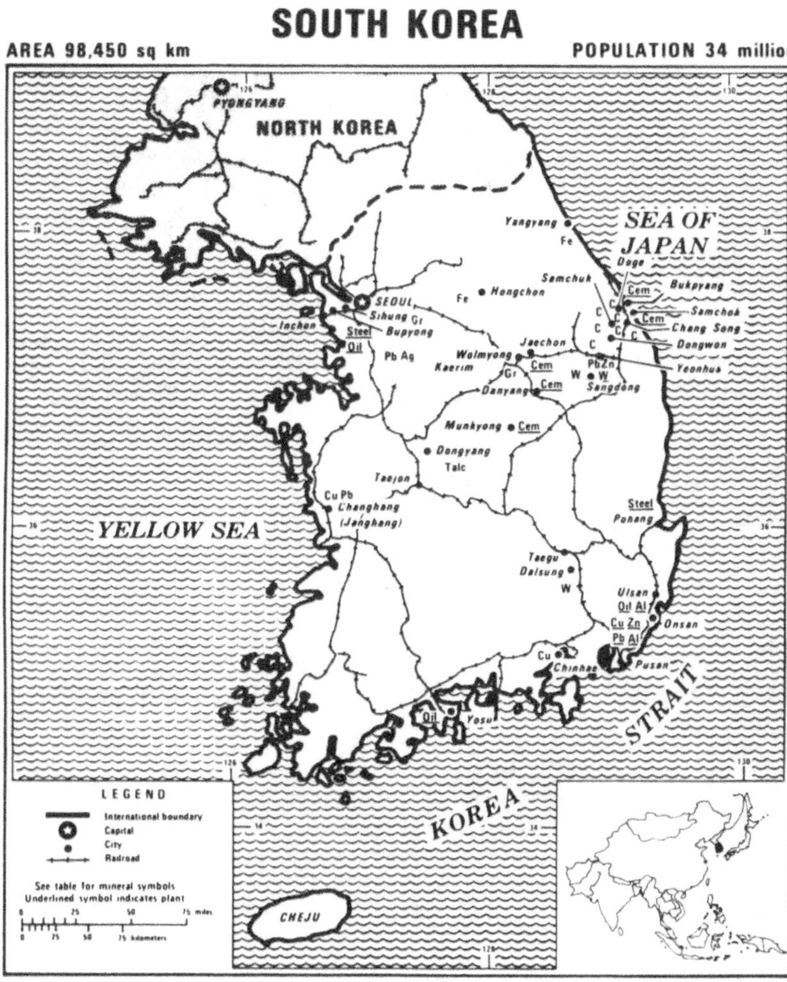

Figure 122 Map of South Korea

National Museum in Seoul

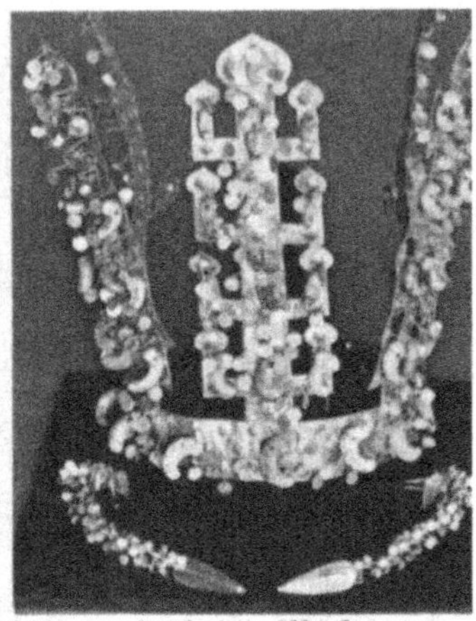

Golden crown from Tomb No. 155 in Gyeongju

Figure 123 Korea's cultural heritage—the National Museum in Seoul

Figure 124 Traditional costumes and rural Korea

Model village near Seoul

MacArthur Park in Inchon

Figure 125 Landmark scenes of South Korea

The heart of Seoul

In the marketplace

Figure 126 New Seoul still has old marketplaces

Figure 127 Blending of South Korea's anthracite

Sangdong tungsten mine

Yeonhua lead-zinc mine

Figure 128 Two of South Korea's famous metal mines

Figure 129 Korea's Pohang Steelworks being built up

Figure 130 One of Ssangyong's large cement plants

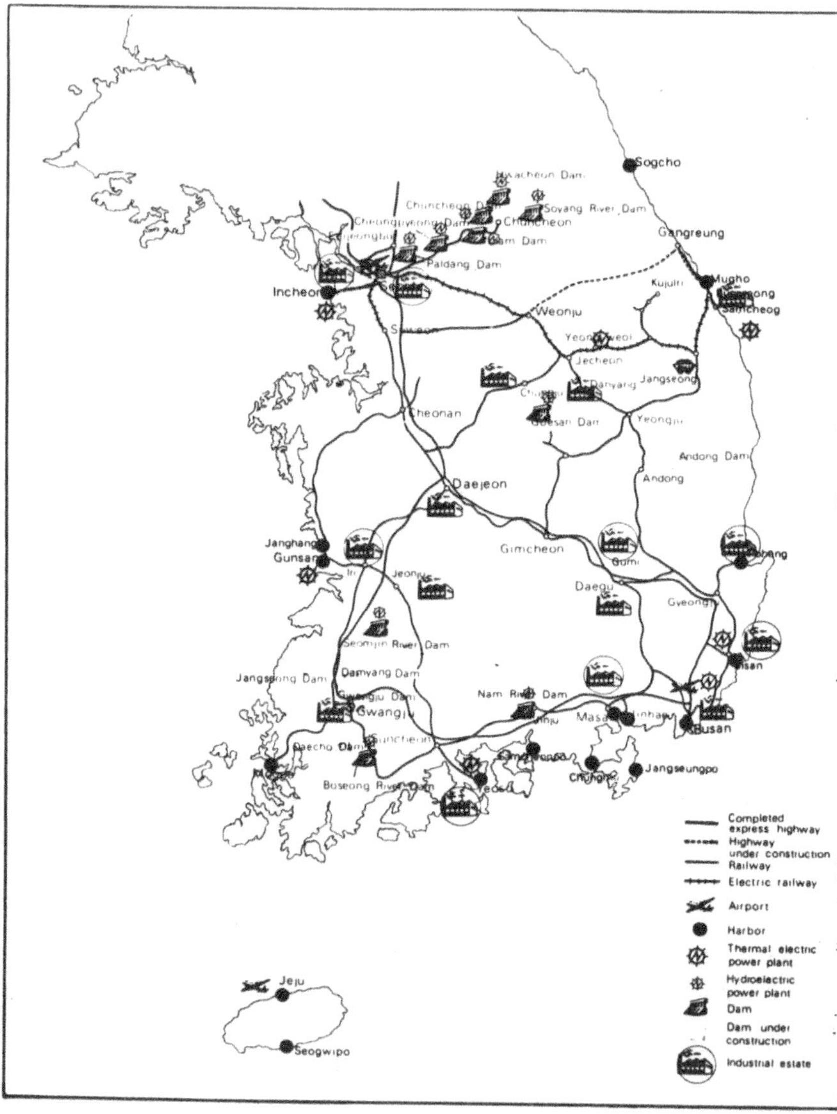

Figure 131 Infrastructure map of South Korea

Figure 132 Industrial facilities in South Korea

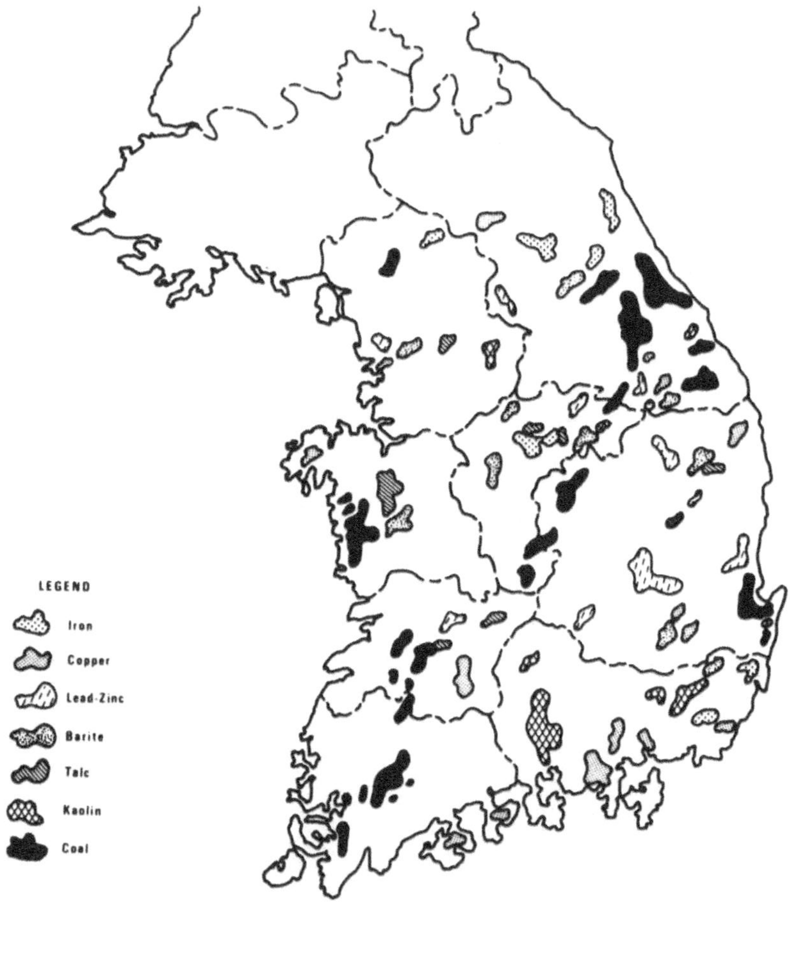

Figure 133 Distribution of major minerals in South Korea

25
Sri Lanka

Sri Lanka is a large island connected to the Indian subcontinent by Adam's Bridge, a chain of shoals. Independent since February 1948, Ceylon was renamed Sri Lanka on May 22, 1972. It is noted for its lush tropical vegetation and tea, coconut, and rubber estates. Few areas in the world produce a greater variety of gemstones—aquamarine, cat's eyes, garnet, moonstone, rubies, and sapphire. Sri Lanka's high-grade amorphous graphite is famous in international markets.

Significance of Minerals

In 1975 GNP was $3.1 billion, and mineral output value was only $39 million. Gemstones represent the most important mineral industry. Gem exports were valued at $22 million in 1975 and $33 million in 1976.

Mineral Supply Position

Sri Lanka has an agrarian economy with limited industry, and mineral fuels and manufactured products are imported. In 1975 oil imports were 1.5 million tons valued at $170 million. Gemstones, graphite, and beach sand products are produced for export; cement, clays, and salt are produced for domestic use. Gems account for up to 5 percent of all exports. Sri Lanka's graphite is unique in purity and is many times

TABLE 16. SRI LANKA: ROLE IN WORLD MINERAL SUPPLY
(Thousand metric tons, unless otherwise noted)

Major Commodities (Map Symbols)	Production 1976	Production 1975	Production 1974	World Output Share, 1975	Trade in 1975 Exports or Imports	Reserves (or Raw Materials)
Metals						
Ilmenite (Ti)..........	56	81	78	2.3%	Bulk exported	Moderate
Rutile (Ti)............	1	3	3.5	1 %	Bulk exported	Small
Nonmetals						
Cement (Cem)...........	500[e]	474	453	Minute	Small imports	(Adequate)
Gemstones (Gem, $$10^6$)...	30	25	20	Moderate	Exports--22 (36 in 1976)	Moderate
Graphite (Gr)..........	8.3	10	10.5	2.5%	Exports--7.8 (7.6 in 1976)	Moderate
Salt...................	140	120	120	Minute	Small imports	Small
Fuels						
Oil, refined (Oil).....	1,500	1,450	1,400	Minute	Neither	(Crude imported)

[e] Estimated

more valuable on a per ton basis than amorphous graphites found elsewhere.

Nature of Mineral Enterprise

Sri Lanka's State Graphite Corp., State Gem Corp., and State Mineral Sand Co. control its three main mineral industries. The graphite industry had only small, scattered mines before it was nationalized. Now there are a few larger, more efficient mines. The Graphite Corp. is also involved in mica mining, processing, and export. The Gem Corp. controls supply and exports, but gem extraction is the work of many "local" entrepreneurs, who simply wash alluvial gravel for gems rather than use mechanical hydraulic techniques. Beach sands are dredged and beneficiated. Most clay, salt, and stone operations are run by private parties.

Principal Mineral Industries

Graphite exports had a difficult year in 1975 because of the world recession. However, development work at the three public mines (Bogala, Kahatagaha, and Kolongsha) proceeded smoothly, and a new mine—Rangala in Yatiyantota—was being built. The Graphite Corp. was also about to complete a flotation plant. The State Gem Corp. ran into financial difficulties in 1975: world gem prices sharply declined, and demand by major buyers (Switzerland, Hong Kong, and Japan) was weak. The Mineral Sand Co. had an average year in producing ilmenite, rutile, zircon, and monazite. Most of the limestone went into cement manufacture at the Kankeoanturai and Puttalam plants.

Mine and Industry Workers

Sri Lanka's unemployment rate may be 20 percent. There is no shortage of industrial labor. The mineral industry employs fewer than 1,500 persons.

Mineral Transport

Sri Lanka's main port and capital is Colombo. Other ports are Galle in the south, Batticaloa in the east, and Kankesanturai, Kayts, and Jaffna in the north. There are over 30,000 miles of roads (half paved), and major truck routes radiate inland from Colombo. The railway network also radiates from Colombo to the major ports and inland cities. Heavy mineral traffic is still limited.

Energy and Power

Sri Lanka has no producing oil or gas wells. It imports crude oil for processing at a 38,000-bpd refinery (to be expanded to 50,000 bpd) at Sapugaskanda on the southwest coast. The Electrical Undertakings Department of the government operated all hydroelectric plants in the country as well as the main thermal power plants. Total electricity generated in 1975 was about 1.3 billion kilowatt-hours.

Summary Outlook

Sri Lanka has opened its continental shelf to international tenders for production-sharing contracts for exploration and development of oil and natural gas. The ten 1,000-square-mile tracts offered cover waters less than 600 feet deep. Two larger tracts off the west coast are deepwater blocks. The State Mineral Sands Company is expanding its beach sands operation at Pulmoddi from the present capacity of 3,500 tons per year of rutile to 13,000 tons of rutile and 8,000 tons of zircon per year by 1980. India is helping to build Sri Lanka's first ammonia urea project (147,000 tpy nitrogen) at Sapugaskanda.

Illustrations for Chapter 25

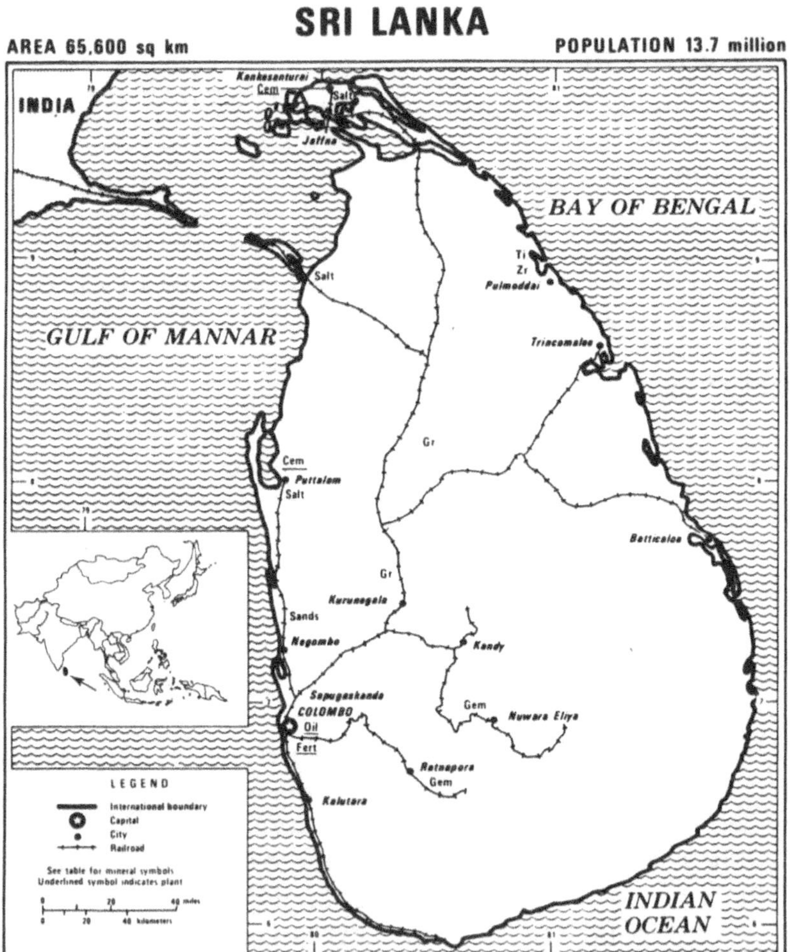

Figure 134 Map of Sri Lanka

Colombo's streets

Native dancers

Small village temple

Figure 135 Typical scenes of Sri Lanka

26
Taiwan

Taiwan is hardly considered a mining country, although it has good facilities for mineral and metal processing. It has a strong agricultural base and ranks about twentieth in world industry and trade. Well-known industries include textiles, food processing, electronics, shipping, shipbuilding, machinery, oil refining, cement, power, and light industries. However, Taiwan's economy is dependent on imported oil, and the consumption of metal products is also steadily rising. Locally produced cement is important to the expansion of the infrastructure. Domestic coal plays a significant, but historic, role. Taiwan has made good industrial and economic progress despite large defense expenditures.

Significance of Minerals

GNP was about $14.3 billion in 1975 and $16.3 billion in 1976. Mine output value in 1975 was estimated at $255 million; it included primarily coal, $102 million; oil and gas, $100 million; and metal ores and cement raw materials, $25 million each. The output value of manufactured mineral and related products was many times greater. Of the $4,130 million credited to this category in 1975, chemical products accounted for $2,076 million; oil and coal products, $1,016 million (including crude oil imports, however); nonmetallic

TABLE 17. TAIWAN: ROLE IN WORLD MINERAL SUPPLY
(Thousand metric tons, unless otherwise noted)

Major Commodities (Map Symbols)	Production 1976	Production 1975	Production 1974	World Output Share, 1975	Trade in 1975 Exports or Imports	Reserves (or Raw Materials
Metals						
Aluminum (Al, tons)......	25,512	28,111	31,320	0.2%	Bauxite imported	Insignificant
Copper, refined, (Cu, tons)	11,660	8,539	9,859	0.2%	Partly imported	(Mainly scrap)
Iron, steel ingot (St)...	597	520	570	0.8%	Imported*	(Scrap imported)
Nonmetals						
Cement (Cem).............	8,749	6,796	6,171	1 %	Exports--243	(Adequate)
Dolomite (Dol)...........	172	136	135	Minute	Neither	120,000
Limestone (Lime).........	9,610	9,480	8,960	1 %	Neither	Sizable
Marble (Marb)............	1,245	531	313	Sizable	Exports--large	300,000
Phosphate rock (P, tons).	500	500	500	Minute	Imports--210,000	Insignificant
Pyrite (Pyr, tons).......	9,400	14,200	11,100	Minute	Neither	1,900,000
Salt.....................	497	268	368	0.2%	Exports--6.6	Seawater
Sulfur (S, tons).........	5,470	5,480	3,310	Minute	Imports--144,000	Insignificant
Talc (tons)..............	15,480	12,050	13,520	0.5%	Neither	2,500,000
Fuels						
Coal, bituminous (C).....	3,236	3,140	2,934	0.1%	Neither	200,000
Natural gas (Gas, 10^6M^3).	1,836	1,575	1,587	Minute	Neither	32,000
Oil, crude...............	213	185	181	Minute	Imports--7,532	3,000
Oil, refined (Oil).......	10,500	8,500	8,500	0.3%	Imports--2,213	Not applicable

* Iron and steel products imports: 1974, 2,577,000 tons; 1975, 1,404,876 tons.

products, $422 million; and metal products, $616 million.

Taiwan is developing a major program of ten large infrastructure projects, including an integrated steel mill, a refinery–petrochemicals complex, and power plant construction. Most of the other projects deal with transport and shipping, which have an indirect relationship with minerals, metals, industry, and trade.

Mineral Supply Position

Except for construction raw materials, Taiwan is greatly deficient in minerals. Large imports are necessary to meet the needs of energy production and manufacture of finished products. All 1975 petroleum imports (refined and crude oil) were valued at $766 million, or 15 percent of all imports, compared with $851 million in 1974. However, crude oil imports in 1975 were 7.53 million tons, compared with 13.74 million tons in 1974.

Imports of iron and steel products were 2.58 million tons valued at $630 million in 1974, and 1.40 million tons valued at $395 million in 1975. Scrap iron imports totaled 786,000 tons valued at $100 million in 1974, excluding obsolete ships coming into the country to be scrapped, and 408,000 tons valued at $53 million in 1975. Nonferrous metals imports were 108,800 tons valued at $147 million in 1974, and 86,800 tons valued at $117 million in 1975. The only other important mineral imports in 1975 were chemical fertilizers, 331,000 tons (338,600 tons in 1974) worth $46 million; phosphate rock, 211,000 tons (251,000 tons in 1974) worth $16 million; and sulfur, 96,000 tons (209,000 tons in 1974), worth $6 million. When the new integrated steel plant is completed at Kaohsiung, most of the raw materials will be imported.

Most of the above imports are consumed domestically. Taiwan also uses by far the bulk of the coal and cement it produces domestically. In 1975 about 343,000 tons of steel products valued at $106 million and 523,000 tons of refined oil (excluding bunkering oil) valued at $54 million were exported. Other exports of lesser value were nonferrous metals, cement, and glass products. Taiwan is also producing increasing quantities of marble for export; 532,000 cubic meters were produced in 1975.

Nature of Mineral Enterprise

Taiwan's imports and processing activities in minerals, fuels, and metals overshadow indigenous extraction. Start-up of large mineral, metal, and power projects is usually by the government, but many of these are turned over to private industry in due time, as has been the case with coal mines, fertilizer plants, and cement plants. Taiwan has small coal mines, small to medium-sized quarries, and medium-sized to large industrial plants.

Some major mineral concerns are the state-owned enterprises: China Petroleum Corp. (CPC), China Iron and Steel Corp. (CI&S), Taiwan Fertilizer Co., Taiwan Aluminum Corp., and Taiwan Metal Mining Corp. Privately owned companies include the Taiwan Cement Corp., Asia Cement Corp., and Tang Eng Iron Works. There is considerable local capital, both government and private; but foreign capital is welcome, and outside loans are obtainable. The Mining Research Service Organization (MRSO) is a mineral-oriented government agency; it has recently added a nonprofit section to work on foreign projects at a fee.

Minerals, metals, and energy are important in government programs and are emphasized in the new six-year economic development plan (1976-1981) now in progress. Policies are directed toward importing needed minerals and metals, processing as much as possible, and exporting finished industrial and agricultural products to pay for the raw materials imported.

Principal Mineral Industries

Taiwan's oil-refining industry is about a tenth the size of Japan's, and it has a whole complex of downstream activities. The Kaohsiung refinery has a throughput of 230,000 barrels daily. With the completion of the new refinery at Taoyuan, Taiwan will be able to produce 500,000 barrels of refined oil daily. Petrochemical plants include two naphtha crackers, one aromatics extraction unit, one ethane cracker, and one cyclohexane plant. In addition, two more aromatic units plus a xylene separation plant, a third naphtha cracker, a fourth reforming unit, and a ninth topping unit are also being built. CPC already has six 100,000-dwt tankers, three buoys, and a large storage capacity. Indigenous oil and natural gas have not proven important as yet, although the gas is useful for making fertilizers. Most crude oil is imported, mainly from the Middle East.

The existing steel industry is centered at Kaohsiung and is based mainly on local and imported scrap. An integrated steelworks being built by CI&S, also at Kaohsiung, will have an annual ingot capacity of 1.5 million tons by 1977 and, it is hoped, 6 million tons by 1983; the bulk of the raw materials needed will be from foreign sources. Meanwhile, large tonnages of finished steel products are imported.

The 38,000-tpy integrated aluminum works in Kaohsiung is being expanded to 70,000 tons with the help of the French firm Pechiney. The bauxite comes from Malaysia and Australia, and local caustic soda is used to convert it to alumina. Power shortages cut output sporadically, and electricity costs are high. Taiwan Aluminum also makes downstream products, and many small private companies also make fabricated products.

The cement industry is booming, with the 1975 output 50 percent greater than that of 1970. Annual capacity will top 11 million tons after 1976. The many large construction projects will need increasing quantities of cement. Taiwan has abundant limestone, but its western reserves are running low, and new plants must be built to tap the huge reserves in the east. There are a dozen cement plants near the major industrial areas throughout the country.

Coal output has been steadily declining—from about 5 million to 3 million tons in the past decade. Mining conditions are increasingly difficult, but the coal is of good quality, often of coking grade. Many small mines work steep and deep seams. The local coal market is good, but the reserves are dwindling.

Mine and Industry Workers

Taiwan does not lack underground mine workers or surface excavation personnel. Adequate industrial workers can also be trained for the mineral processing and refining plants. The universities graduate earth science engineers locally, but many go abroad because of lack of work. There are about 50,000 mining and quarry workers and over a million workers in manufacturing.

Mineral Transport

Taiwan has good railroads, roads, and ports close to areas of mineral and fuel consumption. The coal mines are located near the markets, and cement plants are built near resources and the major consuming areas. Oil and steel products come in at the major ports. Kaohsiung is by far the most important industrial center and port, and it is connected to many outlying areas and places by roads. The Suao harbor is being built to accommodate industry and commerce in the northeast and to complement Keelung. Taiwan has a good north-south railroad along the west coast, and highways run around the island and cross from the east to the west in the north.

Energy and Power

The economy has been increasingly dependent on imported oil, but there is local coal and 1.2 million kilowatts of hydropower (another 1.5 million kilowatts will be added at Sun Moon Lake). A 1.8-million-kilowatt thermal plant was recently completed at Taling near Kaohsiung. Taiwan produced about 23 billion kilowatt-hours of electricity in 1975, mainly through the Taiwan Power Company, which now has a 6.5-million-kilowatt capacity. The big thrust is nuclear power, and the hope is to install 5.1 million kilowatts capacity (six generators at three plants) by 1985. Taiwan is often short of power, which is also relatively expensive. The present power expansion program may cost $3 billion.

Summary Outlook

Sedimentary nonmetallics show fair potential, but even these incur land-use problems. The country must look abroad for future coal supplies. There may be some offshore oil, but problems of jurisdiction of international waters complicate matters. The alternative is to buy more foreign oil as demand increases or to help develop occurrences abroad. In regard to oil-producing countries, Taiwan has very good relations with Saudi Arabia. To cope with greater metal use, the policy has been to cut down import cost by smelting and processing foreign raw materials. In this instance, steel and aluminum production are good examples, and Taiwan has started to build new copper and zinc smelters. Taiwan does well in agriculture but earns more foreign exchange from industries and trade. Thus, any minerals, metals, and fuels needed by the industrial economy must continue to be obtained at any reasonable cost. Taiwan has recently been working to improve its mineral and industrial technology.

Illustrations for Chapter 26

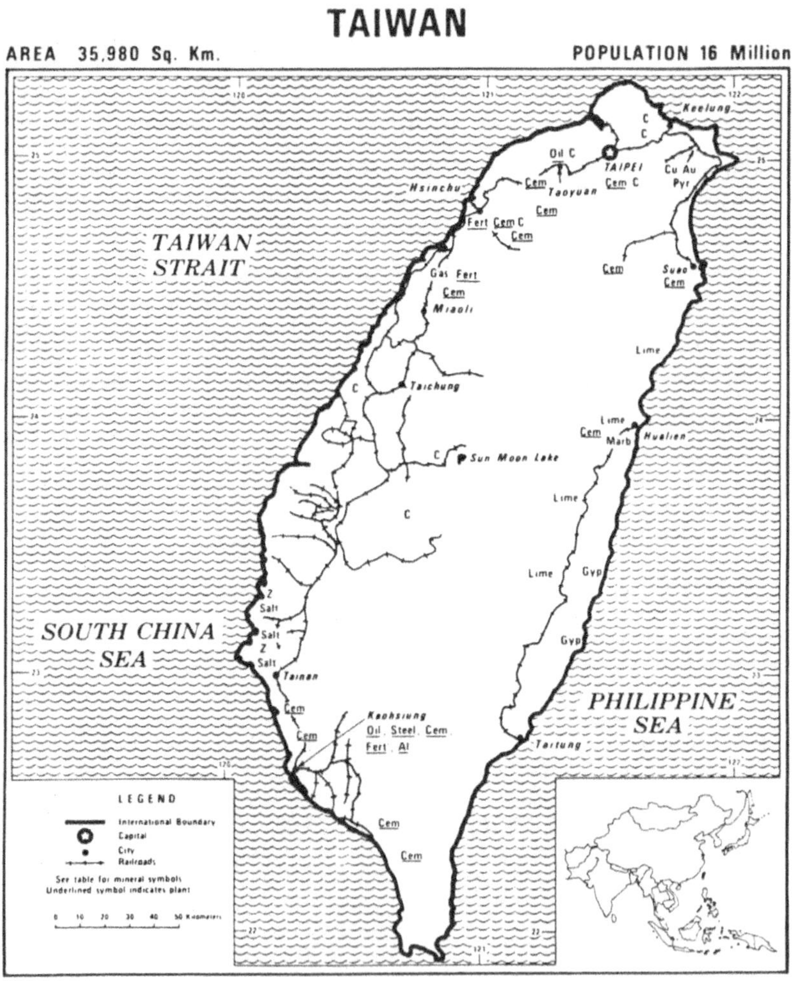

Figure 136 Map of Taiwan

Yehliu seascapes in northern Taiwan

North-south freeway

Rock Island off the coast at Chia Lau Sui

Cross-island highway

Wen Wu Temple at Sun Moon Lake

The 234,000-kw Techi power project on the Tachia River

Figure 137 Taiwan's mountains, highways, lakes, and coasts

Figure 138 Farms and agricultural products of Taiwan

Figure 139 Views of Taipei and temple at Sun Moon Lake

Figure 140 Taiwan Metal's Chinkwashih copper operation

No. 2 Naptha cracker at Kaohsiung, with No. 3 being built

Northern refinery at Taoyuan under construction

Figure 141 Refining and petrochemical facilities in Taiwan

RAW MATERIAL UNLOADING FACILITIES Two ship unloaders each average capacity 1000 metric tons/hr. Shown here is the erection in progress

COKE OVEN PLANT Two batteries each having 39 coke ovens. A blend of coking coals is fed into the coke ovens to produce coke with suitable porosity and hardness for the use in the blast furnace

SINTER PLANT: Fine ores are fused into sinter before they are charged into the blast furnace

STEEL MAKING PLANT: There are two basic oxygen furnaces each having a capacity of producing 145 metric tons of liquid steel per heat. Besides, one slab caster and two bloom casters are installed within the plant

PLATE MILL: The plate mill has an annual capacity of 400,000 metric tons. Maximum width of plate is 3.8 meters. The picture shows the installation of the mill stand and roller table

Figure 142 New integrated steelworks of China Steel at Kaohsiung (Courtesy of China Steel)

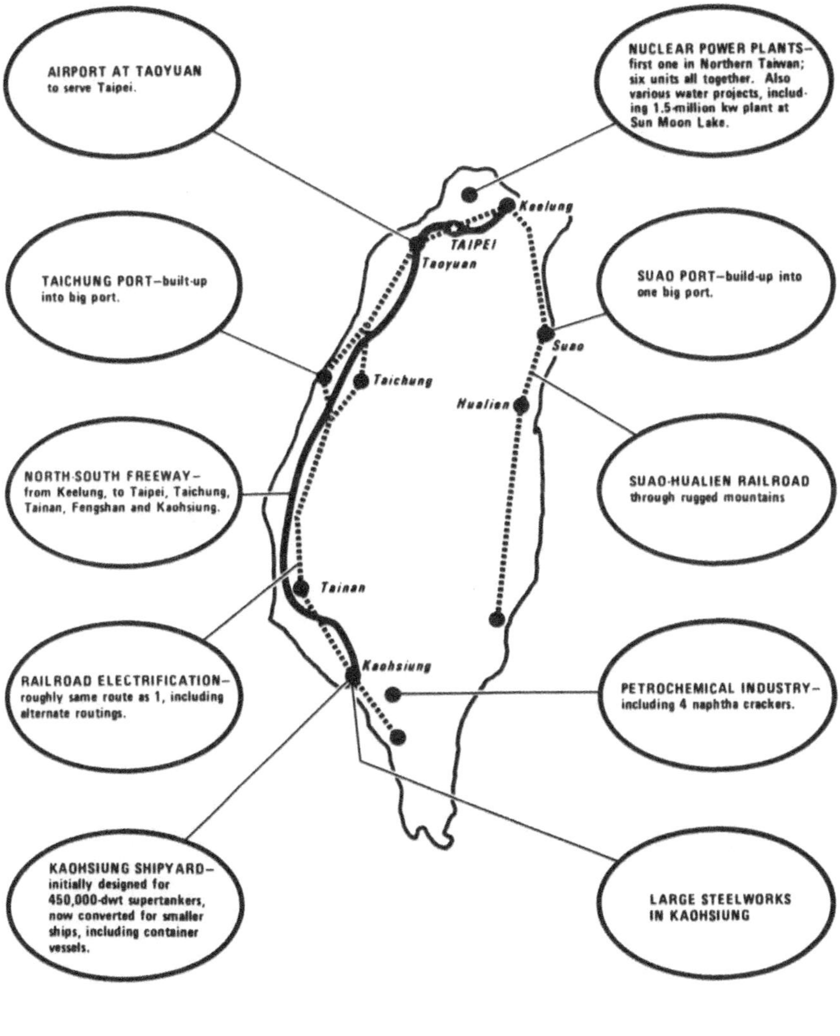

Figure 143 Ten major development projects in Taiwan

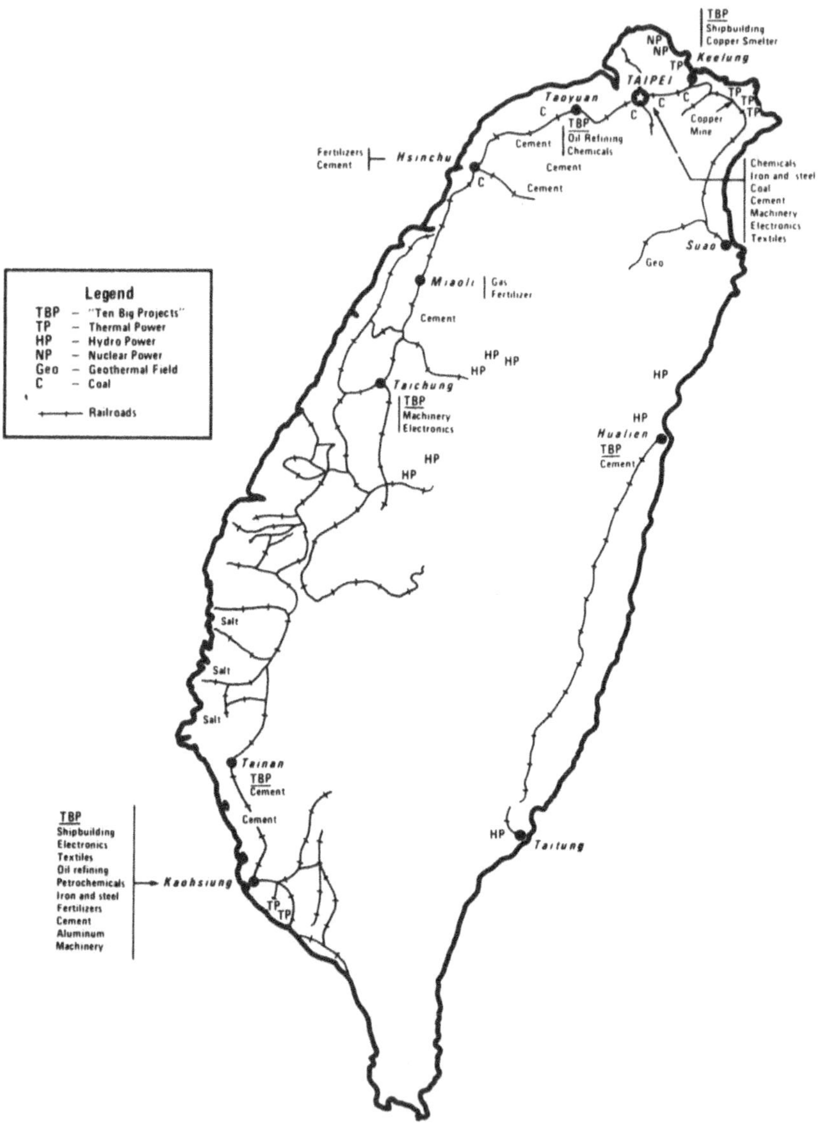

Figure 144 Infrastructure and basic industries in Taiwan

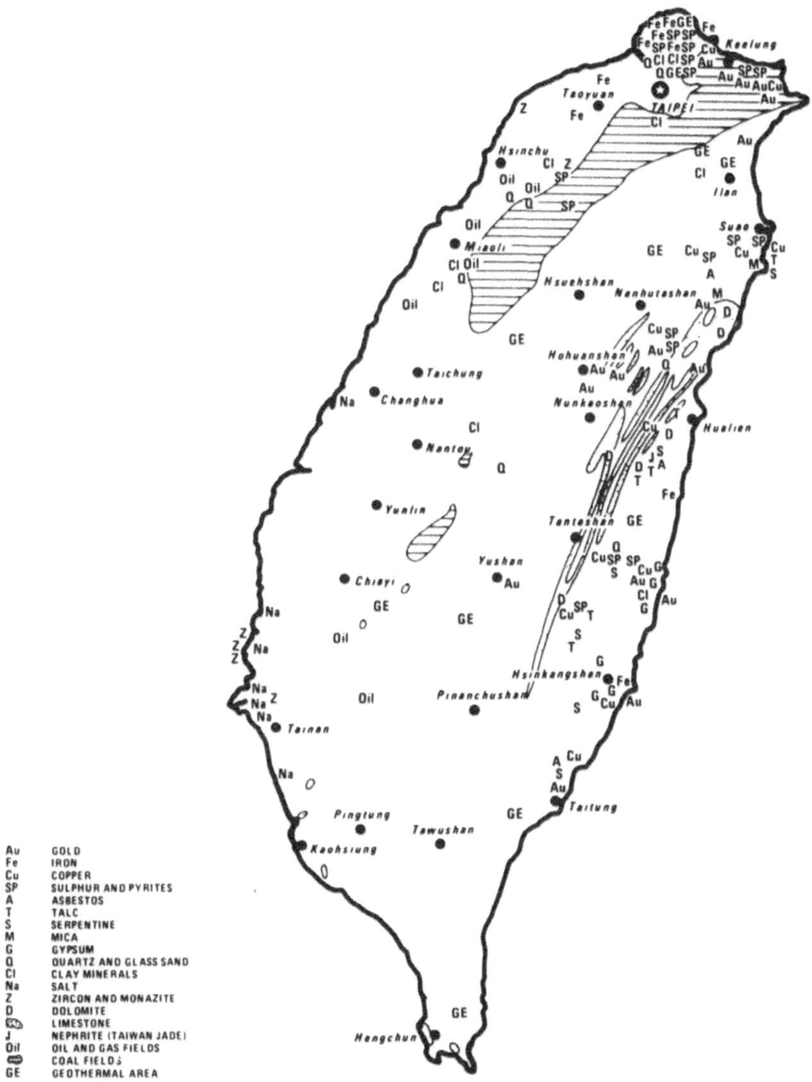

SOURCE: MINING RESEARCH & SERVICE ORGANIZATION, OCTOBER, 1975

Figure 145 Mineral distribution in Taiwan

27
Thailand

Thailand produces two minerals of great world importance: tin and fluorspar. Both occur in the granites of the Malay Peninsula. It has been said that fluorspar is often found in tin-barren granites and vice versa. Wolfram, stibnite, and barite have also emerged as significant minerals. Yet the value of agricultural production, headed by rice, tapioca, maize, sugar, and rubber, overshadows the minerals sector. Thailand exports most of the minerals it produces but is totally dependent upon foreign sources for petroleum and hard coal. The fuel supply situation may change, however, in view of the commercial quantities of natural gas found not long ago. Thailand has had several changes of government recently, and its policy toward foreign investment and mining and industrial development is unclear. The Fourth Five-Year Plan was initiated in September 1976 to cover 1976-1981. Thailand's economic growth rate in 1976 was about 10 percent.

Significance of Minerals

In 1975 GNP was $14.8 billion, with the mining industry contributing 1.2 percent. The total value of mining output of $170 million in 1975 was down 27 percent from 1974, and the total value of mineral exports of $155 million was down 26.5 percent. Limestone is included in the above figures, but

TABLE 18. THAILAND: ROLE IN WORLD MINERAL SUPPLY
(Thousand metric tons, unless otherwise noted)

Major Commodities (Map Symbols)	Production 1976	Production 1975	Production 1974	World Output Share, 1975	Trade in 1975 Exports or Imports	Reserves (or Raw Materials)
Metals						
Antimony, mine (Sb, tons).	4,000	3,200	4,300	5 %	Exports--2,200	Considerable
Iron, ore (Fe)...........	35	33	36	Insignificant	Neither	50,000 - 100,000
Iron, steel..............	250	236	220	Insignificant	Imports--700 (1973)	(Based on scrap)
Tin, mine (Sn, tons)......	20,453	16,406	20,339	9.5%	Locally smelted	1,200
Tin, refined (Sn, tons)...	20,337	16,630	19,827	9.5%	Exports--16,552	(Local mine tin)
Tungsten, concentrates (W, tons)..................	3,976	3,441	4,276	5 %	Exports--3,354	100
Nonmetals						
Barite (Ba)..............	151	258	201	5.5%	Exports--110	Extensive
Cement (Cem).............	4,422	3,952	3,923	0.5%	Exports--685	(Adequate)
Gypsum (Gyp).............	269	255	312	0.4%	Exports--89	Extensive
Fluorspar, (F)*..........	129	175	341	3.5%	Exports--210 (315 in 1974)	10,000 - 30,000
Fuels						
Coal, lignite (C).........	680	462	465	Insignificant	Neither	Can support output
Oil, crude (Oil)..........	0	0	0	0	Imports--6,500 (6,700 in 1976)	None so far
Oil, refined (Oil)........	6,500	6,000	6,500	0.2%	Imports--2,500 (1974)	(Imported crude)

NOTE: Most 1976 data are rounded.
* Production data covers high-grade metspar only. Thai Department of Mines figures report "low-grade materials" separately and acidspar not at all.

cement is not. Thailand's export minerals are primarily foreign exchange earners. Tin and tungsten prices were rising in 1976, but production was below normal.

Certain mineral products, either little produced or hardly produced at all, are consumed in large quantities by the economy. In 1975, the oil import bill was about $700 million, and the iron and steel import bill was perhaps $200 million. Imports of nonferrous metals and fertilizers were also considerable. Thus, mineral imports correspond to perhaps 6-7 percent of the GNP. Local lignite and cement are essential to Thailand's power and construction activities.

Mineral Supply Position

Thailand is an important exporter of various minerals and a growing consumer of fuels and construction materials. Its metal exports are significant by world standards, but they are not outstanding in gross value because of the small tonnages involved. In 1975, tin exports were valued at $110 million ($150 million in 1974), tungsten exports at $16 million ($19 million in 1974), and antimony exports at $3 million ($5 million in 1974). Fluorspar exports declined from $15 million in 1974 to $10 million in 1975. Barite exports increased from $1.8 million in 1974 to $3.3 million in 1975 because of better prices and higher demand (it is used as an oil drilling mud in Southeast Asia). Thailand exported 140,000 tons of zinc oxide ore in 1974 for experimental and testing purposes. The country has traditionally been famous for its semiprecious stones, particularly zircon.

Mineral imports have averaged about a billion dollars annually in the last three years; they are mainly the petroleum and metals needed by the increasingly flourishing economy. Cement consumption has steadily risen, thus cutting down on the surplus available for export.

Nature of Mineral Enterprise

Thailand has an export-oriented mining industry and a consumption-oriented mineral processing industry. Almost all of the mineral industries, with the exception of some in the energy field, are privately owned and operated. The tin industries of southern Thailand were started by Occidentals in the case of large operations and by Orientals in the case of small operations. Most other mining industries have been developed by Thais working on small properties. Under a special arrangement, foreigners can have controlling interest in developing minerals in the north, too. The state-owned Electricity Generating Authority of Thailand (EGAT) controls various facets of the energy industry, including lignite and power projects.

Mineral and metal refining and processing facilities are also predominantly privately owned. A few larger and technically difficult enterprises were started by foreigners. The most famous are the Thailand Smelting and Refining Company (Thaisarco), which built the tin smelter, and the Thailand Exploration and Mining Company (Temco), which was involved with offshore tin. Management of Thaisarco has gone to Billiton N.V., and management of Temco has been temporarily assigned to the state-owned Offshore Mining Organization (OMO).

Various foreign concerns have shown interest in a zinc project, the latest being New Jersey Zinc Co., which apparently has become fully committed. A 4-million-ton oxide deposit (Mae Sot) near Burma, with ores of 25-35 percent zinc, will be mined to feed a 60,000-tpy zinc smelter at Tak sixty miles away—all at a cost of about $90 million.

Most cement and steel plants are headed by Siam Cement Co., which deals with both commodities and is Thai-owned. The Thais are affluent, enterprising, and would be willing to get more involved in minerals production if they knew the business. There is considerable domestic capital for small-scale tin operations, yet there is little capital for hard-rock mining.

The government is inclined to strengthen its role in resource development. It controls mineral extraction rights and is generally the Thai entity for joint ventures. Of late, it has become interested in the discovery and development of raw materials for the fertilizer, steel, and energy industries.

Principal Mineral Industries

Tin holds a unique position in Thailand's mineral economy. In recent years, it has contributed about two-thirds of the total value of minerals produced (excluding cement). Despite a serious drop in output during 1975 because of the Temco affair (when the mineral rights of Union Carbide were revoked), Thailand's share of world tin output was still nearly 10 percent. The management change did not greatly affect the output of Thaisarco, which smelts the bulk of the country's tin and produces by-product columbite-tantalite as well. However, the former Temco operation will never be quite the same; there are indications that some illegally mined tin was being smuggled from its concession off Phuket into Malaysia. In January 1977, OMO engaged Billiton N.V., Aokim Tin, and Phairor Sawakhom to dredge offshore tin along the Phangnga coast. Other large tin-dredging companies had fairly normal years in 1975 and 1976, but some small marginal producers had to shut down when prices were low. The Chasintr Mining Co. opened Thailand's first open-pit tin mine (1,000 to 2,000 tons of concentrates per year) in Ban Juai Wan Khao near Kanchaneburi and the Burma border in 1976.

Thailand's extensive fluorspar resources can support high-level production for decades. However, the average grade is only fair, and Japan, the principal market, is playing the field for better-grade material. World prices are down, and there appears to be an oversupply. Thus, the Thai fluorspar industry, which was in the doldrums in 1975 and 1976, may not soon return to the prosperity of a few years back. At its peak, the fluorspar industry had over 150 small mines, mostly near Chiengmai. There is only one heavy media plant (at Lamphun), owned by Universal Mining, and one flotation plant (at Petburi), owned in part by Kaiser Cement. Thailand's 1976 output of metspar was very low, but the production of acidspar established a record. Exports of acidspar during 1976 were 90,622 metric tons.

Thailand's important tungsten industry, centered at Doi Mok in Chiang Rai Province and at Khao Sun in Nakon Si Thammarat Province, may be on the decline. The easily minable shallow ores of known deposits have been partially stripped, and mining deeper ores will involve difficult techniques and higher costs. It is rumored that some Khao Sun ores are transported covertly out of the country.

Barite is the only important Thai mineral showing increased production, which is due to the expanding market in oil drilling mud in Southeast Asia. Deposits are widespread, and there are about three major producers, with the largest mine in Petburi. In late 1976, Dresser Industries opened its new barite-mud processing plant at Amphoe Tha Sala in southern Thailand.

Thailand's oil industry consists of three major refineries in the delta area and exploration activities offshore in the Gulf of Thailand. The three refineries—Thai Oil Refining Co., Esso Petroleum, and Summit Industrial Corp.—together satisfy the bulk of the Thai market by processing about 170,000 barrels per day of imported crude. The government will take over Summit shortly and Thai Oil by 1981. The most important natural gas discoveries have been made by Union Oil of California about 180 kilometers off the east coast of Thailand in Blocks 10, 12, and 13.

Mine and Industry Workers

The Thais know how to work hydraulic and gravel pump tin operations and are learning dredging techniques as well. They are also becoming familiar with construction and road-building activities. There are many graduates from Western mining schools. However, the Thais are not very familiar with hard-rock mining, particularly underground mining, owing mainly to the general lack of such operations. Thailand does not have adequate industrial workers to man new smelting and refining plants, but the necessary personnel can be trained. There are about 50,000 mine and quarry workers.

Mineral Transport

For high-unit-value metals such as tin, tungsten, and antimony, transportation cost is not a big factor. For fluorspar, which is mainly produced in the north, shipping charges to the port area in the south are relatively high. Barite is trucked on fairly good highways to the markets. Cement does not have such difficulties, since plants are located near the markets and highways, particularly around the Bangkok area. The outer port of Bangkok is Thailand's only good port. It is difficult to move low-unit-value minerals occurring in the northeastern plateau and western hill areas to the markets and the coastal region. Most potential mining areas require totally new access roads to tap the minerals. Thailand does have fairly modern truck highways and a growing fleet of relatively new trucks.

Energy and Power

EGAT controls much of Thailand's energy and power industries, with the exception of oil. Its generating capacity near the beginning of 1975 was about 2.2 million kilowatts, roughly half-thermal and half-hydropower. The thermal facilities are run mainly by imported heavy oil and domestic lignite. Additional facilities being built include the 360,000-kilowatt Ban Chao Nen hydroproject, the 150,000-kilowatt Mae Moh Lignite thermal project, and the first unit of the 600,000-kilowatt nuclear power plant at Ban Aow Phai. Two other hydroprojects are being investigated. Meanwhile, energy and power are generally in short supply and expensive. The Thai government now subsidizes petroleum in order to hold prices and fuel costs down. The newly found offshore natural gas is expected to be very important for use in energy and metal smelting and for use as a feedstock for chemicals.

Summary Outlook

The uncertain political situation is holding back foreign investment and industrial development. The Temco affair has further discouraged start-up of new large mining projects, at least momentarily, but the government has been making serious efforts to reverse this trend. Although the prospects for developing nontin mines are reasonably good, the Thais have yet to learn about hard-rock mines. World commodity prices are a matter of great concern to Thai mineral exporters, which partially explains why Thailand generally supports international associations and agreements. In order to cut the fuel import bill, Thailand is attempting to interest foreigners in more oil and gas exploration. Establishing diplomatic relations with the People's Republic of China means not only the importation of Chinese oil but additional commercial and trade dealings as well.

Illustrations for Chapter 27

Figure 146 Map of Thailand

Figure 147 General scenes in Thailand

Figure 148 Additional scenes in Thailand

Figure 149 Drilling for oil in record depths off Thailand's west coast (Courtesy of Exxon Corp.)

Modern sea dredge in Phangnga Bay

Fishing boats turned tin dredges in Ao-Kham Bay, Phuket

Tin palong structure just north of Phuket

Tin-dredging apparatus on small boats in Phuket-Phangnga

Typical hydraulicking operation in Phuket

Gravel pump operation in Phuket, showing sump and palong

Figure 150 Tin operations in Thailand

Selective mining in open pit

Examining the selectively mined product

View of open pit benches

Drilling and benching

Hand-sorting shed

Closeup of sorting shed

Figure 151 Fluorspar operations southwest of Chiangmai, Thailand

Figure 152 Where Thailand produces its tin and fluorspar

28
Vietnam

Vietnam officially became one nation on July 2, 1976, although warfare had ceased in April 1975. The country's 45 million inhabitants traditionally have been engaged in agriculture, and most of what little industry there is, is in the north. Wartime disruptions and bombings were severe, and production data and the status of facilities are difficult to ascertain. However, there is enough information to evaluate Vietnam's general resource position, the characteristics of its mineral industries, and its efforts to rehabilitate and expand facilities. Agriculture has the highest priority, but basic industries are important, and the government is placing considerable emphasis in this area.

Vietnam plans to expand its production of coal, cement, fertilizers, metals, and electric power. The current output of coal is more than 5 million tons annually, and outputs of cement and phosphate rock (mainly apatite) are over 1 million tons each. Oil had been found offshore in the south before unification, and the present government is apparently trying to interest foreigners in developing it. The construction of a 460,000-tpy (crude steel) integrated steelworks reportedly has been planned. The Second Five-Year Plan (covering 1976-1980) will not be effectively started until 1977, since progress in 1976 was extremely sluggish, particularly with regard to capital construction.

TABLE 19. VIETNAM: ROLE IN WORLD MINERAL SUPPLY
(Thousand metric tons, unless otherwise noted)

Major Commodities (Map Symbols)	Production 1976	1975	1974	World Output Share, 1975	Trade in 1975 Exports or Imports	Reserves (or Raw Materials)
Metals						
Chromite (Cr)............	35	36	30	0.4%	Mostly exported	Moderate
Tin, mine (Sn, mine)......	300	300	200	0.1%	Mostly exported	Small
Zinc, refined (Zn).......	10	10	8	0.2%	Partly exported	Small
Nonmetals						
Apatite (P)..............	1,400	1,300	1,200	1 %	Partly exported	1,000,000
Cement (Cem).............	1,500	1,200	1,000	0.2%	Neither	(Adequate)
Salt.....................	500	500	400	0.3%	Neither	Moderate
Fuels						
Coal (C).................	6,000	5,300	4,000	0.2%	Exports 504 (Japan)	3,000,000

NOTE: All data estimated.

Significance of Minerals

Even an agricultural-based economy requires increasing quantities of mineral products in order to grow. Coal is very useful locally for power generation and industrial consumption, and the surplus earns welcome foreign exchange. Cement will become more and more important in Vietnam's reconstruction program. The need for fertilizers is obvious. Vietnam has an important phosphate rock deposit near the China border; it supplies both the Chinese and Vietnamese markets. Petroleum requirements are rising, and the development of indigenous production will be very significant. In 1975 GNP rose by about 11 percent over that of 1974, industrial output by 17 percent, and coal output by 31 percent, according to Vietnamese broadcasts.

Mineral Supply Position

Vietnam has for many years sold anthracite to Japan and sporadically has shipped moderate quantities of good white silica sands to Japan. All its small tin output is destined for the international market, and Vietnam can become a significant exporter of crude phosphates.

Small amounts of indigenous iron ore are converted to steel domestically, and some zinc is produced as well. Metal consumption should increase under peaceful conditions, and this must be either produced or imported. The Hanoi government undoubtedly used considerable quantities of imported liquid fuels during the civil strife.

Nature of Mienral Enterprise

The northeast corner of Vietnam (the area north of Lao Cai, Hanoi, and Haiphong) seems to have most of the country's known minerals and basic industries. Many areas across the country have limestone and other sedimentaries, and a few areas in the south have special nonmetallics. Generally, southern Vietnam does not have much in the way of minerals, although the offshore oil potential is better in the south.

Historically, the French played a significant role in developing minerals in the north. In particular, they examined the Lao Cai (Laokay) apatite deposit many times before abandoning Indochina. Various other deposits and industrial plants were first discovered, evaluated, or built by the French, such as the Hong Gay (Hongay) anthracite mine, Cho Dien zinc mine, Tin Tuc tin mine, Lang Hit phosphate rock deposit, Lang Son bauxite deposit, Co Dinh chromite deposit, and various chemical, metallurgical, power, and oil facilities. The small steel complex at Thai Nguyen was heavily bombed and may still be being rebuilt and expanded. The Vietnamese have rebuilt a cement plant of about 300,000 tons in Haiphong—the largest such plant in the country.

The Vietnamese are thinking of producing 10 million tons of washed coal, 2 million tons of cement, 1.3 million tons of chemical fertilizers, 300,000 tons of steel, and 5 billion kwh of electricity by 1980.

In early 1976, Vietnam formulated a long-range geological plan for the country and started to explore "dozens of forests" and make geological maps for minerals, including anthracite, iron, bauxite, and tin. The government has also divided the country into seven economic zones for the purpose of developing raw materials for industry and export.

Principal Mineral Industries

Coal remains the main fuel for northern Vietnam's power network. The country's coal production target for 1975 was 5.3 million metric tons (virtually all in the north). Much emphasis has been given recently to new washing plants and to additional roads and port facilities for the export of coal to France and Japan (Japan imported 664,410 metric tons of Vietnamese anthracite in 1974 and 503,654 tons in 1975). The Hongay anthracite combine (with the open-pit mines of Deo Nai, Ha Lam, Coc Sau, and Ha Tu) may also be going underground—to tap extensive reserves said to comprise several billion tons. A Japanese company is helping to build a coal calcining plant for Hongay. A new 600,000-tpy coal combine (Mao Kye) near Quang Ninh may be in the process of substantial expansion. Bac Thai is a new mining area and may be supplying coking coal to the main steelworks.

The Thai Nguyen steel complex, which draws its iron ore from Trai Ca, may have a capacity of 200,000 tpy. Its three small blast furnaces were repaired by the Chinese, and $60 million worth of machinery was being purchased from the French. A new steel rolling mill was recently completed at Gia Sang with East German aid, and another rolling mill (120,000 tpy) was being built at Luu Xa. The East Germans are also helping to build a construction materials plant at Dao Yu, and the Soviets and Bulgarians are helping to build the Bim Son cement and tile works. There is a 10,000-ton zinc smelter at Quang Yen in the north, which is supplied by the Co Dien Mine. The Hungarians are investigating the feasibility of building an alumina plant, which would presumably use bauxite from Lang Son and elsewhere. Chromite is produced at Co Dinh and tin at Cao Bang and Tin Tuc.

Fertilizer production reportedly increased 22 percent over that of 1974. The large Lao Cai apatite deposit is world-famous, and annual output can easily be increased to over 1.5 million tons. In fact, its mine and mill are being expanded. The apatite goes to the Lam Thao plant and no doubt to China also. A new phosphate works is being built at Van Dien. The Japanese are trying to secure a contract to build a 189,000-ton phosphoric acid plant (including a 292,000-ton sulfuric acid unit and a 90,000-ton diammonium phosphate unit) in the suburbs of Hanoi. Vietnam also has regular phosphate rock deposits at Thanh Hao, Ham Rong, and Lang Hit. The Chinese are helping to build a large nitrogenous fertilizer plant at Ha Bac; it is now nearing completion. So far, Vietnam needs to import about 300,000 tpy of chemical fertilizers.

The French, Canadians, Americans, and Japanese have been involved in offshore oil exploration southeast of Saigon. A French subsidiary of Shell struck oil in a block shared with Cities Service in late 1974, and in February 1975 a Mobil consortium (including the Japanese company Kaivo Oil and others) struck oil again (2,400 bpd initial flow) in the area, about 190 km (120 miles) southeast of Saigon. Hanoi is keeping its options open in trying to interest foreigners, and the Japanese sent a delegation to Vietnam in the fall of 1976 to discuss oil exploration. In February 1977, nine Western oil companies (includes Japanese, but no American firms) were negotiating with the Vietnamese for rights off Vung Tau. U.S. companies cannot be directly involved in exploration and drilling until U.S. foreign policy is clarified. Onshore oil may have been found by the Soviets, for it was announced that a Vietnamese Oil and Natural Gas Commission was formed in August 1975.

Mine and Industry Workers

The Vietnamese have a small core of miners and industry workers in existing operations, and many learned the rudiments of mechanics in dealing with vehicles, engines, and pumps during the war. When the need arises, adequate workmen can be trained in basic technology for specific purposes.

Mineral Transport

Vietnam has a short east-west railroad from Lao Cai (connects into southwest China) to Hanoi, Haiphong, and Hongay. The north-south railroad extending all the way from Lang Son south to Saigon along the coast was reopened in early 1977. Theoretically, the whole coastal area can be served by this railroad. However, more railroads or roads will be needed to serve the mineral-industrial complex in the northeast.

Vietnam's road system is badly in need of repair and

basically inadequate. The smaller ports also have to be built up. It is believed that the country's mineral traffic will remain relatively light for some time yet. Vietnam has two good ports for exporting coal—Hon Gay and Cam Pha.

Energy and Power

Vietnam's power output in the north may have been about a billion kwh in 1975, a reported 29-percent increase over 1974. The gain in 1976 was similar. Two-thirds of the energy is derived from coal, and the rest mainly from hydropower. In 1975 the major Uong Bi and Ninh Binh thermal stations went into partial operation, and various small and medium-sized hydropower stations were developed. The thermal power stations at Cao Ngan and Viet Tri will also be expanded. Preparations were made in 1976 to build various hydropower stations on the river Da and thermal stations in Pha Lai and Dap Cau. A major dam is planned for an area southwest of Hanoi to complete an irrigation system for the Red River delta and to produce 1.6 million kilowatts of electricity.

Summary Outlook

By the end of 1975, nearly all the war-devastated industrial bases had been "substantially restored." The government's stress on promoting industry, mining, metallurgy, chemicals, fertilizers, and fuels is unmistakable, and Vietnam has the resources to increase output greatly. For 1976 alone, the plan was to raise production of electric power by 23 percent, cast iron by 30 percent, phosphate fertilizer by 11 percent, coal by 13 percent, and cement by 21 percent. Construction will begin on two new cement plants at Buu Son and Phu Xuan. Output of steel, tin, ferroalloys, chromite, and phosphate rock will also be increased.

Most railroad bridges, road bridges, and railway stations have already been restored, including the main north-south coastal railroad. The problem in the south will be more complicated, since totally new transport facilities must be built to serve new industries.

Vietnamese planners seem to have an open mind about

seeking foreign assistance; obviously, it would be difficult to go it alone. Both the East and West Europeans are helping to develop resources and industry, and the Japanese are making a strong bid to become a major force.

Illustrations for Chapter 28

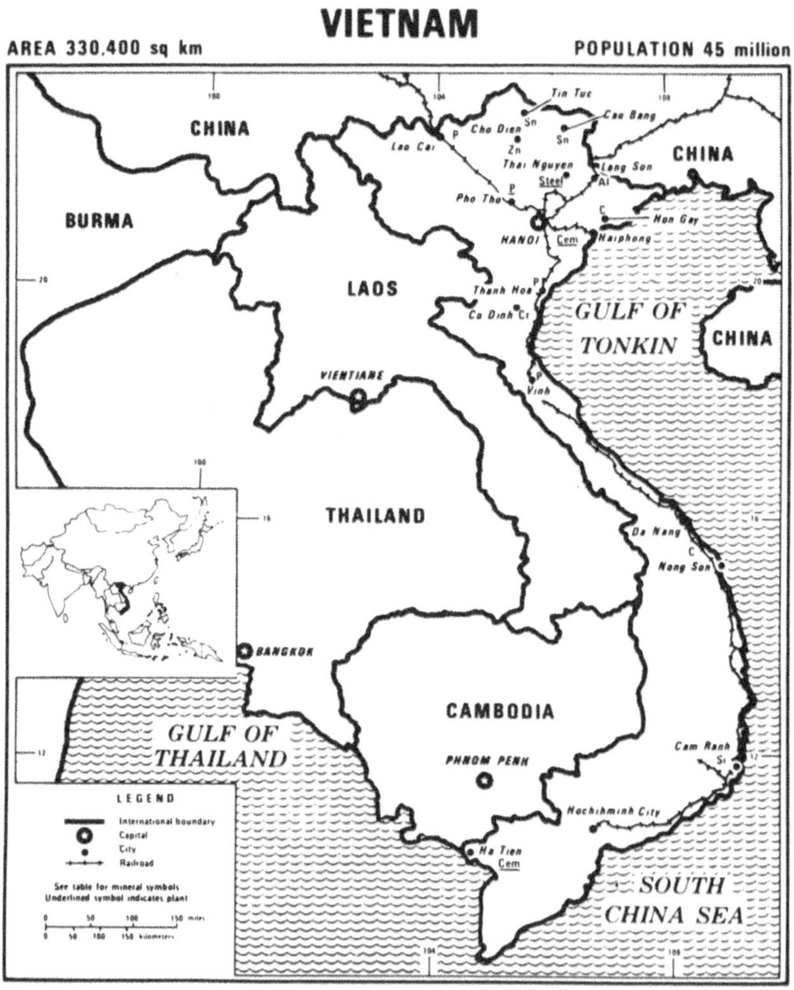

Figure 153 Map of Vietnam

Building from the ashes

Street scene of Hanoi

Figure 154 Scenes from northern Vietnam

Figure 155 The Ha Bac fertilizer plant in northern Vietnam

Deo Nai coal mine

Hatu coal mine

Figure 156 The Hongay anthracite operations in northern Vietnam

Drilling at a new site

Open-pit excavation

Figure 157 The world-famous Lao Cai apatite operations near the China border

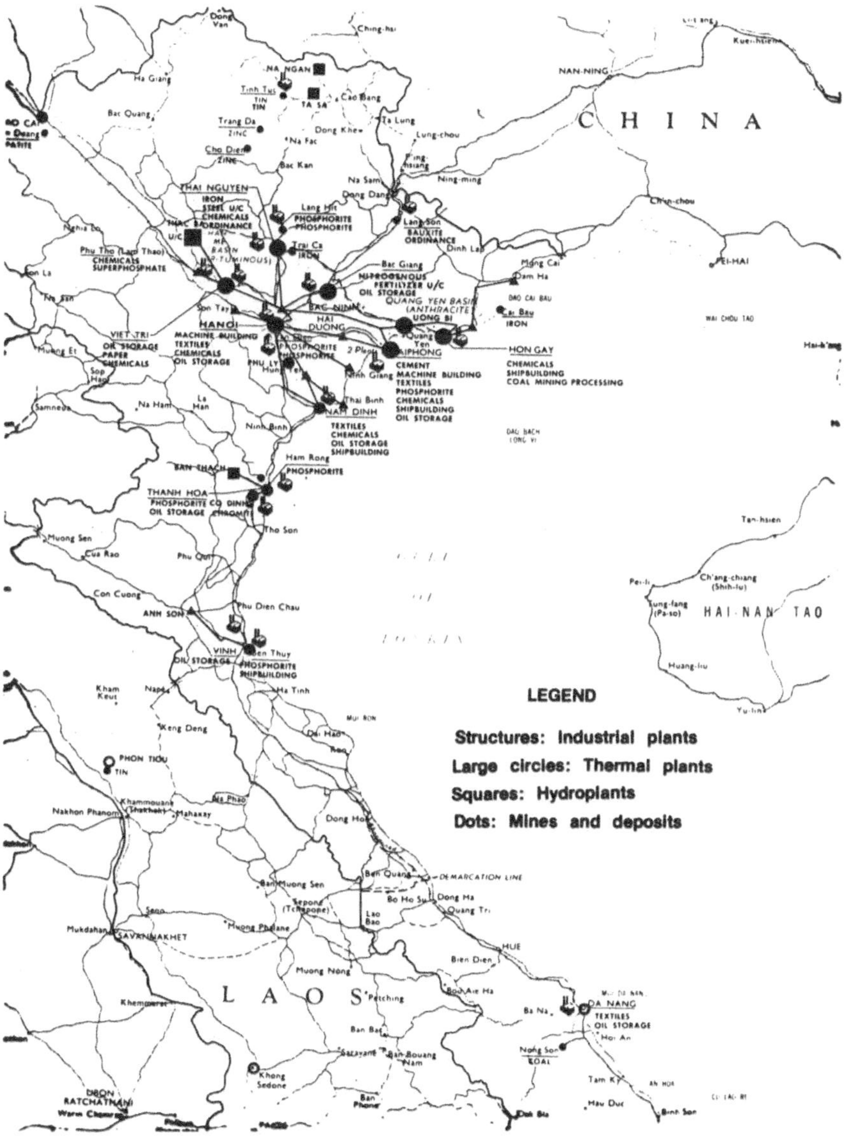

Figure 158 Major industries of Vietnam as of 1970

Selected Bibliography

General

Commodity Data Summaries 1977. Annual. U.S. Bureau of Mines. Washington, D.C. 1977.

Economics of Mineral Engineering (papers from a United Nations seminar held in Ankara, April 1976). London: Mining Journal Books, Ltd., 1976.

Energy Perspectives 2. U.S. Dept. of the Interior. Washington, D.C. June 1976. 224 pp.

Engineering and Mining Journal. Monthly. McGraw Hill. New York. 1975-77.

Industrial Minerals. Monthly. Metal Bulletin Ltd. London. 1976-77.

International Coal 1976. National Coal Association. Washington, D.C. 1977. 31 pp.

International Petroleum Encyclopedia 1976. Annual review by country. Petroleum Publishing Co. Tulsa. 1976. 456 pp.

Mineral Facts and Problems 1975 Edition. U.S. Bureau of Mines Bulletin 667. Washington, D.C. 1976. 1,266 pp. and 203 diagrams.

Mining in the Outer Continental Shelf and in the Deep Ocean. National Academy of Sciences. Washington, D.C. 1975. 119 pp.

Mining Industry and the Developing Countries. World Bank (Bosson, Varon). Washington, D.C. 1977.

Mining Journal. Weekly. Mining Journal Ltd. London. 1976-77.

Nitrogen. Bi-monthly. The British Sulphur Corp., Ltd. London. 1976-77.

Rock Products. Vol. 80, no. 4. Maclean Hunter. Chicago. April 1977. 194 pp.

Tungsten Statistics. Quarterly. UNCTAD Committee on Tungsten. Geneva. 1975-77.

World Coal. Monthly reviews on coal developments, with country reviews around midyear. San Francisco. 1975-77.

World Metal Statistics. Monthly. World Bureau of Metal Statistics. London. 1975-77.

World Mining. Monthly reviews on mineral developments, with country reviews around midyear. San Francisco. 1975-77.

World Mining and Metals Technology. 2 vols. American Institute of Mining, Metallurgical and Petroleum Engineers, Inc. New York. 1976. 1,107 pp.

Regional

ADB Quarterly Review. Information Office, Asian Development Bank. Manila. 1975-77.

ASEAN: Association of South East Asian Nations. Commission of European Communities and Asean Mission to the European Communities. Dec. 7, 1975. 172 pp.

Asia Mining. Asiaworld Publishers. Manila. Monthly. 1976-77.

Asia Yearbook. Far East Economic Review. Hong Kong. 1975, 1976, and 1977.

Asian Wall Street Journal. Daily. Hong Kong. 1977.

Background Notes. Periodic reviews on individual countries. U.S. Department of State. Washington, D.C. 1975-77.

Bain, H. F. *Ores & Industries in the Far East*. New York: Council on Foreign Relations, Inc., 1933. 288 pp.

Far East Economic Review. Weekly reviews on Far East countries. Hong Kong. 1975-77.

Foreign Economic Trends and Their Implications for the United States. Periodic reviews of countries. U.S. Department of Commerce. Washington, D.C. 1975-77.

Minerals Yearbook. Vol. 3. Annual reviews of individual countries. U.S. Bureau of Mines. Washington, D.C. 1974-75.

Mining Annual Review of the London *Mining Journal*. Reviews by industries and countries. London. 1975-76.

Modern Asia. Monthly. Johnston International Publishing Corp. New York. 1975-77.

Summary of World Broadcasts (Part 3 is the weekly economic report on the Far East). Weekly. British Broadcasting Corporation. Caversham Park, Reading. 1975-77.

Torgasheff, B. P. *The Mineral Industry of the Far East.* Shanghai: Chali Company, 1930. 510 pp.
Wang, K. P. *Mineral Perspectives: Far East and South Asia.* U.S. Bureau of Mines. Washington, D.C. May 1977.

China

China Pictorial (English Edition). Monthly. Peking. 1975-77.
China Reconstructs (English Edition). Monthly. Peking. 1975-77.
China Trade Report. Monthly. Far Eastern Economic Review. Hong Kong. 1976-77.
China's Construction & Mining Industries. The National Council for US-China Trade. Washington, D.C. March 1977. 431 pp.
China's Foreign Trade. Monthly. 1976, no. 1. Peking. 1976. 53 pp.
The China Business Review. Bi-monthly. National Council for US-China Trade. Washington, D.C. 1975-77.
Phipps, J. *Coal Mine Equipment (China).* U.S. Department of Commerce, Bureau of East-West Trade. March 1977. 20 pp.
Tien-Kung, K'ai-Wu. *Chinese Technology in the Seventeenth Century.* University Park, Pa.: Pennsylvania State University, 1966. 372 pp.
Wang, K. P. *Mineral Resources and Basic Industries in the People's Republic of China.* Boulder, Colorado: Westview Press, 1977. 225 pp.
Wang, K. P. *The People's Republic of China—A New Industrial Power with a Strong Mineral Base.* U.S. Bureau of Mines. Washington, D.C. 1975. 96 pp.

India

Coal After Nationalization. Coal Consumers Association of India. Calcutta. 675 pp. plus 107 pp. of tables and statistics.
Indian Fertilizer Year. 1975-76. Fertilizer International (monthly), no. 85. British Sulphur Corp., Ltd. London. July 1976. pp. 4-5.
India's Oil Potential. The Himachal *Times.* Dehra Dun (UP). July 1976. 122 pp.
Iron and Steel Industry in India. 1974. Hindustan Steel Ltd. Ranchi. 1974. 617 pp.
Mica Pegmatites (in India). Bulletin no. 5. India Bureau of Mines. Nagpur. April 1976.
Shaffer, Francis E. U.S. Embassy, New Delhi, India. Various mineral industry reports on India, including iron and steel, coal, petroleum, nonferrous metals, and bauxite-aluminum. 1976-77.

Indonesia

Carlson, Sevinc. *Indonesia's Oil.* Boulder, Colorado: Westview Press, 1977. 200 pp.

Indikator Ekonomi. Monthly. Central Bureau of Statistics. Jakarta. 1976-77.

Indonesia Mining Yearbook 1975 (in Indonesian with English summary). Indonesia Ministry of Mines. Djakarta. 1977. 67 pp.

Mining in Indonesia. Australia Mining. Vol. 69, no. 4. April 1977. pp. 30-33.

Petroleum & Natural Gas Industry of Indonesia. Monthly. Direktorat Jendral. Djakarta. 1976-77.

Japan

Energy in Japan. Monthly. Institute of Energy Economics. Tokyo. 1975-77.

Industrial Review of Japan 1977. Annual. Nihon Keizai Shimbun. Tokyo. 1977. 146 pp.

Japan Chemical Week. Weekly. The Chemical Daily Co., Ltd. Tokyo. 1975-77.

Japan Company Handbook First Half 1977. Semiannual. Toyo Keizai Shinposha, Ltd. Tokyo. 983 pp.

Japan Exports & Imports. Monthly. Japan Tariff Association. Tokyo. 1975-77.

Japan Metal Bulletin. Three times per week. Sangyo Press. Tokyo. 1975-77.

Japan Metal Journal. Weekly. Tokyo. 1975-77.

Japan Petroleum Weekly. Japan Petroleum Consultants, Ltd. Tokyo. 1975-77.

Japanese Finance and Industry. Quarterly Survey. The Industrial Bank of Japan. Tokyo. 1975-77.

Roskill's Letter from Japan. Monthly reviews drawn from the Japan Society of Newer Metals. London. 1977.

Malaysia

Bank Negara Malaysia. *Quarterly Economic Bulletin.* Vol. 9, no. 4. December 1976. 155 pp.

Malaysia Department of Mines. *Quarterly Bulletin of Statistics of the Mining Industry.* Kuala Lumpur. 1976-77.

States of Malaya. *Chamber of Mines Yearbook 1974.* Charles Grenier Sdn, Berhad. Ipoh-Perak. 1975. 119 pp.

Tin News (on Malaysia). Monthly. The Malayan Tin Bureau. Washington, D.C. 1976-77.

Philippines

Amcham Journal. Monthly. American Chamber of Commerce of the Philippines, Inc. Manila. 1975-76.

Annual Reports. Philippine Bureau of Mines. Manila. 1974-76.

Annual Review. Minerals News Service. No. 71. Philippine Bureau of Mines. Manila. August 1976. 37 pp.

Philippine Mining & Engineering Journal. Monthly. Published by Luciano B. Quitlong. Manila. 1975-76.

Philippines Mining Yearbook. Annual. Philippines Mining Yearbook Publications. Quezon City. 1974-76.

The Philippine Economic Horizon. Monthly. Private Development Corporation of the Philippines. Makati. 1976-77.

South Korea

Korea Statistical Yearbook 1976. Annual. Bureau of Statistics of the Economic Planning Board. Seoul. 1977.

Korean Business Review. Bi-monthly. The Federation of Korean Industries. Seoul. 1976-77.

Korea's Economy Past and Present. Korea Development Institute. Seoul. May 1975. 367 pp.

Korea's Energy Program and Policy. U.S. Embassy, Seoul. Dispatch A-14. February 1, 1977. 8 pp. and 8 tables.

Mineral Industry in Korea. Korea Mining Promotion Corp. Seoul. January 1975. 189 pp.

Taiwan

Industry of Free China. Monthly. Economic Planning Council. Taipei. 1975-77.

Mineral Resource Development in Taiwan. 1945-1974. MRSO Report 150. Mining Research and Service Organization. Taipei. October 1975. 33 pp.

Taiwan Industrial Production. Statistics Monthly. Department of Statistics, Ministry of Economic Affairs. Taipei. 1975-77.

Ten Major Development Projects (in Taiwan). Ministry of Economic Affairs. Taipei. March 1976. 48 pp.

Thailand

Bank of Thailand. *Monthly Bulletin.* Bangkok. 1976-77.

Business Review (Thailand). Monthly. The Nation Co., Ltd. Bangkok. 1975-77.

Mineral Resources Gazette (in Thai with some English captions). Monthly. Thai Royal Department of Mineral Resources. Bangkok. 1975-77.

Scholla, Paul F. & Assoc. Various reports on specific mineral industries of Thailand, including tungsten, barite, fluorspar, copper-lead-zinc, antimony, and tin (to be published). Bangkok. 1975-77.

Other Countries

Hong Kong 1977. Hong Kong Government Publications. February 1977. 282 pp.

Mongolia. Bi-monthly pictorial magazine. Ulan Bator. 1976-77.

Area Handbook for North Korea. Foreign Area Studies. The American University. Washington, D.C. 1976. 394 pp.

Democratic People's Republic of Korea. Monthly pictorial magazine. Pyongyang. 1976-77.

Progress. A monthly publication of Pakistan Petroleum Limited. Karachi. 1976-77.

Monthly Digest of Statistics. Department of Statistics. Singapore. 1976-77.

Annual Report of the Ministry of National Development of Singapore (1975). Singapore. 49 pp.

Sri Lanka Yearbook 1975. Department of Census and Statistics. Colombo. 1976. 365 pp.

Indochina. Vietnam. Incorporated in *China Trade Report.* Monthly. Far East Economic Review. Hong Kong. 1976-77.

For Product Safety Concerns and Information please contact our EU representative GPSR@taylorandfrancis.com Taylor & Francis Verlag GmbH, Kaufingerstraße 24, 80331 München, Germany

Batch number: 10726009

Printed by Printforce, the Netherlands